Operational security management in violent environments

Good Practice Review 8
Revised edition

Good Practice Review

Operational security management in violent environments

December 2010

Good Practice Review 8
Revised edition
Humanitarian Practice Network
Overseas Development Institute

Contents

Authorship and acknowledgements   xi
Disclaimer   xv
Glossary of security terms   xvii
Introduction   1

SECTION 1
KEY CONCEPTS AND PRINCIPLES

Chapter 1 **Key concepts and principles of security management**   7
1.1 Why manage security risks?   7
1.2 Organisational security management   12
1.3 Interagency security management   17
1.4 Transferring security risks   21
1.5 The host country and security management   23

SECTION 2
STRATEGIC AND OPERATIONAL APPROACHES TO SECURITY MANAGEMENT

Chapter 2 **Risk assessment**   27
2.1 The importance of systematic risk assessment   27
2.2 Key definitions   28
2.3 Context analysis: know where you are   30
2.4 Programme analysis: know who you are and what you want to do   35
2.5 Threat assessment   38
2.6 Vulnerability assessment   42
2.7 Risk analysis   46

Chapter 3 **Security strategy**   55
3.1 Developing a security strategy   55
3.2 Acceptance   57
3.3 Protection   71
3.4 Deterrence and armed protection   73

Chapter 4 **Evacuation, hibernation, remote management**   83
programming and return
4.1 Evacuation and relocation   83
4.2 Hibernation   93
4.3 Remote management programming   94
4.4 Return   99

Chapter 5 Incident reporting and critical incident management 101
5.1 The importance of incident reporting and monitoring 101
5.2 Critical incident management 103
5.3 Post-incident management 107

SECTION 3
PEOPLE IN SECURITY MANAGEMENT

Chapter 6 People in security management 111
6.1 Field-level security managers 111
6.2 Personal competence 115
6.3 Team competence 118
6.4 Differentiating threats and risks for different types of staff 120
6.5 Human resources 125
6.6 Stress and stress management 128

SECTION 4
COMMUNICATIONS SECURITY

Chapter 7 Managing communications security 141
7.1 Telecommunications 141
7.2 Protecting communications equipment 153
7.3 Information security 154
7.4 Dealing with the media 159

SECTION 5
MANAGING SPECIFIC THREATS AND RISK SITUATIONS

Chapter 8 Travel and movement security 165
8.1 Security on arrival 165
8.2 Vehicles and security on the road 167
8.3 Road travel: incident preparedness and incident response 176
8.4 Travel by aircraft and boat 178
8.5 A checklist for staff preparation 179

Chapter 9 Site security 181
9.1 Site selection 181
9.2 Physical perimeter reinforcement 184
9.3 Site security management 187
9.4 Areas under terrorist threat 192
9.5 Counter-surveillance 194
9.6 Distribution sites 195

Chapter 10 Crowds, mobs and looting   197
10.1 Situational monitoring and analysis   197
10.2 Preventive action   198
10.3 Protection   199

Chapter 11 Cash security   203
11.1 Reducing the use of cash   203
11.2 Discretion   203
11.3 Limiting exposure   204
11.4 Electronic money security   206
11.5 Cash programming   207

Chapter 12 Sexual aggression   209
12.1 Definitions and scope   209
12.2 Risk reduction   210
12.3 Surviving sexual assault   213
12.4 Crisis management   215
12.5 Preparation and training   223

Chapter 13 Detention, arrest and abduction   225
13.1 Terminology   225
13.2 Risk reduction   226
13.3 Incident response and crisis management   226

Chapter 14 Kidnapping and hostage situations   229
14.1 Definitions   229
14.2 Risk reduction   229
14.3 Surviving a kidnapping or hostage situation   232
14.4 Critical incident management   235
14.5 Communicating and negotiating with the captors   243
14.6 Managing the aftermath of a kidnapping   247
14.7 Preparation and training   249

Chapter 15 Combat-related threats and remnants of war   253
15.1 Core questions   253
15.2 Shelling and bombing   253
15.3 Crossfire and sniper fire   258
15.4 Mines, booby traps and unexploded ordnance   260
15.5 White phosphorus   268
15.6 Remnants of war: a reminder   268

Annexes

Annex 1 Global trends in aid worker security   273
Annex 2 The United Nations security management system   278
Annex 3 Saving Lives Together: a framework for security collaboration   282
Annex 4 Private security providers   286
Annex 5 Insurance   291
Annex 6 Donor funding and security management   295
Annex 7 Additional resources   298

Authorship and acknowledgements

This revised GPR is the product of many specialists in the field of operational security management.

Koenraad van Brabant, the lead author of the 2000 edition, wrote working notes and extensive working documents for many chapters and annexes of the revised edition. Adele Harmer, Abby Stoddard and Katherine Haver project managed and co-edited the GPR. Adele, Abby and Katherine are all partners in Humanitarian Outcomes. Wendy Fenton, the HPN Coordinator, oversaw the production of the GPR, and Matthew Foley, HPG Managing Editor, edited the manuscript.

Significant input and advice was also provided by an Advisory Group, comprising:

Frédéric Bardou	Security Adviser, Action Contre la Faim (ACF)
Shawn Bardwell	Safety & Security Coordinator, USAID Office of Foreign Disaster Assistance
Oliver Behn	Executive Coordinator, European Interagency Security Forum (EISF)
Alexandre Carle	Africa Security Advisor, CARE
Pascal Daudin	Safety and Security Director, CARE International
Christopher Finucane	Research Consultant, Humanitarian Policy
Anthony Val Flynn	European Commission Directorate General for Humanitarian Aid and Civil Protection
Pierre Gallien	Technical & Development Director, Solidarités
Andrew Gleadle	Independent Consultant
Heather Hughes	Security Adviser, Oxfam GB
Melker Mabeck	Deputy Security Delegate, International Committee of the Red Cross (ICRC)
Maarten Merkelbach	Project Director, Security Management Initiative (SMI), New Issues in Security Progamme at the Geneva Centre for Security Policy (GCSP)
Mamadou Ndiaye	General Director, OFADEC
Erin Noordeloos	Director, International Programmes, RedR UK
Michael O'Neill	Senior Director, Department of Global Safety and Security, Save the Children

Robert Painter	Senior Security Specialist: NGO Liaison, Division of Regional Operations, United Nations Department of Safety and Security
Jean S. Renouf	Researcher and Consultant in conflict and security issues
Mike Tomkins	Associate Director (Operations), Office of Corporate Security, World Vision International
Security Unit	International Federation of Red Cross and Red Crescent Societies

We would also like to thank our contributors and peer reviewers:

Yan Bui	Account Executive, Commercial Insurance, Clements International
Pete Buth	Independent Consultant
Andries Dreyer	World Vision International
Patricia Dunbar	Security Advisor, UNICEF
Ben Emmens	Director of HR Services, People In Aid
Matthew Freedman	CEO, Indigo Telecom USA
Bruce Hickling	Country Director Somalia, International Rescue Committee
Ian Howard-Williams	Team Leader, Humanitarian Preparedness and Response Deputy Director, Conflict Humanitarian and Security Department, Operations Team (CHASE OT), DFID
Trevor Hughes	Director of Global Security, International Medical Corps
Rafael K. Khusnutdinov	Associate Director, Department of Global Safety and Security, Save the Children
Gerald Kloski	Director, Global Security, CHF International
Terry Lewis	Training and Publications Director, Mango
Randy Martin	Director of Global Emergency Operations, MercyCorps
Steve McCann	Director, Armadillo At Large
Auriol Miller	Country Director for Oxfam GB in the Russian Federation
Josh Miller	General Manager, Mexico, Central America and the Caribbean, Control Risks Group
Julian Neale	Conflict, Humanitarian and Security Division, DFID
Michael Niedermayr	Zonal Security Coordinator Asia Pacific, International Federation of Red Cross and Red Crescent Societies (IFRC) (Michael extensively peer reviewed multiple chapters)
Manual Novoa	Stress Counsellor, GTZ

Rupert Reid	Managing Director, Security Exchange Ltd.
Norm Sheehan	Global Security Director, Academy for Education Development (AED)
Julie Spooner	Security Awareness Trainer (for Women), World Food Programme
Simon Springett	Regional Humanitarian Coordinator for the Middle East, Eastern Europe and the Commonwealth of Independent States, Oxfam GB
Hine Sullivan	Security Manager for Pacific Development Group (Papua New Guinea, Solomon Islands and Vanuatu) and Timor-Leste, World Vision
Hernan del Valle	Head of Mission, Médecins Sans Frontières (MSF), Papua New Guinea
Amy West	Program Manager, Academy for Education Development (AED)

Finally, we would like to thank the following, who generously gave their time in interviews:

Felix Ackebo	Interim Head of Eastern Zone Office, UNICEF, DRC
John Adlam	Team Director, CHASE OT, DFID
José Luis Barreiro	Protection Programme Manager and in charge of security for Colombia, Oxfam GB
Sophie Battas	Technical Assistant, ECHO, Chad
Tom Karl Bil	GTZ
Reiseal Ni Cheilleachair	Somali Programme Support Officer, Concern, Nairobi
Robin Coupeland	Insecurity Insight
Marie-Jose D'Aprile	Researcher, SMI
Michel Emeryk	Global Security Adviser, British Red Cross
Paul Farrell	UNICEF HQ
Susannah Friedman	Emergencies Director, Save UK, Somalia (based in Nairobi)
Anne Garella	Head of Mission, ACF Afghanistan
Eric le Guen	Global Safety and Security Advisor, IRC
Patrick Hamilton	International Committee of the Red Cross
Roland Van Hauwermeiren	Country Director, Oxfam GB, Chad
Kevin Henry	Vice President, Global Response, Hiscox USA

Alfred Kamara	Programme Coodinator, 'Hands empowering the less privileged (HELP)', Sierra Leone
Sureka Khandagle	Country Rep, OFDA/USAID, Sudan
Kai Leonhardt	GTZ
Christoph Leudi	Head of Regional Delegation, ICRC, Nairobi
Sean McDonald	International Safety Advisor, Joint NGO Safety Office, Timor Leste
Rebekka Meissner	Medair International Headquarters
Perry Metaxas	NGO Liaison, UNDSS, Darfur
Ron Mortensen	Acting Regional Adviser, OFDA/USAID, Dakar
Abdi Rashid Hadi Nur	Country Director, Somalia Programme, Concern
John Prideaux-Brune	Oxfam GB, Country Director, Occupied Palestinian Territories and Israel
Lara Puglielli	Formerly Director, Staff Safety and Security, Catholic Relief Services
David Richards	SPAS, Somalia
Tom Rogers	USAID/OFDA
Hussein Ali Salad	Policy Adviser, ICRC, Somalia
Nuwa Serunjogi	Humanitarian Advocacy Adviser, Christian Aid
Stefanie Sobol	OFDA/USAID, Dakar
Alain Ondias Souna	Security Manager, WVI Sri Lanka
Barry Steyn	CARE Bangkok
Marcel Stoessel	Country Director, Oxfam GB, DRC
Hine Sullivan	Security Manager for Pacific Development Group (Papua New Guinea, Solomon Islands and Vanuatu) and Timor Leste, World Vision
Nathan Taback	Insecurity Insight
Fergus Thomas	Head of Office, Goma, Concern, DRC
Christina Wille	Insecurity Insight
Nigel Young	Humanitarian Support Personnel, currently acting Country Director for North Sudan, Oxfam GB

Disclaimer

No condition is made or to be implied nor is any warranty given or to be implied as to the quality, life or wear of this GPR published in December 2010 or that it will be suitable for any particular purpose or for use under any specific conditions. Any information in this GPR is presented by ODI as a security management guidance of a general nature only, and must not be regarded as an adequate or valid statement about any standard operating procedures and/or threat patterns in a particular country and/or the security management of one or more agencies.

Although ODI has endeavoured to ensure the accuracy and quality of the information presented in this GPR, ODI will not be liable to the fullest extent permitted by law for any loss, damage, or inconvenience arising as a consequence of any use of or the inability to use, or interpretation of, any information contained within. ODI will not assume responsibility and will not be liable to you, or anyone else, for any damages whatsoever incurred for any decisions made or action taken in reliance on the provided information in this GPR.

This GPR may include the views or recommendations of third parties and does not necessarily reflect the views of ODI or indicate a commitment to a particular course of action.

Glossary of security terms

Abduction: the taking of a person against his or her will. Distinct from 'kidnapping', which implies a demand made (e.g. a ransom) for the victim's return.

Acceptance approach: an approach to security that attempts to negate a threat through building relationships with local communities and relevant stakeholders in the operational area, and obtaining their acceptance and consent for the organisation's presence and its work.

Ambush: a sudden attack made from a concealed position. Often used in the context of road/vehicle attacks.

Battlefield survival: measures to lessen the risk of death or injury when under fire, or in an area which is under fire from any sort of weapon.

Booby trap: an improvised or custom-made explosive usually attached to or concealed under ordinary objects, which acts as a mine to deter or harm people approaching the booby trap area.

Car-jacking: the stealing of a car by armed force, while the driver is in the car.

Civil–military coordination: the interface between military actors (including peace operations) and civilian actors deployed in the field, particularly those from the humanitarian and development community.

Clan: a social grouping of people united by kinship, defined by perceived descent from a common ancestor.

Communications tree: an arrangement to spread information rapidly, such as a security alert, whereby one person or agency informs a predetermined list of others, who in turn then inform those on their lists, and so on.

Compound mentality: the tendency of an organisation to discuss and analyse the external environment from within the protective confines of its 'compound', with little reference to or interaction with actors in the external environment.

Contingency planning: a management tool used to ensure adequate preparation for a variety of potential emergency situations.

Convoy: a group of vehicles (or ships) travelling together in an organised manner for mutual support and protective purposes.

Counter-surveillance: watching whether you are being watched. A strategy to detect whether your movements or facilities are being studied by people with malicious intent, e.g. for kidnapping, bombing or armed robbery.

Critical incident: a security incident that significantly disrupts an organisation's capacity to operate; typically life is lost or threatened, or the incident involves mortal danger.

Critical incident management team (CIMT): a group created for the purpose of managing the organisational response to crisis situations. Typically will involve staff members who have been pre-identified and trained, and who are familiar with the critical incident management procedures and protocols of their organisation.

Danger habituation: a usually unconscious adjustment of one's threshold of acceptable risk resulting from constant exposure to danger; the result is a reduction of one's objective assessment of risk, possibly leading to increased risk-taking behaviour.

Detention: the holding of a person by someone acting under authority (e.g. police, border guards) where the person is not free to leave.

Deterrence approach: an approach to security that attempts to deter a threat by posing a counter-threat, in its most extreme form through the use of armed protection.

Evacuation: the withdrawal of staff across an international border.

Extortion: the use of coercion or intimidation to obtain money, property or patronage.

Gender-based violence (GBV): violence directed against a person on the basis of gender. It includes acts that inflict physical, mental or sexual harm or suffering, threats of such acts, coercion or other deprivations of liberty. While both sexes and all ages can be victims of gender-based violence, because of their subordinate status women and girls are the primary victims.

Harassment: abusive conduct, verbal or physical, directed at a person, which causes distress or discomfort.

Hibernation: the process of sheltering in place until danger passes or further assistance is rendered.

Hostage situation: where a person or group is held in a siege situation in a known location. Similar to a kidnapping scenario, their safety and subsequent release is usually dependent on the fulfilment of certain conditions. These conditions may include: the publicising of a political cause; the exchange of hostages for political prisoners; or the evasion of prosecution by criminals when their activity has been discovered by the authorities.

Improvised explosive device (IED): a bomb which can be placed more or less anywhere, for instance on a roadside or in a vehicle, bag, parcel, letter or clothing.

Incident analysis: deeper and more critical inquiry into the structural and contextual factors that allowed a security incident to happen; questioning the effectiveness of security management, and asking whether or to what degree the agency or one or more of its staff members could have been perceived to be 'provoking' anger or aggression.

Incident inquiry: the collection of situational and circumstantial information about an incident beyond the basic facts stated in the incident report.

Incident mapping: the visualisation, usually on a map but potentially also in a timeframe, of when and where and what type of incidents happened in an attempt to find patterns and identify high-risk areas and high-risk times.

Kidnapping: the forcible capture and detention of someone with the explicit purpose of obtaining something (money, materials or certain actions) in return for their life and release.

Medevac: medical evacuation. The transfer of a patient by road, sea or air for the purpose of obtaining medical treatment in another location.

Mob: an aggressive group of people with destructive or violent intent.

Neighbourhood watch: a more or less formalised scheme among neighbours to keep an eye open for suspicious people and crime.

Post-traumatic stress disorder (PTSD): a psychological condition that may affect people who have suffered severe emotional trauma; may cause sleep disturbances, flashbacks, anxiety, tiredness and depression.

Private security provider/contractor/company: a private entity providing remunerated security services to individuals or organisations. These services can range from 'soft' security (e.g. consultancy, training and logistical support) to 'hard' security (e.g. guarding services, armed protection) to crisis and risk management, training of armed forces and even operational command and combat.

Prodding: a key technique used in extraction from a suspected minefield, whereby the soil is carefully examined for possible mines before a foot is set on it.

Protection: used here as distinct from 'safety' and 'security' to refer to the protection of civilians and non-combatants who are not aid agency staff.

Protection approach: an approach to security that emphasises the use of protective procedures and devices to reduce vulnerability to existing threats; does not affect the level of threat.

Relocation: the withdrawal of staff from an area of operations to a safer location, usually within the same country.

Risk: the likelihood and potential impact of encountering a threat.

Risk assessment/analysis: an attempt to consider risk more systematically in terms of the threats in the environment, particular vulnerabilities and security measures to reduce the threat or reduce your vulnerability.

Risk reduction: the purpose of your security management, by reducing the threat or reducing vulnerability.

Rules of engagement: guidelines to soldiers or armed guards regarding the conditions under which they can use force, and stipulating how much force may be used.

Safety: freedom from risk or harm as a result of unintentional acts (accidents, natural phenomenon or illness).

Scenario planning: forward planning about how a situation may evolve in the future, and how threats might develop; reviewing the assumptions in plans and thinking about what to do if they do not hold.

Security: freedom from risk or harm resulting from violence or other intentional acts.

Security (alert) phases: a summary classification of various possible levels of risk and insecurity in the environment, each of which requires a specific set of mandatory security procedures.

Security auditing: an evaluation of the strengths and weaknesses in an organisation's security management and infrastructure in order to assess its effectiveness and identify areas for improvement.

Security strategy: the overarching philosophy, application of approaches and use of resources that frame organisational security management.

Sexual aggression: the act or threat of rape, sexual assault and intimidation, sexual harassment or unwanted touching.

Small arms: weapons used for self-protection and close or short-range combat.

Social reference: a recommendation or personal guarantee about a potential recruit from someone who has not necessarily had any professional involvement with the recruit but knows their standing and reputation within a community.

Standard operating procedures: formally established procedures for carrying out particular operations or dealing with particular situations, specifically regarding how to prevent an incident happening, survive an incident or follow up on an incident as part of the agency's crisis management planning.

Stress: a state of emotional strain or severe or prolonged worry.

Terrain awareness: being attentive to the physical and social environment, where potential dangers may come from and help or cover might be found.

Terrorism: acts intended to inflict dramatic and deadly injury on civilians and to create an atmosphere of fear, generally in furtherance of a political or ideological objective.

Threat: a danger in the operating environment.

Threat assessment/analysis: the attempt to examine more systematically the nature, origin, frequency and geographical concentration of threats.

Threat mapping: visualising and illustrating threats on a geographical map.

Threshold of acceptable risk: the point beyond which the risk is considered too high to continue operating; influenced by the probability that an incident will occur, and the seriousness of the impact if it occurs.

Triangulation: cross-checking information or details by comparing different sources.

Unexploded ordnance (UXO): any type of munition (bullet, hand grenade, mortar shell, etc.) that has been fused (prepared for firing) but not used, or that has been fired but has not gone off and is considered unstable and dangerous.

Warden/warden system: one or more focal points, typically with responsibility for a set of people in a defined geographical area; the warden is an important node in the communications tree and will also ensure that all those under his or her responsibility follow agreed security procedures.

Note: A useful reference point for terminology is the International Organisation for Standardization (ISO 31000) Guide 73:2009 on 'Risk Management – Vocabulary', available at www.iso.org.

Introduction

The first edition of this Good Practice Review on *Operational Security Management in Violent Environments* (also known as GPR 8) was published in 2000. Since then it has become a seminal document in humanitarian operational security management, and is credited with increasing the understanding of good practice in this area throughout the community of operational agencies. It introduced core security management concepts and highlighted good policy and practice on the range of different approaches to operational security in humanitarian contexts. When it was published, the majority of aid agencies were only just beginning to consider the realities and challenges of operational insecurity. Few international or national organisations had designated security positions or policies and protocols on how to manage the risks of deliberate violence against their staff and operations. The GPR thus filled a significant gap in the policy and practice of security management.

Although a good deal of the original GPR 8 remains valid, the global security environment has changed significantly over the past decade. Increasing violence against aid workers, including more kidnappings and lethal attacks against humanitarian aid workers and their operations, has had serious implications for international humanitarian assistance. Attacks have been both politically motivated and an expression of rising levels of banditry and criminality. This growing violence has generated a deeper awareness of the security challenges faced by operational agencies, giving rise to new adaptations and strategies in security management and growing professionalism and sophistication in humanitarian security practices and interagency coordination. Overall, the changes in the operational and policy environment in the last decade suggest that a review and update of the first GPR is warranted.

This revised GPR both updates the original material and introduces new topics. In particular, it presents a more detailed and refined approach to undertaking risk assessments specifically oriented to field practitioners. It also outlines a more comprehensive means of implementing an 'active acceptance' approach, as well as examining in detail deterrence and protective approaches, including maintaining a low profile and using armed protection. New topics include the security dimensions of 'remote management' programming, good practice in interagency security coordination and how to track, share and analyse security information. It provides a significantly more comprehensive approach to managing critical incidents, in particular kidnapping and hostage taking. Issues relating to the threat of terrorism are discussed in a number of chapters within the revised edition and have been purposefully mainstreamed rather than siloed into one chapter. A series of annexes examines issues such as the changing security environment for humanitarian action, the role of private security providers, insurance provision, and the role of official donors in supporting security management.

Target audience

The original GPR was used by a multitude of individuals and organisations, both as an operational reference manual and as a base or template for organisation-specific security management policies and procedures.

This revised GPR is written primarily for senior operational managers who directly oversee and support operations in violent environments. This includes not only field security advisors but also senior representatives in a given operating environment, including programme managers and coordinators. A wide range of others, from local staff to senior policy managers, may also make use of it as well. Although the content is oriented particularly to non-governmental organisations (NGOs), both international and national, other organisations may also find it useful.

This GPR focuses on security defined as relating to acts of politically and economically motivated violence and crime. Insecurity, however, is not the only type of risk to the life and wellbeing of aid workers. Health and safety risks, including illness and accidents, fires and environmental hazards, are also serious threats, but these are covered in other guidelines. Local communities receiving assistance and other civilians may be at equal or greater risk of violence and in need of major assistance and protection. This GPR does not address these protection challenges, not least because the strategies used to protect civilians are often quite different from those used to protect aid workers.

Good practice and best practice

This GPR describes good practice, not best practice, and does not offer much by way of standard operating procedures and checklists. This is deliberate. There are undoubtedly a number of security measures that are almost always applicable, such as locking doors at night, having effective antivirus protection on computers, informing someone where you are going and when you should be back and reporting every security incident and every near-miss. Getting such basics right is already a good step. The basic checklists included in this guide should be seen as memory aids to ensure that basic measures are and remain in place.

But a significant part of operational security management is about acting appropriately under the given circumstances. Depending on the circumstances, that may mean doing something very different from – even contrary to – what might be considered good practice in most parts of the world. In other words, a significant amount of security management depends on situational judgment, awareness and the ability to assess the relative effectiveness of different security options.

Good practice in security management also means responsible management. Responsible management (of oneself and others) means not putting people and assets at unnecessary risk or at a risk that is disproportionate to the potential impact of the aid you might be seeking to deliver. Mountain rescuers do not go out to search for people caught in an avalanche if the weather or the snow conditions are such that the rescuers themselves would be at very high risk. Good operational security management means asking whether the risk is justified in light of the potential benefit of the project or programme, and whether everything possible has been done to reduce the risk and the potential impact of an incident.

Finally, good practice means integrating security management across the organisation. It is not an add-on or a luxury. Lack of time is often given as a reason for not devoting enough attention to lots of things, including security management. This must be challenged. It should not be acceptable for someone to be seriously injured or killed because their agency has failed to take the time to implement good practice. Organisations without exception take the time to implement financial checks and controls. Why should protecting the lives of agency staff not merit similar attention? And is time really that scarce and are workloads really that heavy, or is this simply a reflection of an organisational culture that encourages staff to see themselves as forever under pressure, rushing from crisis to crisis with no time to pause and draw breath? Ultimately, security management in high-risk areas is both a moral and a legal obligation, and agencies must make the time to see that it is done properly and well.

More importantly, good practice in security management is closely linked with, builds on and reinforces good practice in programme and personnel management more broadly. These are not separate tasks and workloads; there is an important positive multiplier effect. Good programme management requires an understanding of the operating environment and the impact of your agency's presence and its work, building good relationships, managing international and national staff well and collaborating effectively with other agencies.

How to use this GPR

The manual is structured as follows. Part I (Chapter 1) explores the key concepts and principles of security management. Part II (Chapters 2–5) highlights strategic and operational approaches to security management, including risk assessment and an organisational security strategy. Part III (Chapter 6) looks at personnel issues, including recruitment, staff composition and dealing with stress. Part IV (Chapter 7) covers communications management. Part V (Chapters 8–15) examines a variety of specific threats and risk situations and ways to manage them, including travel, site and cash security and dealing with mobs and crowds. It also considers issues of sexual aggression, detention, arrest and abduction and kidnapping and hostage situations.

Some users will have extensive security management experience, or are part of organisations with a strong security culture and related capacities. Others will have little or no such experience, or work in organisations that have not given much thought to security management. Potential users of this GPR will find themselves in very different positions and therefore will be looking at the question of operational security management from different angles and with different needs and priorities. We hope this guide is able to meet the needs of many kinds of readers.

Section 1
Key concepts and principles

Chapter 1

Key concepts and principles of security management

1.1 Why manage security risks?

Managing security is not an end in itself. The primary concern is to be able to deliver humanitarian assistance in an impartial manner, which may require establishing and maintaining a presence in highly insecure contexts. High insecurity jeopardises or impedes the achievement of that goal. Security management is therefore a means to an operational end. At the same time, security management is about protecting and preserving the lives and wellbeing of agency staff (and possibly partners) – and about protecting the organisation's assets, as well as its programmes and reputation. This point holds true from two perspectives:

- Pragmatically speaking, the temporary or permanent loss of assets or injury of a staff member reduces operational capacity and may even lead the agency to suspend its programme or withdraw.
- Morally, agencies have a duty of care towards their employees and colleagues. While aid work implies a certain level of risk, agencies need to be sure that all reasonable measures are taken to mitigate this risk.

The legal requirement of duty of care of the employer is becoming increasingly important. Many countries have labour laws that impose obligations on employers to ensure safety in the workplace. Although such obligations have rarely been considered in the context of international aid work, aid organisations are open to growing legal challenges if they fail to properly inform staff about the risks associated with a particular assignment, or fail to take all necessary measures to reduce those risks.

Effectively managing security risks is therefore essential from an operational, moral and legal point of view. The aim is to protect staff and assets, while enabling assistance to reach some of the world's neediest people.

1.1.1 Combining security risks with other risks

Not all risk management concerns security risks: organisations and individuals take other factors into account when they consider risks. There may be financial incentives for an organisation to decide to go into or stay in an environment with very significant security risks. Reputational considerations often also come into play. In some cases organisations have strong reputational and financial reasons to be present in a high-profile crisis, even if it is a very dangerous one. Individual staff, particularly national staff, may agree to work in very dangerous environments because of the economic incentives that might not otherwise be available to them. A different type of consideration, which merits greater attention, concerns the need that agencies are trying to address. What would the consequences be for people in need if a programme is discontinued? How effective can a programme be under these conditions? How many people can realistically be reached? How severe are their material and protection needs? These issues are discussed in detail in the following chapters.

1.1.2 A basic framework for security risk management

Figure 1 shows the basic framework for security risk management.[1] Its fundamental logic is the same as that of the project management cycle: assess, plan, implement (and adjust if needed), review and reassess. Note that built into the model is the possibility of not implementing a programme should the risks be deemed too high, radically altering it should risks change, or discontinuing it.

The main steps of the security management process are:

- Identify a potential programme: a need exists and the organisation has the mission or mandate and the capacities to respond to that need.
- Thoroughly assess the security risks and the organisation's capacities (human, financial, time resources) to manage those risks. (The risk assessment process is covered in detail in Chapter 2.)
- Determine the threshold of acceptable risk. This may differ depending on the potential benefits of having a presence and a programme, and on the mandate of the organisation.
- Ask whether the risks are beyond the organisation's ability to manage: if so, do not proceed with the programme (or alternatively 'transfer' the risk to another actor that can manage it). If there is sufficient security management capacity that the risk can be reduced to an acceptable level, initiate the programme.
- Develop a context- and situation-specific operational security strategy (the concepts of acceptance, protection and deterrence are explained in Chapter 3).
- Responsible security management requires not only taking preventive measures to avoid an incident, but also investing in the capacity to

1 This figure incorporates elements of the InterAction's Security Risk Management guide (Washington DC: InterAction Security Advisory Group, 2010), p. 7.

Figure 1

Security Risk Management Framework

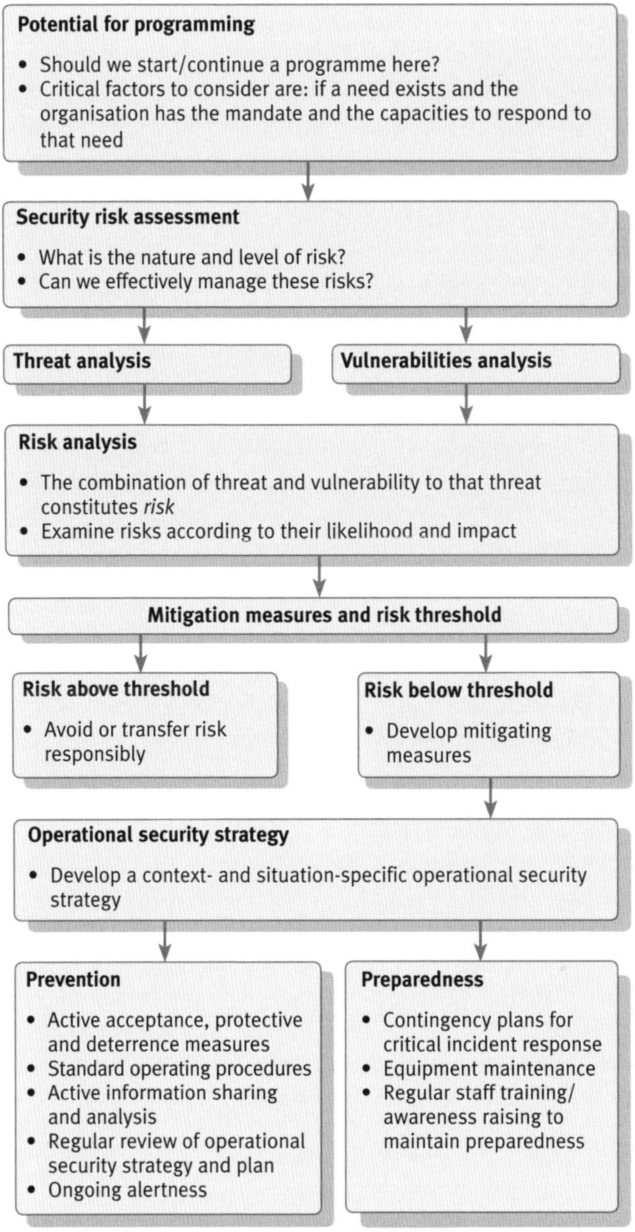

Key concepts and principles

1

Potential for programming

- Should we start/continue a programme here?
- Critical factors to consider are: if a need exists and the organisation has the mandate and the capacities to respond to that need

Security risk assessment

- What is the nature and level of risk?
- Can we effectively manage these risks?

Threat analysis   **Vulnerabilities analysis**

Risk analysis

- The combination of threat and vulnerability to that threat constitutes *risk*
- Examine risks according to their likelihood and impact

Mitigation measures and risk threshold

Risk above threshold

- Avoid or transfer risk responsibly

Risk below threshold

- Develop mitigating measures

Operational security strategy

- Develop a context- and situation-specific operational security strategy

Prevention

- Active acceptance, protective and deterrence measures
- Standard operating procedures
- Active information sharing and analysis
- Regular review of operational security strategy and plan
- Ongoing alertness

Preparedness

- Contingency plans for critical incident response
- Equipment maintenance
- Regular staff training/ awareness raising to maintain preparedness

manage an actual crisis situation and the consequences of a critical incident. This also requires ongoing assessment of security conditions to determine whether the security strategy remains appropriate to the threats in that environment, and whether the risks remain acceptable.

- Establish critical incident procedures. Even with the best preventive approach and measures, an incident may happen. Those caught up in the incident will have to do their best to survive it (in which their preparedness – or lack thereof – will be a significant factor), while the organisation will mobilise an immediate critical incident response.
- Provide post-incident support. Support will be required by the survivors of a critical incident, and possibly also by other staff and/or the families of affected staff.
- Perform post-incident reviews ('after action reviews'). Objectively and honestly analyse how the incident came to happen, how the risks were assessed and how appropriate and effective the security measures were. Evaluate the quality of the critical incident response and overall preparedness. These reviews and evaluations may result in adjustments to the operational security management strategy, or they may lead to the conclusion that the risks have become unmanageable and that more significant programme changes need to be made, or activities suspended.

1.1.3 Main actors in security management

National authorities are responsible for the security of all civilians in their territory. In practice, however, many governments are unable to meet this responsibility (see the discussion below in Section 1.5). That does not mean that the authorities should be ignored. It does mean that additional measures will be needed to manage security effectively.

As noted, organisations have a formal responsibility as employers towards all their staff. A key concept in that regard is 'duty of care'. An organisation's duty of care towards its employees should be defined in its security policy. It is also the responsibility of the organisation to proactively inform employees, potential employees and associated personnel such as consultants about security risks. This allows individuals to exercise 'informed consent' – i.e. to accept a degree of risk after having been made fully aware of the extent of the risk. The organisation is also responsible for ensuring that risks are reduced to a reasonable level.

Managers within an organisation also have a responsibility towards their staff. If the organisation is accused of negligence with regard to security, as a result of which a staff member has been hurt or killed, senior managers or field-level representatives can in some cases be individually pursued for legal redress. An 'accountability framework', which may cover issues beyond security, is one means to make these responsibilities and accountabilities clear to managers at all levels. It should also be made very clear to *all* staff, from guards and drivers to senior programme managers, that each individual has a responsibility for their own security – and for the security of the team as a whole, as well as the organisation's assets. All staff should be involved in regular security-related discussions and activities, including training. An organisation may also have to exercise responsibility on behalf of those other than its staff. Dependents are one such category, certainly for international staff. Define responsibilities carefully and clearly, and make sure that people understand the extent of their responsibility, and the security procedures they must follow. For international staff, home country embassies may have a role to play in alerting their citizens to possible risks. As a general rule, embassies maintain a very low risk threshold for visitors and those who do not operate under any security framework. While the embassy's guidance should be sought, an organisation may still be able to operate securely outside of this guidance if it has an effective security management system. Organisations also have a responsibility to communicate vital security-related information to other agencies operating in the same location. Failure to alert others that a staff member has narrowly escaped an ambush attempt on a particular road, for example, may mean that others unnecessarily become the victims of a violent incident.

Many international organisations employ global security advisers to provide support to field offices. Some also have regional security advisers, who oversee a specific high-risk operational area and provide surge capacity to the country programme. In other organisations, security management is integrated into line management, and no separate security advisors exist. In-country, it is the responsibility of the senior representative (i.e. the Country Director) to ensure that organisational policies and procedures are implemented and adhered to, though in practice many security management tasks may be delegated to a Security Advisor or security focal point (given the sensitivities around the word 'security', in some countries the title Safety Advisor is used instead). The decision to appoint a Security Advisor (either full-time or, where the security focal point has other responsibilities, on a part-time basis) should be based on a range of considerations, including the risk rating for the location, the scope of work and the resources available.

Many organisations devolve decision-making authority to the Country Director or his or her field staff, rather than maintaining responsibility in a regional office or international HQ. Ultimate responsibility, however, lies with the Executive

Director, or in some cases the Board of Trustees. These responsibilities must be clearly articulated in job descriptions. Specific decisions may also need formal approval from a higher authority than the senior field representative. These include:

- to downgrade the risk rating of a country or an area in a country;
- to return to an area from which staff have been relocated because of security risks;
- to adopt a 'low-visibility' approach and remove logos and flag from offices and vehicles;
- to use armed protection; and
- to use a private security provider.

Major incidents, such as a kidnapping or hostage-taking, also usually require the ongoing involvement of the organisation's senior leadership. Official donors may have imposed contractual obligations regarding the visibility ('branding') of assistance they fund, in which case the organisation may have to seek their formal approval to forego this requirement.

1.2 Organisational security management

While most organisations delegate decisions as closely as possible to the field, the operational management of security is intricately linked to wider organisational practices and decision-making. This includes:

- The development of an organisation-wide safety and security policy and practical guidance on security management.
- Organisational skills and responsibilities for certain serious incidents, including the establishment of a critical incident management team in the regional office and/or global headquarters (for international organisations).
- The establishment and maintenance of a centralised reporting system so that all security incidents and near-misses are gathered together in a central point, to enable a global analysis of security incidents affecting the organisation.

Decisions about whether to initiate operations in a certain country, and what type of programme to undertake, are usually the responsibility of headquarters. The organisation may also require that senior headquarters staff make decisions on certain major security issues, as outlined above. In addition, much of the media and communications as well as fundraising for field programmes may be done at headquarters, and other human resource issues such as the establishment of insurance policies are also often handled organisation-wide, rather than at the individual operational level.

An aid agency that deploys people to high-risk areas should have the policies, procedures and capacities to manage such operations. The following is a list of documents in which these policies could be spelled out. These documents have an organisation-wide remit, are developed at and by HQ and constitute general reference resources.

- Agency mandate, general mission statement or statement of values and principles.
- General agency-wide security policy and, where relevant, policy statements on specific security-related issues, such as the use of armed protection, private security providers and information protection.
- Management accountability structure, spelling out where responsibilities for security management and critical incident management and decision-making lie (differentiating between HQ and the field).
- General reference guides and handbooks, for instance on radio use.

1.2.1 Security planning and preparedness

At the field level, the cornerstone of security management is the security plan. The quality of a good operational security plan is dependent on the quality of the planning process. Team planning – with national and international staff – is preferable to individual planning, as it brings to bear collective knowledge and experience and facilitates ownership of the final product. A good planning process needs to be followed up with periodic reviews – as the environment changes, there is a need to adapt the plan.

Different organisations produce different security plans to reflect their organisational needs, the context and their organisational policies and procedures. A good security plan might include the following major components:

1. A synopsis of the country context, including conflict, if relevant.
2. Specific mission objectives in the country.
3. A security risk assessment (see Chapter 2).
4. A threshold of acceptable risk. Such a statement should include a commentary on how that threshold was arrived at (see Chapter 2).
5. A statement of responsibilities in terms of security management.
6. Preventative measures. Some measures will be covered in standard operating procedures (SOPs), as they will involve issues such as site security, movement and communications (see Parts IV and V). Some of

these SOPs can translate into checklists. Other preventive measures do not exist as SOPs or checklists, for example efforts to increase acceptance among local actors.

7. A clarification of the roles and responsibilities for incident response and crisis management. In some cases, involvement by a regional office or HQ may be required or mandatory (see Chapter 5).
8. Procedures for incident reporting, as well as incident response analysis.
9. Retreat plans (hibernation, relocation, evacuation).
10. A statement of principles or policy regarding collaboration on security with others operating in the same environment, such as acknowledging the inter-dependencies between aid providers and the resulting minimum responsibilities, including communicating 'alerts' to others and possibly collaborating in areas such as risk analysis and assessment, pooling or sharing of resources or logistics in case of a withdrawal.
11. A statement on when the plan was produced or last reviewed, how it was produced (the planning process and who was involved), who signed off on it and when it will be reviewed again.
12. Maps of the operating environment, including office locations.

There are a number of issues to bear in mind with regard to security plans:

- A plan is a piece of paper. Paper does not reduce any risks. Plans need to be shared, explained and implemented.
- A good plan today may no longer be appropriate six months from now. If the situation evolves, review the analysis and plans.
- People not familiar with security plans and procedures cannot adhere to them. All staff and visitors need to be briefed as soon as they arrive and after any important changes are made.
- Good implementation depends on competencies. The best possible plan falls apart without the knowledge and skills to implement it. Some aspects of security management require specialised knowledge or skills.
- Effective security management depends to a degree on practice. Practicing – through simulations and training – is vital.

1.2.2 Reviewing security plans

Even in a quiet and secure environment, security plans should be reviewed annually. In higher-risk environments, they should be reviewed more frequently to ensure that they reflect prevailing risks, and that the information they contain is up to date.

When to review
- When there are significant changes in the external context, especially as a result of the actions of the major protagonists.
- When another agency has been affected by an incident, especially in or near the same operational zone.
- When someone else is affected by an incident that in its nature or intensity appears to introduce a new element into the original risk assessment.

What to review
Virtually everything can be a potential candidate for review:

- The wider context and situational analysis.
- The threat assessment.
- The risk assessment.
- The security strategy.
- The preventive/risk-controlling standard operating procedures.
- Programme choices and/or implementation strategy.
- Staffing policy and recruitment criteria.
- Vehicle and transport choices.
- Interagency security information-sharing arrangements/practices.
- The contacts and connections used to maintain acceptance.

If the review suggests a significant deterioration in security, staff may be assembled and briefed on the new assessment of the situation and what realistically can be done to mitigate the risks. Staff need to be able to reassess the situation in light of their own personal threshold of acceptable risk, and reconfirm their 'informed consent' – or not.

1.2.3 Developing a security culture

Much of the focus in security management tends to be on specific operational needs, such as security policies and plans, but there is also a need to take a step back and look at how to develop a culture of security within the organisation, including developing capacity. One of the most important priorities is to make sure that all staff know the organisation and its mission in any given context. It is not uncommon for many staff, including national staff, not to know much about the agency that they represent. Staff need to be told what the organisation is about. Key questions include:

- Why is this organisation here?
- What is it doing here?
- Where does it get its money from? What does it use that money for?

- Who directs its activities?
- Is it serving foreign political interests?
- What is its political agenda?
- Does it want to change local society, culture, values or religion?
- Is it on the side of the government (or another political actor in that environment)?

Consider providing staff with some written material in their own language(s), and go through it with them in an interactive way, periodically bringing staff together to hear from them what sort of questions and comments they most regularly get from those in the community and how they answer them. In addition, treat security as a staff-wide priority, not a sensitive management issue to be discussed only by a few staff members behind closed doors. Specifically:

- Make sure that all staff are familiar with the context, the risks and the commitments of the organisation in terms of risk reduction and security management.
- Make sure that all staff are clear about their individual responsibilities with regard to security, teamwork and discipline.
- Advise and assist staff to address their medical, financial and personal insurance matters prior to deployment in a high-risk environment.
- Be clear about the expectations of managers and management styles under normal and high-stress circumstances.
- Make security a standing item (preferably the first item) on the agenda of every management and regular staff meeting.
- Stipulate reviews and if needed updates of basic safety and security advice, as well as country-wide and area-specific security plans, as described above.
- Invest in competency development. It is not uncommon for aid agencies to scramble to do security training when a situation deteriorates. Investment should be made in staff development, including security mitigation competences, in periods of calm and stability.
- Ensure that security is a key consideration in all programme planning.
- Perform periodic inspections of equipment by a qualified individual, including radios, first aid kits, smoke alarms, fire extinguishers, intruder alarms and body armour.
- Carry out after-action reviews (AARs). The focus is on assessing what happened and how the team acted in a given situation, not on individual responsibilities. It is a collective learning exercise.

Mainstreaming a security culture, both at the level of individual staff members and as an organisation, means considering the security implications involved in everything the organisation does (or chooses not to do), from discussions about programme design and public messages to funding decisions and the hiring of external contractors. People 'think security', and act accordingly because they understand the importance of it, and are respected for doing so. The importance of security is continually reinforced, not just in written policies but also in actions. Senior staff are held accountable for decisions that impact positively or negatively on overall staff security. Organisations have also started to undertake annual security audits of their field offices against a series of benchmarks. This is usually announced in advance, but may not be. Audits can take place after a critical incident, in times or places of heightened risk, or periodically in any dangerous environment.

1.3 Interagency security management

1.3.1 Interdependence and collaboration

Security management in the aid world is largely agency-centred. There are obvious reasons for this: as an employer, the agency must assume responsibility for the safety and security of its personnel, and resources will naturally be directed to this end; different agencies have different mandates or missions, and may therefore establish different thresholds of what they consider 'acceptable risk' and pursue different security strategies. At the same time, however, there are good reasons why agencies in the same violent environment should cooperate. Modes of cooperation include:

- Collective alert: if one agency suffers or narrowly avoids a security incident, unless there is proof that the agency was directly targeted it must be assumed that other agencies are at risk of a similar incident. Rapid reporting to other agencies in the area is a collective responsibility.
- Direct interdependence: if one agency has the capacity to bring in a plane or ship to evacuate staff and others do not, they should meet in advance to agree on evacuation criteria and procedures.
- Indirect interdependence: the security strategies of one agency can have repercussions for others. If one agency pays bribes at checkpoints, for example, this will create problems for those that do not. If a number of agencies operate in a district and the majority of them decide to adopt armed guards, this will increase the vulnerability of the remainder, who have now become a comparatively 'soft' target. If an agency decides to suspend aid to a certain district because one of its vehicles has been stolen at gunpoint, this may affect other agencies working there.

Interagency collaboration can offer some significant advantages:

- A better alert system: agencies receive a fuller picture of actual or possible security threats or alerts in their environment, which increases the chances of avoiding an incident. This can be supported by a 'communications tree' using mobile phones, email and radio. It can also be supported by a common emergency radio channel.
- Better risk assessment: a central record of all incidents and near-misses in a given operating environment is a better basis for a risk assessment than a partial or incomplete record.
- Strategic and tactical monitoring and analysis of the operating environment and its security implications: every agency has to do this, and will normally contact others informally to obtain information. Where there is trust and confidentiality is respected it is possible to collaborate in a more structured way.
- Cost-effective extra capacity or services: rather than each agency individually carrying the costs of bringing in or hiring additional skills, specialists can be brought in on a collective basis. The costs for a training event on security can also be shared.
- Liaison and engagement with the authorities: rather than negotiating individually, agencies can potentially make a stronger and more consistent case together.
- Advocacy with donors: if the security situation deteriorates and several agencies conclude that they need extra financial resources for additional mitigating measures, they may be able to make a more effective case with donors collectively.

1.3.2 Interagency security mechanisms
Headquarters

At headquarters level, coordination between NGOs, and between NGOs and the UN, has moved forward in recent years. There are now two regional NGO interagency security fora: Interaction's Security Advisory Group (SAG), based in Washington DC and serving the US NGO community, and the European Interagency Security Forum (EISF), which is based in London and serves the European NGO community. These platforms serve as information-sharing, awareness-raising, advocacy and training forums. They are seen as valuable for encouraging and promoting good practice as well as sharing lessons learned and providing country-specific information in near to real-time. The 'Saving Lives Together' initiative provides a framework for security collaboration between the UN and NGOs (see Annex 3). Since 2007, UNHCR and OCHA have co-chaired an IASC working group on challenges to humanitarian space.[2]

---

2 V. Tennant, B. Doyle and R. Mazou, *Safeguarding Humanitarian Space: A Review of Key Challenges for UNHCR* (Geneva: UNHCR, 2010).

Field-level security mechanisms

There is no standard model for an interagency security mechanism. In practice collaborative mechanisms have taken various forms, including:

- Informal networking, for example periodic meetings or an informal network of security focal points.
- Interagency security measures, such as a shared residential guard network, sharing of field-level security focal points or security training.
- Introducing security as a theme in existing interagency working groups.
- Interagency security and safety offices, which can be independently resourced and led, or hosted by NGOs.

An interagency security mechanism may have several functions, including:

- Convening security meetings.
- Providing security alerts, cross-checking unconfirmed information and facilitating information dissemination.
- Carrying out risk assessments and pattern and trend analysis, and communicating the results in threat reports.
- Providing introductory security briefings, as well as technical assistance and advice to individual agencies, and training.
- Crisis management: providing support with contingency planning and facilitating in-extremis support; for example if an agency suffers a critical incident such as a kidnapping, the platform might be able to provide additional analysis and support through local networks.
- Liaison with governmental authorities, international and national military forces, including UN peacekeeping forces, and private security companies.

Often, an interagency platform will be hosted by a particular agency, giving it the legal identity it needs to receive and spend funds. The host agency signs contracts and assumes legal responsibility. Most such field-level security platforms operate between NGOs and tend not to include UN agencies, though information and analysis can be shared. In cases where collaboration is more formal the relationship can be more direct, particularly where UN security staff have been designated as NGO liaison points. Alternatively, under the Saving Lives Together initiative, NGOs may identify a Security Focal Point to participate in UN Security Management Teams.

Some highly principled agencies are inclined to stand outside formal security platforms, although they may share information to varying degrees. Most field-level security platforms operate between international NGOs, and it is unclear the extent to which national NGOs participate and benefit.

Examples of field-level interagency security mechanisms[3]

- The Afghanistan NGO Safety Office (ANSO). ANSO was set up in late 2002. It comprises international and national security personnel.
- The NGO Coordinating Committee in Iraq security office (NCCI). NCCI is an autonomous body which grew out of a general coordination forum for INGOs working in Iraq in 2003. In late 2004, NCCI relocated to Amman in Jordan for security reasons, along with most international aid organisations, and the security office suspended its incident tracking. As of early 2010 NCCI had built up an extensive information network among local NGOs inside the country, as well as a new security incident tracking system. Along with some international NGOs, NCCI is beginning to redeploy personnel inside Iraq.
- The Balochistan INGO Consortium-Security Management Support Project (BINGO) was created in early 2004 by agencies based in Quetta, Pakistan. The consortium used both national and international security officers. In late 2005 BINGO closed down, partly due to pressure from the Pakistani authorities and partly because INGO resources were reprioritised in the earthquake response. In 2010, in response to the emergency operations, a new country-level security coordination platform called PAKSAFE was established. PAKSAFE will initially be hosted/chaired by IRC, and will serve as the main liaison point for NGOs.
- The NGO Safety Program (NSP) in Somalia. The NSP was established by a larger Somalia NGO Consortium in late 2004. It is based in Nairobi, but has links in Somali regions. The project uses both international and national security officers.
- The Initiative ONGs Sécurité (IOS)-Haiti. IOS-Haiti was created in late 2005, and was staffed by a national security officer. The IOS closed down in 2009, but was revived in response to the earthquake in January 2010.
- The Gaza NGO Safety Office (GANSO). GANSO was established in 2008 to provide information and analysis to NGOs working in Gaza.
- Chad OASIS provides software, helps manage incident data, develops lessons learned and supports information flows between agencies working in Chad. It is currently hosted by iMMAP, and uses its specially developed mapping software. It is supported by international donors.

3 Most of these security mechanisms are hosted by an INGO and financial support is provided by international donors.

Impediments and enabling factors

The factors that can impede or facilitate interagency collaboration around security are largely the same factors that impede or facilitate aid agency collaboration in general, albeit security as a topic can raise particular sensitivities.

Table 1: Impediments and enabling factors for security collaboration

Factors that can impede security collaboration	Factors that can facilitate security collaboration
• Lack of agency commitment and support. • Differences in approaches, for example in relation to armed security. • Ineffective governance. • Lack or loss of transparency and trust, for example because sensitive information is not handled discreetly. • Suspicion and interference by the authorities. • Staff recruitment and retention problems. • Competing priorities and heavy general workloads. • Inadequate funding.	• NGO-driven and -managed, providing good buy-in. • Shared, realistic aims and objectives. • Appropriate for the situation. • Effective leadership and governance. • The right staff, capacities and resources. • Easy-to-use reporting mechanisms. • Information is treated sensitively and confidentially. • Timely, detailed analysis is provided to participants. • A deterioration in the security environment leads NGOs to question their security management. • Access to adequate and predictable security funding.

It is important to be aware that an agency could develop an over-reliance on an interagency mechanism to the extent that it replaces internal efforts to actively maintain the agency's own security management. It is important to ensure that the mechanism provides an organisation with additional capacity, but doesn't displace it.

1.4 Transferring security risks

In aid work it is common for part or all of a programme to be designed and 'owned' by one agency, but implemented by another. Working with and through other organisations or associations – whether NGOs, community-based organisations or private contractors – may be more cost-effective, or part of a deliberate strategy to strengthen local capacities. Risk transfer becomes a component of an operational security strategy when an agency consciously seeks someone else to carry out certain activities in a highly insecure context.

There is a fundamental distinction between risk transfer to national staff of the organisation (for whom that organisation has a clear legal responsibility) and risk transfer to entities that have their own legal identity. In the first case, the organisation may conclude that the risks to national and international staff are similar and that neither international nor national staff should be deployed to areas deemed too dangerous. Alternatively, based on a solid risk assessment the organisation may determine that national and international staff face different risks. An agency's risk assessment may confirm a higher risk for international staff. The decision may be to withdraw international staff, and leave national staff to manage and oversee the programme. National staff will then often have greater authority, which may increase the pressures on them and the risks they face. It is important for agencies to assess when this goes beyond the threshold of what constitutes acceptable risk. This is significantly more difficult to do if international staff (and possibly non-local nationals) are no longer present. Equally it is difficult to determine when the security situation has improved sufficiently for international and non-local national staff to return.

Entities that have their own legal identity are solely responsible for the security management of their staff and assets, as well as the mitigation of risks. In this sense the transferring organisation has no legal responsibility to provide support on security matters. This does not, however, preclude a possible ethical and moral responsibility, alongside the practical responsibility to ensure that operational and security needs are addressed so that the work can be carried out. Options for providing support to an implementing partner include:

- A joint assessment with the implementer of the security risks and the threshold of acceptable risk, so that both actors have a clear picture of what the risks are likely to be, allowing the implementing partner (and its staff) to give their informed consent. This should involve a joint periodic review of the evolving risk picture.
- A joint assessment of the capacity of the implementer to manage security risks, and if need be capacity strengthening, for example through training, the secondment of a security advisor and periodic joint reviews of security mitigation measures and critical incident management procedures.
- A sustained effort to extend appropriate medical and malicious act insurance coverage to the staff of the implementer, or at least those staff most at risk.
- An effort to transfer security capacities to the implementer in the form of material inputs (such as communications equipment and vehicles), information and analysis and training.

A process will also need to be agreed in cases where either agency believes that the threshold of acceptable risk has been reached. If the controlling agency is concerned about the potential risks to its implementing partner but cannot offer practical help to mitigate them, it might well decide not to ask its partner to undertake the work.

1.5 The host country and security management

One often overlooked aspect of security management is the role of the host country. Nominally, state authorities are responsible for the security of their citizens and any other (law-abiding) persons passing through or residing in their national territory. In contexts of war, this protection is enshrined in the Geneva Conventions and the principles of International Humanitarian Law (IHL). States have a duty to disseminate IHL, train military and other personnel in how to apply it and deal with individuals suspected of violations. A number of other key conventions and frameworks, primarily driven by the UN, seek to outline the security situation for aid workers and state responsibilities in this area.

Key conventions, frameworks and resolutions on aid worker security

- Convention on the Safety of United Nations and Associated Personnel (1994)
- Security Council Presidential Statement on the Protection of UN Personnel in Conflict Zones (2000)
- Safety and Security of United National Personnel – Report of the Secretary General (October 2000)
- Security Council Resolution 1502, which condemns all forms of violence against those participating in humanitarian operations and urges states to ensure that crimes against such personnel do not go unpunished (2003)
- General Assembly Resolution 59/211 on the safety and security of humanitarian personnel and the protection of UN personnel (2004)
- General Assembly Optional Protocol 60/123 (2006)

The relationship between aid agencies and the state can be a sensitive one, particularly where the state is a belligerent in a conflict. For the most part, agencies do not want the state to provide protection for humanitarian workers directly; rather, they prefer to distinguish between the provision of ambient security (the general security environment in which humanitarian work takes place) and proximate security (such as travel escorts and the protection of property). Overly protective state arrangements for aid agencies can increase insecurity due to perceptions of partiality, and can make it more difficult for agencies to respond impartially to needs by making access dependent on state police or military escorts. Bear in mind that aid agencies do not have to accept armed protection from the authorities, may feel that the local police are not able or willing to act against criminal gangs, and may feel reluctant to involve the authorities in the resolution of a kidnap or hostage situation. Other key issues to be aware of include:

- Context analysis may be perceived as an unduly political activity.
- Security assessments and threat monitoring may be perceived as implying that the authorities cannot maintain law and order. More problematically, such assessments may be perceived as intelligence gathering.
- Government forces engaged in battlefield operations can create security risks for aid agencies.
- The authorities may refuse an aid agency permission to deploy tele-communications equipment, especially radios, which the agency considers essential for its security management.
- Poorly equipped and badly paid governmental security forces may resent aid agencies for their relative wealth and may seek to requisition or loot their assets.
- The decision to evacuate staff, especially international staff, has political connotations, and may cause the authorities concern.

Section 2
Strategic and operational approaches to security management

Chapter 2
Risk assessment

Proper assessment of risk is a critical component of good security management, and an area where aid organisations have advanced significantly in recent years. Current thinking on good practice holds that organisations should conduct a security risk assessment (SRA) before starting operations in a new location, and that this should inform programme design from the very beginning. The goal of the exercise is to help determine the level of risk in undertaking a programme, and weigh this risk against the benefits the programme brings to the population being helped. The SRA is not something to be completed and put on the shelf, but should be treated as a living document that is frequently revisited and revised as the situation changes. The SRA, and the resulting risk–benefit analysis, will therefore change along with any major changes in the operating context (political, economic, demographic), when programmes begin, end or expand into new areas, or before special events.

This chapter provides guidance on risk assessment, based on the latest thinking in the sector. It draws on a number of models currently in use, in particular the UN SRA, which has been adopted (and adapted) by major operational NGOs.

2.1 The importance of systematic risk assessment

Risk assessment needs to be done in a structured and disciplined manner because, as human beings, we are normally inclined to be subjective. That subjectivity can create a distorted picture reflecting our unconscious bias. Psychological research has shown that human beings:

- Exaggerate spectacular but rare risks, while downplaying more frequent, more common risks.
- React intensely to immediate threats and under-react to long-term threats.
- React quickly to sudden, dramatic changes, whilst being slow to adapt to changes that occur slowly and over time (the 'frog-in-the-pot' syndrome).
- Have trouble estimating the risk in unfamiliar situations and experiences.

- Overestimate risks that continue to be talked about, and underestimate risks that are so common that they hardly get attention (for instance car accidents).
- Underestimate the risks they are willing to take, and overestimate the risks in situations they cannot control.
- Overestimate the risks that affect their own community, and underestimate the risks that affect others.

The purpose of this manual is to help field practitioners to manage risks. Managing risks starts with an attempt at a disciplined and reasoned assessment. Gut feeling is not good enough. At the same time, risk assessment should not become rarefied as the exclusive, specialised domain of the manager responsible. That person must ensure that the system is inclusive, eliciting perspectives and information from all staff, in order to create a common understanding of the risk and a sense of shared responsibility for the necessary security measures.

2.2 Key definitions

2.2.1 Understanding the concept of risk

Risk is a measure of vulnerability to threats in the environment. In other words, risk is about the potential for harm: the likelihood of something harmful happening, and the extent of that harm if it does. Fundamental concepts here are 'threat', 'vulnerability', 'risk' and 'risk mitigation/reduction'. In the context of security management, a *threat* is anything that can cause harm or loss, while *vulnerability* refers to the *likelihood* or *probability* of being confronted with a threat, and the *consequences* or *impact* if and when that happens. The combination of threat and vulnerability to that threat constitutes *risk*.

Risk mitigation or *risk reduction* measures are actions to reduce the risk. There are basically three ways of doing this, none of which is mutually exclusive:

- Removing or diminishing the threat itself.
- Reducing exposure to the threat.
- Taking measures to ensure that, when confronted with the threat, the impact will be limited.

Identifying the threats that may be faced, and vulnerabilities to them, calls for a full appreciation of the environment in which the agency is working, and what can be achieved there. The following sections cover the basic components of this analytical process:

1. Contextual analysis, as essential background for understanding potential threats.
2. Programme analysis, to clarify the priority objectives of the organisation in the location and determine its capacities.
3. Threat analysis, to identify and understand those who could cause the organisation or its programmes harm.
4. Vulnerability analysis, to understand the organisation's exposure to threats, points of weakness and the ways in which the organisation may be affected.

All of this information is used to produce a risk analysis, which is designed to enable the organisation to determine whether the level of risk in a given environment is acceptable. The assessment process described in this chapter culminates in a matrix which plots risks according to their likelihood and impact; an example is given below.

Table 2: Risk analysis

		Impact				
		Negligible	Minor	Moderate	Severe	Critical
Likelihood	**Very likely**	Low	Medium	High	Very high	Very high
	Likely	Low	Medium	High	High	Very high
	Moderately likely	Very low	Low	Medium	High	High
	Unlikely	Very low	Low	Low	Medium	Medium
	Very unlikely	Very low	Very low	Very low	Low	Low

Source: InterAction, Security Risk Management: NGO Approach 2010.

Risk assessment models vary in complexity and level of detail from agency to agency, and there is no one-size-fits-all. This section aims to explain the basic building blocks and present tools that have been found useful by security managers and field staff in aid organisations. The appropriate risk assessment model for your agency is that which you determine can be both understood and consistently employed by your staff in the field, and which will add value to their security management process.

2.3 Context analysis: know where you are

Good security management, like good programming, requires a solid understanding of the local environment and of the role – both actual and perceived – that aid agencies play in it. Ideally, the organisation will already seek a deep contextual knowledge base for every setting for the benefit of programming, but if not, security management can be a legitimate impetus for doing this. Such an understanding can contribute greatly to an organisation's ability to anticipate threats.

Developing and maintaining in-depth knowledge of the context has practical implications. For example, it means investing staff time in initial analysis and ongoing monitoring, and building this into briefings for newcomers and handovers to successors. Lack of time during an acute emergency and continuous staff turnover are constraints to be overcome, not excuses. In practice, the development of contextual knowledge is an ongoing and iterative process, but in this exposition it is presented in steps. (Note that most operational risk assessment models omit the deep contextual knowledge-building that is suggested here, and begin with the second step, programme analysis/assessment. However, it is included in this volume as an example of good practice, albeit arguably only achievable over an extended period of time in a given setting.)

Investing in good context analysis does not mean becoming 'politicised' or compromising the principle of neutrality that underpins the humanitarian enterprise. The critical issue is not an agency's self-proclaimed 'neutrality', but how its actions and words are perceived by the actors that matter. If agencies want to be perceived as neutral, they need to be savvy and understand the interests, concerns and perceptions of the many actors in their operating environment – and actively and constantly manage their own position and image.

2.3.1 General context analysis

General context analysis begins with a basic knowledge of the origins of the modern state and its history, including colonial legacies, if any; its relations with key neighbours and great power states; and the overall domestic political situation, including the nature of the government, the party political situation, the conduct of elections and the way in which average people interact with and experience government in their lives. Other issues to consider include:

- Any social struggles between groups or regions over resources, territory or control of government, or discrimination or exclusion grievances.
- Identity groups (based on religion, caste, class or ethnicity, for instance), and how ideology, myths and symbols have been used to mobilise these groups.

- Religion and social and political ideology: key beliefs, symbols and areas of sensitivity and respect.
- The traditional social structures used to manage conflict and uphold norms, and whether they are they still functional or influential.
- Social norms and codes governing public behaviour, dress and the interaction between men and women.

2.3.2 Detailed conflict and violence analysis

Once the 'big picture' is in place, a more detailed conflict and violence analysis will help to illuminate motivations and sources of threat. That said, the roots of a conflict can often appear baffling to foreigners, and in any case understanding how a conflict first began does not always fully explain what is happening today. Conflict analysis must also locate other, more immediate issues. Thus, the root cause of the Palestinian struggle in the occupied territories does not explain what has driven the violent confrontation between Hamas and Fatah in recent years. Sometimes, multiple conflicts are interwoven. Tensions and outbreaks of violence in a city like Karachi in Pakistan can turn on Shia–Sunni dynamics, tensions between autochthonous and 'immigrant' (i.e. those who came during Partition) city dwellers, the arms and drugs trade, Pakistani national politics or radical Islam. Any and all of these can be a source of threat. Good conflict analysis does not focus just on where violence is visible. Violence is preceded by tensions that may be less visible: the 'deep divisions' and 'fault lines' in a society. These too must be explored and understood.

Analysing violence in Algeria

Aid agencies responding to flooding or an earthquake in Algeria, or which have an office in the country, would do well to understand the complex nature of social and political violence. One of the obvious critical episodes in Algeria is the violent civil war (1991–2002) between the Western-backed state and Islamist insurgents following the Islamists' victory in local elections in 1990. The conflict, which left large numbers of Algerians dead, also included attacks on Western targets. Yet there are other important chapters to political violence in Algeria. These include the brutal war between the French and the Algerian independence movement, and the treatment of 'collaborators' at the hands of the Algerian state once independence had been secured. Another aspect relates to the recent emergence in Algeria of Al-Qaeda's wing in North Africa, which has its roots in the Algerian civil war but which is also connected to global radical Islamist networks. Al-Qaeda claimed responsibility for the bombing of the UN office in Algiers in December 2007.

Understanding the nature and structure of violence helps in anticipating where it might erupt, how intense it might be and the likelihood that aid workers will be caught up in it. This is not, however, an exact science. In 'traditional' conflict contexts where the lines of battle are clear, such as Ethiopia–Eritrea, Angola and the Balkans, threats are easier to anticipate than in a guerrilla insurgency: while the risk of an unexpected ambush, a hit-and-run attack, a mine planted on a road or a massacre of civilians exists in both cases, it is likely to be easier to judge and anticipate in the former than the latter. The point is to ask questions that will lead to a better understanding of the particular context in question, going beyond a generalised impression of violence as always and everywhere the same.

One key question is whether the violence is random and decentralised, or organised and targeted. Who does it target and why? Does it tend to be perpetrated by organised armed groups, small groupings or single individuals, or mobs? Is it motivated by politics or criminal/economic gain or both? Has the intensity or lethality of violence increased? Raiding (of homes and offices) and road banditry are two different types of threat, and each can involve varying levels of violence, ranging from little or none to murder. In Darfur, many aid organisations noticed an increase in the severity of violence against their drivers by bandits as the conflict wore on, whereas the majority of incidents had previously left the victims unharmed physically.

In the Balkans, rape was used as a weapon of ethnic cleansing to demoralise the opponent. In general, international staffers were at less risk than local staff. By contrast, in Sierra Leone rape was widespread, less as a tactic of war and more to subjugate and terrorise civilian communities and to brutalise the (child) soldiers committing it. In such a setting international staff will be just as much at risk as national staff, particularly if there is little regard for international political (Western) opinion. Although few in the reported number of incidents, violent sexual assault against aid workers in eastern DRC and Darfur indicated a deliberate targeting/terrorising of the international aid community.

Violence is not always linked to conflict. For example, although Guatemala is no longer in active conflict, the homicide rate is higher than during the civil war, and violence, most of it linked to crime, is widespread. Research general crime patterns in the setting and determine what the principal criminal threats are (kidnapping, rape, armed robbery, car-jacking). In some places there can be a seasonality to violence. In Chad, for instance, major attacks tend not to be launched during the rainy season. Paradoxically, the period just after the end of a conflict could be particularly difficult to manage as some former fighters may be left without a source of income.

2.3.3 Actor analysis

Actor analysis focuses on the principal actors/groups potentially affecting security. It can proceed in two steps: first, list all the relevant actors, then visualise their relationships with each other. This is an exploratory exercise. It should be ongoing and will certainly initially raise more questions than it yields answers. The relevant actors will include the various armed groups fighting each other, and the national and international participants formally trying to mitigate and mediate the conflict. For each of these actors list their stated goals (if known). National or local actors could also include the urban middle class, radical student groups, trade unions, large landowners, militant religious or nationalist radicals, the local media, local NGOs and traditional leaders. Potentially relevant regional and international actors might be neighbouring powers, intergovernmental organisations, transnational corporations, diplomats and human rights and humanitarian organisations, as well as diaspora groups.

To illustrate the interactions between the various actors, lines can be drawn between them to represent different types of relationships – to show, for instance, who funds whom, which groups are hostile to each other and who is competing for territory in a particular region. Again, while the answers may not be known, the first step is to ask pertinent questions. Do not be surprised if different people give different interpretations of these relationships. Relationships are complex, and different dimensions will come to the fore at different times.

As the analysis deepens it may become apparent that groups of allies, or single actors, are not as monolithic or homogeneous as they first appeared. There may be factionalism and power struggles within the government or within a resistance movement; different UN organisations and NGOs may have different opinions and perspectives; international political actors may be jostling with each other to take the lead in the conflict management process. The more that can be known about where an organisation or individual stands within what appears to be a common interest group, the more nuanced the relationship that can be cultivated. This exercise will also provide a handy tool for briefing newcomers and successors.

2.3.4 Understanding armed groups

Understanding armed groups is a difficult and highly sensitive subject. It is also vital to understanding how and why your presence and programmes might be manipulated or threatened. Again, insights may come only gradually. Look at:

- The ideology of a movement/organisation. Understanding something of the worldview of the key actors in the conflict will help in discussions and negotiations, and perhaps also in reading and interpreting public statements and communications that may include an implicit 'warning' to the agency and its activities. What do they claim as the reasons and justification for their struggle, and how do aid agencies and international political actors appear in that perspective? What symbols and myths do they use?

- The organisation and structure of command and control. Try to determine how a certain group is organised: whether there is a clear hierarchy, who the leaders are and how centralised decision-making is. Who are the appropriate individuals to negotiate with, and what sort of practical outcomes can be expected from a formal agreement with them?
- The 'social contract' between an armed group and the civilian population. The more abusive armed groups are against civilians under their control, the more difficult and dangerous it is likely to be for the aid agency.

Finally, if an aid agency's presence and programmes are perceived as threatening to or undermining the control of an armed group over a civilian population, they may well seek to intimidate that agency or retaliate against it.

2.3.5 The resource base and the war economy

Being present in an area can contribute to, or threaten, the resource base of an armed group. In addition to weapons and ammunition, armed groups need food, medicine, transport and other supplies, and money to pursue their objectives. Many modern conflicts have been underwritten and sustained by 'war economies', including the illegal and quasi-legal trade in weapons, drugs, diamonds, oil, minerals and other materials. An aid agency may be threatened with a direct attack to seize its assets, or may face a situation where beneficiaries and their local communities are under threat by the armed group for control over local resources. Where there are few alternative resources aid agencies assume a greater importance in the war economy; this will make them more vulnerable. If their presence or activities take place in a sensitive area where natural resources that support the war economy are exploited, or along export/import routes, they could be perceived as a hindrance or an undesirable witness. Aid programmes may also complicate the recruitment drive directly, for example by introducing income generating programmes for ex-fighters, or indirectly, for example by supporting schooling and agricultural rehabilitation and thereby offering alternative 'livelihoods' to young males.

2.3.6 The history of aid interventions in the country

Many contexts have had a long history of international aid work. Afghans may have known violence and war for 30 years, and many have been experiencing international aid for a good 25 years, in Afghanistan and in refugee camps in Pakistan and Iran. People in Haiti have seen repeated international interventions to stabilise the country and get it politically and economically on track. And yet many Afghans and Haitians would complain that they remain as poor as ever. Many populations will acknowledge that, at one time or another, they have received some tangible benefit, but are sceptical if not cynical about the longer-term effectiveness of aid and the motives of aid organisations. In addition, local political elites may resent the predominance of an 'international community' that pays lip-service to national ownership and national priorities, but which can also at times feel more like a colonising power. The history of aid and how historically it has been perceived by the beneficiaries and host community is thus another important consideration, as is the past practice of individual aid organisations in the country or locality in question. Some organisations have been operating in the same settings for decades, so this history will be vital to understanding the context and for programme analysis, covered in the next section.

2.4 Programme analysis: know who you are and what you want to do

A general appreciation of security risks should factor into the decision to initiate or continue programme work in a given environment. The next critical considerations are mission and mandate, specific programming priorities and capacity to manage the security risks. The following subsections cover the essential why, where and what components of programme analysis.

2.4.1 Mission and mandate

There is some confusion about the distinction between 'mandate' and 'mission'. Non-governmental organisations typically have a self-ascribed purpose reflecting the underlying values of the organisation and its raison d'être. We can call this the 'organisational mission', often reflected in a 'mission statement'. A mandate differs from a mission in that it is given by someone else. Multilateral entities such as the UN or the Organisation for Security and Cooperation in Europe (OSCE) have a mandate from their member states. That mandate can be quite specific: UNHCR, for instance, has a mandate to work for refugees, and the Office of the High Commissioner for Human Rights (OHCHR) has a mandate to work on human rights. Clarifying this is not just a distraction: if an organisation has a mandate, the expectation that it must be present in a particular place is stronger; for agencies with a self-ascribed mission, the choice of staying away from a difficult and dangerous situation is more squarely in their hands. Where a significant refugee population exists, UNHCR *must* be present; where there are gross violations of human rights, OHCHR *must* pay attention to it; where there are significant numbers of children in need, UNICEF *has* to get involved in some way.

How agencies understand their mandate or organisational mission has an influence on their general tolerance for risk. When a situation heats up, some actors may flock there – the ICRC, MSF, UNHCR, journalists and human rights defenders, for instance. Others whose purpose is essentially developmental and based on working through governmental structures may suspend operations or withdraw. Some UN agencies and many of the large NGOs undertake aid programming in both humanitarian and development contexts. These organisations will typically shift modes of programming when an emergency strikes or instability grows, often necessitating a shift in operations and staffing profiles to bring in the appropriate skill sets. Missions and mandates may also create vulnerabilities.

The term 'mission' is also used in a more precise sense to describe what agencies want to achieve in a particular context. We can call this the 'field mission'. This too provides some criteria on what to do: if the mission is to provide emergency health services in a conflict zone or vocational training in an unstable area, agencies may decide to suspend operations or withdraw when the circumstances become such that they can no longer fulfil their mission: too much medicine and health equipment is being looted, or the situation has deteriorated to a point where the jobs for which the agency is offering training can no longer be pursued.

2.4.2 Objectives

From a security point of view, an agency may or may not have the option of asking whether it needs to enter or remain in a dangerous environment. Choosing to be in a danger zone entails asking how the risks incurred relate to what the agency wants to do. Who goes and who stays, and where existing resources should be directed, should be decided based on the urgency and severity of humanitarian needs, balanced against the duty of care to keep staff secure. If the intended mission is neither life-saving nor seeking to address acute suffering, it is reasonable to think hard about whether it is worth continuing to operate in conditions of extreme insecurity. Assess the criticality of programmes in terms of the aid being provided. Is the work actually saving lives, or supporting wellbeing? What would be the consequences for the direct beneficiaries if it were suspended? What would be the consequences for other organisations (e.g. other NGOs, local health facilities) that rely on this programming? These questions are also relevant for the decision to enter a country, re-enter after an evacuation or expand geographically (and thematically) within a country.

2.4.3 Location

Where will programmes be undertaken? It is vital to be clear about the geographic radius of the operational presence. Group activities by their geographic location, being sure to consider all facilities supported or visited by staff, and residences and routes used. Additionally, it is important to note what other aid agencies (and how many, with rough staff sizes) and other international and national actors are present and operating in the same environment, and what types of programmes they are running there.

2.4.4 Capacities

A core set of capacities is relevant for security risk management, notably financial resources, key competencies and staff and management time.

- *Financial resources.* Managing security risks is not a cost-free enterprise. The financial costs associated with effective security management will have to be budgeted for adequately. Planners will also have to be confident that they will be able to mobilise the necessary funds when needed.
- *Competencies.* While it is possible to contract out for specific competencies in the form of consultants, when it comes to security management it is important to develop some core competencies in-house. A distinction has to be made between awareness and knowledge on the one hand and real, experience-based skills on the other. Giving management responsibilities to someone who has awareness but only limited knowledge and no real hands-on experience is irresponsible in a high-risk environment. Having a low ratio of experienced staff to inexperienced staff in a high-risk environment is also not a good idea – and would certainly suggest a need to pay attention to staff development.
- *Staff and management time.* Even if the money and staff are available, this will mean little unless people are also going to devote time to security risk management as a key responsibility built into their job description. Out-sourcing security planning to a consultant is no substitute for taking the time to develop and maintain an effective security strategy and plans.

2.4.5 Stay – or go?

The above considerations can be summarised in a simple question sheet:

- Does the agency's 'mandate' or 'organisational mission' suggest that it should be operating in this environment?
- By being present and operational, will programmes be meeting critical human needs?

- If it is necessary and appropriate for the agency to be there, does it have the capacities (financial and competencies) to manage the security risks?
- If not, can these be developed or brought in quickly enough?
- Once financial and human resources are in place, can enough staff and management time be devoted to managing security risks?

If anywhere along this question sheet the answer is 'no', think seriously before deciding to go ahead, at least until the situation improves or adequate capacities (money, competent people and time) are available to manage the risks. There are valid alternatives to a physical programming presence, including channelling available funding or other resources through organisations that are better placed to securely operate in the setting in question.

2.4.6 Drivers for decision-making

All of the above may seem like simple common sense, yet plenty of aid organisations initiate programmes in high-risk environments without the money and competencies they need (where there is significant human need, agencies are likely to have a higher tolerance for risk). And then there are agencies that have the money and competencies in-house, but other priorities constantly take attention away from the management of security risks. The reality is that there are other considerations that – rightly or wrongly – can take precedence in a situation of high security risks and low risk management capacities. But another frequent and influential factor in decision-making is financial opportunity. Agencies go somewhere because there is need, but also because there is money available. Ignoring risks because of financial opportunity may be justified from the perspective of organisational survival and growth, but is it responsible towards staff and colleagues, especially if the needs are not that acute? An honest appraisal of an organisation's motives would necessitate adding a final question to the checklist above:

- Is the organisation being unduly influenced by donor pressure or financial incentives to operate in the setting?

It may help in this exercise to use a programme analysis matrix, such as the sample one set out at right, used by the NGO World Vision International.

2.5 Threat assessment

So far we have examined the operational context – the general background, the nature and level of violence and the relevant actors involved – and clarified mission and priority objectives in that context and capacities to

Table 3: Programme Analysis Matrix

Programme description	Location	Activity	Timeframe	Positive impacts	Negative impacts
	• Where are we working? • What threats are present or could evolve? • Humanitarian space: shrinking or stable?	• Criticality • Relevance • Urgency • Needs • Methods of delivery	• Current and future operations • How long have we been there?	• Enhances credibility and acceptance? • Reduces risk by stabilising community? • Meets community needs?	• Perceived to only benefit some parts of the community? • Requires staff to travel to 'high-risk' areas? • Funding sources

Source: World Vision International. (Note: this material is used with the permission of World Vision International and any reproduction outside this publication (GPR) requires the express permission of World Vision International.)

manage security. The next step is to look specifically at the threats that the organisation and its programmes are likely to face, and its vulnerabilities. Threats are understood as *external* factors and events that can cause harm, while vulnerabilities are more *internal*, and can stem from the way an organisation is perceived, how it operates, the people it hires and its procedures and facilities.

Threats can be divided into two broad categories: general and specific. Contextual analysis provides an idea of general threats, such as crime, terror attacks and combat or military activity. Beyond this there may be specific threats. Examples of specific threat scenarios are given below.

- Crime
  - Car-jacking
  - Road banditry
  - Street robberies/mugging
  - Armed raids/robberies
  - Kidnapping

- Terror attack
  - Roadside improvised explosive devices (IEDs)
  - Car/truck bombs
  - Suicide bombers in vehicles
  - Bombings or gun attacks in public places
  - Grenade attack into compound
  - Hostage-taking

- Combat/military activity
  - Shelling
  - Infantry crossfire
  - Landmines

Some threats may be directed against a specific agency (or against aid agencies in general), and some may be indirect; staff may not be directly targeted in an attack on a government facility or UN office, but they may still be injured if they happen to be present when the attack takes place. When assessing a potential threat from a human source (adversary), determine whether they display the following three key characteristics:

- History – a past incidence or pattern of attacks on similar organisations.
- Intent – specific threats, a demonstrated intention or mindset to attack.
- Capability – the wherewithal to carry out an attack.

2.5.1 Sources of information and analysis

A threat assessment will only be as good as the information it is based on. This information can come from a range of sources, not all of them necessarily reliable.

Incident trending and analysis from a comprehensive monitoring of security incidents (your own agency's and others') in the location can play a vital role in identifying threats and determining patterns of violence and the likelihood of attack (see Chapter 5). A second source includes the UN and NGO security coordination platforms: UN country offices, UN Department of Safety and Security (UNDSS) field officers and NGO field security consortia, where they exist, as well as international peacekeepers. The field offices of human rights organisations may also monitor incidents involving aid workers.

Local officials and the authorities should also be consulted. These include government officials, the local head of the police, embassy staff, army commanders, commanders of armed groups and village leaders/elders. Some of these sources may be well-informed and willing to share what they know, while others may be poorly informed or will give a deliberately distorted picture. This is also an opportunity to inform others about the agency and what its aims and roles are.

Local intelligentsia – academics, journalists, teachers, missionaries, social activists, religious leaders, political activists – tend to be consulted by human rights and conflict-resolution organisations more than humanitarian agencies, but they may have useful things to say. Some may be among the agency's own staff. Again, some will be better informed and will give a more insightful and objective analysis than others, and will probably know more about the broader context than about more precise security risks. In some areas, local networks, such as taxi drivers, traders and merchants, banks and insurance companies, may monitor security conditions in their neighbourhood, and are likely to have similar concerns about risk and security. Locally recruited staff may know of such networks, or may know individuals who are well-connected and able to obtain a good current assessment of particular areas.

The local and international media are another important resource. The international press, especially the websites of major outlets, sometimes present analysis of security incidents over time, using graphs and maps. The local media can be reliable or sensationalist, but finding out whether an incident has been correctly reported is relatively straightforward, whatever further embellishment may occur. Monitoring the local-language media is very useful because it may give a better sense of what local people are likely to hear and read than local media that use an international language and therefore reach only a small part of the population. Finally, international security corporations provide analysis of patterns and trends in violence. This can be helpful for macro analysis, though this tends not to give the kind of day-to-day detail agencies in the field require.

2.5.2 Information and rumours

Rumours are something of a special category of information source. A practical problem with rumours is knowing whether to trust them or not. With any piece of privately acquired information, the question needs to be broken down into two parts:

- Is the source of the information reliable?
- Is the information valid?

Table 4: Assessing information sources

Reliability of the source	Validity of the information
• Knowledgeable with direct access to information • Knowledgeable but no direct access to information • Usually reliable • Source is not usually reliable • Don't know	1. Suggested by several independent sources 2. Very likely 3. Likely 4. Not likely 5. Probably wrong 6. Don't know

Source: InterAction Security Action Group.

Over time, and probably with the help of reliable local people, it is possible to learn to appreciate both. Do not forget to brief successors on who is a reliable source and who is not to be trusted. The grid on p. 41 is a useful way of assessing the reliability of information that is 'heard about' rather than directly experienced or witnessed.

2.6 Vulnerability assessment

Vulnerabilities are factors that increase an organisation's exposure to threats, or make severe outcomes more likely. Specific examples may include:

- Having a very visible presence in a high-crime area.
- Having valuable assets.
- Having no perimeter wall or fence.
- Having multiple access points to the building/compound.
- Communications difficulties.
- Lack of experienced personnel.
- Lack of support from hostile or uncooperative authorities.
- Transporting staff, goods or cash on a regular basis.
- Not varying travel routes.

Key questions include:

- *People.* Who in the organisation is likely to be exposed to threats or targeted, when and where? A differentiated analysis (explained in Chapter 6 on 'People in security management') will be necessary for this analysis. Key here is the concept of differentiated risk. Different types of staff will face different threats and hence different levels of risk (expatriates; nationals/locals of different political, religious or ethnic affiliations; males; females; different positions in the organisation).
- *Places.* Does the location of operations (and movements between them) increase exposure to threats?
- *Assets.* What assets are likely to be vulnerable, and where? Assets are typically vulnerable to theft, looting, damage or destruction (by natural disasters, acts of war, criminal acts and acts of terror). Consider different locations where assets may be targeted: in the office, in residences, in warehouses, while being moved (the physical movement of cash, vehicles on the road, supplies on the road, distribution points).

The flip-side of vulnerabilities, of course, is strengths. These are factors that reduce exposure to threats or mitigate the outcomes. It is useful to detail these as well as part of the risk assessment. For instance, are staff well-trained and security-conscious? Are security issues discussed on a regular basis? Has the organisation had a longstanding presence in the area, and does it have strong local networks to keep it apprised of changes in conditions?

The following aspects of an agency's work may be sources of vulnerability.

2.6.1 Presence/location

The location of offices, main movement routes and/or main programme activities can generate a risk, simply because they put the agency in or near a (potential) danger zone. Consider:

- Do programmes put staff in the path of military or insurgency and counter-insurgency operations? Are operations too close to potential political or military targets? Can entry and exit routes be affected?
- Is the organisation operating in refugee camps that are also serving as rear bases for insurgents?
- Are programmes taking place in areas that are important to the war or illicit economy or the illegal trade (e.g. illegal logging) that is part of it?
- Are programme activities taking place in high-crime areas (e.g. opium or cocaine cultivation areas), or in transit routes used by drug- or people-traffickers?
- If sectarian violence is a problem, are offices or programme activities close to a place that has high social and symbolic value for an identity group and therefore could become a target?

2.6.2 Identity, presence and programming

Security vulnerabilities can also arise from the substance of missions and mandates, as well as from programmes and how they are implemented. These 'inherent' vulnerabilities are often harder to recognise. Some aspects of this question are given below.

- *Mission/mandate.* An organisation may face threats due to a lack of acceptance of its mission or mandate, particularly if its religious or social-political values are seen as extraneous to the act of providing aid to needy people. Examples include a Christian NGO suspected of proselytizing in a Muslim country, or an organisation mandated by a government to pursue aid objectives associated with supporting specific political outcomes.
- *Perceived identity.* How an organisation is perceived can be enough to create suspicion and even hostility. The founder and director of a national NGO or civil society association can be perceived as having personal political ambitions, or can be an outspoken critic of others in society,

prompting animosity towards the national agency as a whole. In fact, *any* religious identification – or conversely an avowedly secular stance – can have negative connotations in certain settings.

- *Controversial programmes.* Are programmes potentially controversial, and if so why and for whom? Do they touch on a source of conflict, such as the reconstruction of houses in ethnically cleansed towns (the Balkans), agricultural rehabilitation where there are disputes about land ownership (north Iraq), or water supply in water-scarce environments (the Sahel or Somalia)? Alternatively, can programmes become a new source of conflict in an already contested environment, for instance a proposal to build a health centre on territory controlled by one group or authority, which will then be contested by a rival? Does the programme challenge social and cultural norms or religious principles, for instance programmes to empower women, schooling for girls and the expansion of secular education? How can legitimacy for this type of programme be gained?

2.6.3 Impact on the local or wider political economy

It may be the case that an organisation's work influences the balance of power between different contesting parties, so that those who fear they might be 'losers' become a source of threat. For example:

- Restocking the herds of pastoralists can be contested by agriculturalists who resent animals invading their fields.
- Providing storage facilities and up-to-date market information in isolated rural environments can be contested by the middle-men who control the flow of information and monopolise warehousing.
- Reorganising a distribution system so that goods are handed out directly to the intended beneficiaries may cut out the camp committee, the local 'commander' or the village council, removing opportunities for patronage.
- If human rights abuses and atrocities are committed, the organisation could be seen as an undesirable witness by the perpetrators.
- The very presence of international agencies may be a factor of stability, and may go against the interests of those who benefit from ongoing instability. Programmes that specifically intend to contribute to peace-building and state-building can give rise to antagonism.
- The source of funding for aid programming in a given environment can be enough to generate distrust.

2.6.4 Impartiality in the allocation of limited resources

Most international aid agencies embrace the concept of impartiality in the allocation of assistance. This means that resources should be allocated on the basis of need alone, and not according to political or other considerations. In practice this is seldom the case, and other factors, such as access, visibility and cost-effectiveness, all play a role in allocation decisions. Resources are also limited, whereas needs often are not. Under these conditions, perceived bias and partiality in favour of one group over another can lead to resentment. One way of mitigating this risk is to make plain the basis on which aid is allocated, and the practical constraints imposed by limited resources. It might also be a good idea to ask beneficiary communities themselves what criteria they would use.

A key consideration here is understanding who is being excluded or bypassed, and how they might react. It is generally accepted that agencies cannot focus all their aid on refugee populations at the expense of host communities, for instance. Other groups of concern may include people living along transit routes or in base towns, who may well come to resent being excluded from assistance or the employment opportunities the aid enterprise creates. Likewise, an agency that runs its own logistics operation may come into competition with local transport companies or deprive them of business.

2.6.5 Transparency and accountability of the intermediary

Agencies that implement programmes through an intermediary (a contractor or local partner) may experience disputes with them, or may be held responsible for their acts and omissions. Clear expectations from the outset can help to avoid problems or manage them as they arise, and prevent them from escalating into violence. The clear allocation of tasks and responsibilities will also reduce the risk of being challenged and perhaps threatened because of the actions and omissions of collaborators. Discuss in advance, and perhaps in an open forum with sufficient 'witnesses', what standards of transparency and accountability are expected, and what procedures will be followed if these are not met and/or malpractice or corruption is identified.

2.6.6 Provoking anger and resentment

Besides perceived bias and partiality, other common causes of anger and resentment include:

- Assessment and inquiry fatigue: yet another agency assessment mission asking the same questions, with no tangible programmes to show for them, or another new agency staff member asking the same questions that have already been answered for three of his predecessors.
- Unaddressed offences: for example, an agency vehicle hits and kills a local villager's cow, but does not stop to sort the matter out.
- Real or perceived broken promises: about a project that never materialised, or did so more slowly or on a smaller scale than expected.

- Simple poor programming – incompetence, waste, unmet objectives.
- 'Lavish' lifestyles: staff frequenting bars, clubs or restaurants that are out of reach for most of the population.

Note that other people often fail to make distinctions between aid agencies, so that one agency may experience a problem created by another.

2.7 Risk analysis

Risk is a combination of threats and vulnerability. Assessing risks essentially means ranking threats according to severity on the basis of their *impact* and *likelihood*. To do this systematically, following the steps below can help – though this is not a strictly scientific formula, but rather is intended to bring some structure and discipline to the way the analysis proceeds.

2.7.1 Impacts

It is useful to think about direct and indirect impacts.

Direct impacts:

- For staff/people (which includes families and friends): temporary or permanent physical injury, temporary or longer-term psychological damage, death.
- For organisations: loss of or damage to assets, operational inefficiency, loss of programme quality or outright suspension; loss of reputation; loss of funding.
- To the programme and its beneficiaries: reduced programme quality, temporary suspension of the programme, forced termination of the programme.

There are also longer-term indirect costs to the organisation. These could include:

- Cost of medical treatment and psychological support.
- Legal costs.
- Higher insurance premiums.
- Loss of staff morale; possible loss of staff trust in management, perhaps leading to higher staff turnover.
- Damage to the agency's reputation, with possible consequences for fundraising.

There should be a shared understanding within the organisation of the severity level of potential impacts. To do this, list them and rank them from negligible (for instance a petty theft) to critical (an armed attack on the compound in which staff are killed).

Table 5: Assessing potential impacts

	Expected impact on agency activities		
	Operations	Personnel	Assets
Negligible	Minor disruptions	No injuries	No damage
Minor	Limited delays	Some minor injuries/ possible stress	Possible damage or loss
Moderate	Delays	Non-life-threatening injuries/high stress	Some loss
Severe	Severe disruption	Severe injuries	Significant loss
Critical	Cancellation of activities	Death and severe injuries	Major or total loss

Source: InterAction Security Risk Management: NGO Approach 2010.

2.7.2 Likelihood

Likelihood analysis helps to prioritise potential threats, from what is possible to what is probable. To a large degree this is a judgement call based on the experience of the decision-makers, but the more information the threat assessment provides (including statistical information on incident trends), the better equipped that decision-maker will be. As covered in the section on threat assessment (see section 2.5), it is important to consider whether a particular adversary has demonstrated a history, intent and capability in regard to a particular threat. If they have, the event can be considered likely.

The following table shows categories that can help rank the likelihood of different events.

Table 6: Categorising the likelihood of events

Descriptor	'Likelihood' definitions
Unlikely	The event is considered as not having a realistic probability of occurring
Moderately likely	The event is considered as having a reasonable probability of occurring
Likely	The event is considered as having a high probability of occurring
Very Likely	The event is considered as having a very high probability of occurring
Certain/Imminent	The event will occur and is imminent

Source: World Vision International. (Note: this material is used with the permission of World Vision International and any reproduction outside this publication (GPR) requires the express permission of World Vision International.)

Table 7: A matrix for assessing probability/likelihood and impact of any given threat

Likelihood	Impact				
	Negligible	Minor	Moderate	Severe	Critical
Very likely					
Likely					
Moderately likely					
Unlikely					
Very unlikely					

The likelihood/probability and impact assessment

Try to rank different threats by two criteria: how likely is it that something will happen, and if it happens, how serious would the impact be? In the matrix above, the vertical columns present the likelihood that an incident will happen within a given time frame, say the next six months. The horizontal row represents the severity of the impact. It is important to clarify what impact means in this context. A rape, for instance, will have a critical impact on the individual concerned, but may not lead the agency to suspend its programmes. If rioters damage the homes of international staff, this is likely to be less critical to these individuals (who after all rent the place and have most of their personal assets overseas) than damage to the homes of national staff (who may have invested all their savings in their houses).

This assessment helps identify areas that are priorities for management, namely those risks that are more likely to happen and whose impact if they happen would be moderate to critical. It also helps in determining when a risk has become too high for operations to continue.

2.7.3 Mitigation measures and the risk threshold

The diagram opposite depicts the following conclusions from a field team discussion:

- The likelihood of civil disorder in the area is fairly high, but its impact on staff and on the programme would be limited.
- The risk of armed robbery may be medium to low, but its impact on the programme would be considerably higher, in terms of severe injuries and high stress to staff, and significant loss of assets.

Both of these factors can be deemed to be within the agency's threshold of acceptable risks, as depicted by the dotted line. By contrast, the threat of landmines, having both a high likelihood and severe to critical impact, is beyond the agency's risk threshold and warrants immediate steps to mitigate the risk. The colours represent overall levels of risk, ranging from low (pale pink) to high (dark pink). The dotted line represents the organisation's 'risk threshold', above which the risk is seen to be too high.

Table 8: Risk analys

Likelihood					
Certain/ imminent	Low	Medium	High	Critical	Critical
Very likely	Low	Medium	High	High	Critical
Likely	Negligible	Low	Medium	High	High
Moderately likely	Negligible	Low	Low	Medium	Medium
Unlikely	Nil	Negligible	Negligible	Low	Low
RISK	Negligible	Minor	Moderate	Severe	Critical

Impact →

(labels on chart: Civil disorder, Malaria, Typhoon, RTA, Landmines, Theft, Car jacking, Armed robbery)

Source: World Vision International. (Note: this material is used with the permission of World Vision International and any reproduction outside this publication (GPR) requires the express permission of World Vision International.)

The next step is to consider what can be done to reduce risks to an acceptable level. In general terms, there are three possible courses of action:

- *Reduce the threat.* If feasible, reach out to or have others negotiate on your behalf with potential adversaries.
- *Reduce the consequences/lessen the impact of the threat.* These might usefully be termed 'contingency measures', such as first-aid protocols, crisis response procedures and in extremis pre-emptive evacuation and guidance on how to behave in the event of a serious incident.
- *Reduce or eliminate exposure* by adopting additional protective measures or changing locations, for instance. The extreme version of this would be 'risk avoidance', i.e. removing the agency entirely from the threat, either permanently or temporarily.

One way of reducing or eliminating exposure is to pass on the risk to another actor (risk transfer).

- *Risk transfer.* Use other entities to take on the work and the risks of the programme, for instance subcontracting to a local partner or vendor. Insurance (of vehicles and other assets) is a form of risk transfer, but only for the financial consequences of an incident. When the risk involves the potential for injury or death, however, transferring it becomes highly problematic from an ethical standpoint.

Now it is time to revisit the earlier analysis of capacities, in order to determine whether the financial resources and competencies are available to implement these strategies and threat-specific measures – and whether the necessary time and attention can be devoted to this. Management responsibility must be specifically assigned, and individuals made accountable. At right is an example of a worksheet that could be used to determine risk mitigation measures based on the risk assessment.

It is important to be realistic about the effectiveness of risk mitigation measures: even well-guarded facilities can be vulnerable to well-planned and determined attacks. In some cases it may be possible to reduce the risk to an acceptable level, but short of quitting the area reducing risks to zero is likely to be impossible. What remains is *residual risk*. Having identified all the risks in the operating environment, and then having objectively and realistically assessed the effectiveness of risk reduction measures, is the residual risk acceptable? Too few organisations have clearly defined risk thresholds and criteria to guide these decisions. Ultimately, if the residual risk is not acceptable, and no additional mitigation measures are feasible, the programming presence will have to be altered or terminated.

Table 9: Determining risk mitigation measures

Realities						Problems				Solutions	
Threat assessment	Programme assessment		Vulnerability assessment			Risk analysis				Recommendations	
Threat	Situation	Location	Activity	Weaknesses	Strengths	Impact	Likelihood	Risk level (current)		Mitigation measures	Residual risk level (future)

Source: InterAction, Security Risk Managament: NGO Approach, 2010

2 Risk assessment

Threshold of acceptable risk

Aid work in conflict-affected environments implies a readiness to take certain risks. Aid agency discourse acknowledges this. An exercise to determine the threshold of acceptable risk seeks to render this risk tolerance concrete and explicit, and to set out the implications of management decisions regarding what to do when faced with risk. Following are three important moments when the threshold of acceptable risk needs to be discussed.

- When deciding to enter or expand into a risky environment.
- To determine individual thresholds of acceptable risk.
- To draw red lines for when a situation deteriorates.

In the first case, an analysis of the threat should provide a more-or-less objective sense of what the risks are likely to be. The question that needs to be asked is whether those risks are acceptable. Deciding what constitutes an acceptable risk requires explicit criteria and conditions to ensure a disciplined and transparent decision-making process.

In the second instance, determining an individual's risk threshold is important because different people have different tolerances for risk. Likewise, the impact of a threat is not necessarily the same for the individual as for the organisation, and can also differ between individuals. It cannot therefore be assumed that all actual and potential staff have the same threshold for what they consider acceptable risk. A climate of trust within the organisation allows people to express unease if a situation exceeds their tolerance of risk, and people entering a higher-risk environment must do so informed about the risks that exist there. At the same time, people may feel obliged to take risks beyond what they are personally able to tolerate, often for economic or career reasons: not going would mean losing the job, or losing an opportunity to distinguish oneself and qualify for promotion, for instance.

In the third case, the purpose is to avoid the 'frog-in-the-pot' syndrome: the water is heated gradually so the frog does not recognise the danger and jump out in time, and when the water reaches boiling point it is too late. 'Danger habituation' is not uncommon among aid workers. Although there is awareness that a situation is deteriorating, people do not withdraw from it or reinforce their security measures until after an incident has occurred. Additionally, there is ample testimony from aid workers that they continuously lower their threshold of acceptable risk as they go along. Such a situation needs external oversight and would only be justifiable if security measures have been significantly reinforced and improved, it is demonstrably the case that needs justify the higher risk (there is high 'programme criticality'), and those staying in high-risk environments can manage the stress and have properly reassessed their personal threshold of acceptable risk.

2.7.4 Security phases

Some organisations, including the UN, manage security on the basis of 'risk ratings', 'levels' or 'phases'. Typically, organisations have four or five security phases, ranging from low risk to very high risk. Each phase comes with a set of predetermined measures or actions to take – the highest one typically requiring the withdrawal of all staff. One way of structuring security management practices according to security phases is given in the following grid.

Indicators	Phase/level	Impact on programme activities	Security measures to take
	Phase 1 ('normal')		
	Phase 2		
	Phase 3		
	Phase 4		

The advantage of working with security phases is that, once declared, they are supposed to trigger a set of actions without further hesitation or discussion. This also brings a level of organisational consistency in the response to increasing risk. It may be particularly useful as a simplified barometer for headquarters to track risk. Typically, the decision to move to a higher security phase is within the authority of senior field-level managers, while downgrading the situation to a lower security phase requires the approval of an organisational authority located outside the operating environment.

Using security 'phases' as a management tool can give a misleading sense of robustness and predictability, and it is important to understand the limitations of this approach:

- Incomplete information and the difficulties involved in correctly interpreting a complex reality may make it difficult to decide whether to move to a different state of alert, and in any case identifying the right security phase is not the same as implementing the plan.
- Phase classifications can sometimes be too broad to capture gradients of threat or categories of those at risk in the same location. For example, some organisations in Somalia have decided to split phase classification into two ratings, one for international and one for national staff (or even broken down between 'local' and 'relocated' national staff), because of the very different risks these groups face.

- Real-life situations do not always gradually worsen or improve: a situation can suddenly deteriorate from conditions corresponding to Phase 1 to conditions corresponding to Phase 5.
- Different agencies may interpret the same situation differently, and consequently put themselves in different security phases with correspondingly different security measures. Evacuations in serious crisis moments usually require interagency collaboration, which may be complicated by different appreciations of the risk, while the fact that some agencies evacuate while others do not may change the risk and increase the vulnerability for those that stay behind.

Chapter 3
Security strategy

3.1 Developing a security strategy

The first edition of this Good Practice Review identified three broad security approaches or postures shaping an organisation's security management strategy, namely acceptance, protection and deterrence.

- An **acceptance** approach attempts to reduce or remove threats by increasing the acceptance (the political and social consent) of an agency's presence and its work in a particular context.
- A **protection** approach uses protective devices and procedures to reduce one's vulnerability to the threat, but does not affect the threat itself. In security terms this is called hardening the target.
- A **deterrence** approach aims to deter a threat with a counter-threat. It ranges from legal, economic or political sanctions (not necessarily by aid agencies) to the threat or use of force.

The concepts of acceptance, protection and deterrence constitute a range of security options and actions for agencies going from 'soft' to 'hard'. They are often used in combination, and will vary according to local security cultures and conditions. The 2000 edition of this Good Practice Review presented the three approaches as a so-called security triangle. Over the years, however, there has been confusion about its meaning and practical application.

The triangle model was not meant to imply that an aid agency simply decides, at an institutional level, which approach is preferable (or where the agency sits on the triangle) and conducts its operations accordingly. The reality is much more fluid. First, a particular approach only has a chance of being effective if it is adapted to its environment, and if the organisation has the capacities and competencies to handle that approach. Second, in any given operating environment an organisation will probably choose a mix of approaches. As risks evolve, the organisation will have to adapt by altering the balance of approaches. Notably, shifting to a protection approach usually will *not* mean abandoning an acceptance approach; rather, the two components will be combined. Hardening the target may require *more* outreach in order to build trust and gain acceptance. Third, the effectiveness of any approach will be influenced by what other aid agencies are doing. Finally, no approach, by itself or in combination, will reduce the risk to zero.

Given their mission and values, aid organisations find acceptance by far the most appealing security strategy. Indeed, acceptance can and should be the foundation of all security strategies. But acceptance will not be effective against all threats. In environments where lawlessness or banditry are pervasive or where belligerents are pursuing national or even global objectives, and where the mission and objectives of aid agencies have little meaning to some actors, an acceptance approach alone may not be viable.

Protection and deterrence approaches are not necessarily more effective in all cases, however, and can bring their own problems. A protection approach focuses attention on the agency as a potential target, and unlike acceptance does not address those who pose the threat. It can also lead to a 'bunker mentality'. This makes it harder to develop relationships with others, which in turn makes it harder to get information about the environment and to communicate effectively with local interlocutors. Poor or non-existent relationships make it easier for suspicion, resentment and hostility to take root.

A deterrence approach can also create additional problems. If agencies display force, for example by driving with armed escorts or hiring armed guards for their offices, it can make it difficult to convey principles of non-violence and independence. Communities or armed actors may believe that the agency is tied in some way to belligerent groups, and acceptance may be compromised. In some environments, such as Somalia, aid agencies have also found that armed guards control a de facto security market and are very difficult to stop using once employed.

In practice, a good security strategy needs a flexible combination of approaches. As a basis for any programming activity, cultivate acceptance and good relationships with the local population and their leaders, as well as relevant state or non-state armed actors. In more insecure environments with identified general risks to aid organisations, certain protective measures, particularly against crime, may be unavoidable. In highly insecure contexts, where there are significant identified risks to the organisation, deterrence measures may be necessary if this is the only way to protect staff and continue providing critical assistance. The point is that security management should be proactive, involving conscious choices about the mix of approaches pursued in the light of the threats identified, and the approaches other agencies are taking.

Finally, it is important to remember that different approaches have different resource implications. All carry a financial cost. Acceptance is perhaps the hardest to measure in financial terms, but should not necessarily be considered inexpensive. If actively pursued, acceptance may require considerable staff time and possibly new programme initiatives, such as media outreach. Protective devices and materials carry a direct financial cost, while protective procedures (for example imposing curfews or always driving with two cars) can add to the budget by restricting operational capacity. A deterrence approach can have small or large resource implications, which may be difficult or impossible to back out of in the long term.

3.2 Acceptance

An acceptance approach has traditionally meant different things to different organisations. Obtaining the consent of the warring parties is part of the historical foundation of Dunantist humanitarian action, in which the modern Red Cross/Red Crescent movement is grounded. Achieving broad acceptance from communities, through good works and adherence to humanitarian principles, is at the heart of the mission and values of a much broader set of humanitarian organisations.

For most humanitarian agencies, acceptance is the most desirable type of security management approach. What is sometimes poorly understood, however, is that acceptance cannot be assumed; it has to be won and maintained. Unlike human rights organisations and journalists, who are more aware that their work is not likely to please everybody, aid agencies have tended to expect that they will be readily accepted, simply by virtue of what they do. However, in parts of the world, for a variety of reasons, this is no longer the case. Since the first analysis of the acceptance approach was undertaken in the 2000 GPR, strong evidence has emerged to suggest that, in a number of contexts, acceptance has become much harder to achieve (see Annex 1). Whether, when and from whom acceptance can be gained is now a serious operational question.

Many agencies today have organisational and security policies that are grounded in the concept of an acceptance approach. However, they often may not have guidelines on the practical steps they should be taking to cultivate and sustain acceptance, or how to assess whether or not they have achieved it. In the past agencies have assumed that simply by not adopting protective or deterrent approaches, or not associating with certain international actors, or not accepting funds from certain donors, they are adopting an acceptance approach. This is misguided; acceptance cannot be defined in the negative or adopted by default. The sections below therefore address the essentials of an 'active acceptance' approach to underscore that acceptance is something to be fostered and continuously worked toward – not a static attitude of the organisation.

3 Security strategy

3.2.1 Key components of an active acceptance approach

What is an active acceptance approach? Key components include active outreach to a wide range of stakeholders; considerable investment of time by staff with excellent social, political, interpersonal and communication skills; and the development and maintenance of core messages regarding the organisation's mandate, objectives and programmes. Perhaps most importantly, it involves acting in accordance with this discourse.

Establishing and maintaining relations with key stakeholders

Key stakeholders in an acceptance approach are anyone who formally or informally can exercise some meaningful influence on whether an agency can operate securely in a given environment. This may include state and non-state armed actors, government officials, local authorities, community leaders, local and international media and business or private sector individuals. Some actors may be hard to identify (sometimes because they do not want to be identified), or they may be hard to reach. Knowing these stakeholders requires mapping and analysing these actors, an exercise which national and expatriate staff should conduct together.

Acceptance needs to be gained from all relevant parties, including those that – for economic, cultural, religious, military or political reasons – may distrust the agency, feel threatened by it or harbour active hostility towards it. These should be identified in the situation/risk analysis. It is important to assess the influence that each party has – in some situations having the acceptance of key influencers might be sufficient if it is impossible to secure the acceptance of all, while in other situations this is not the case. National staff can play a key role in determining the stakeholders to liaise with and getting in touch with them. In difficult environments, dedicated national 'liaison' staff may be needed. In some cases, using a respected intermediary (such as a religious leader or community head) can endow the organisation with local respectability.

An active acceptance strategy may not be limited to local actors. Improvements in telecommunications and transportation have increased inter-connectedness, meaning that key stakeholders may be geographically dispersed. Reaching them requires organisational willingness, competence and financial resources. One NGO, for example, has started to communicate with members of the Somali diaspora about the organisation's mission and values, as a way to promote acceptance.

Completing the following table may be a useful way to ensure that all the key actors are examined. Precision is key here: 'the government', 'the Shia community' or 'the military' is generally not good enough. There are likely to be different opinions and opinion-makers and different centres of power within each category. Even if there are no clear answers, the value of the exercise is very much in the discussion it generates. That discussion may focus attention on a few critical players, or on things that could be done to increase acceptability.

Actor	Level of acceptance (none, low, good enough, high)	Why?	What can be done to gain greater acceptance?

Gaining acceptance from local populations

An active acceptance approach pays attention not only to community members who benefit directly from the aid programme, but also – perhaps more importantly – those who do not. Such people may be found within the programming area, as well as in areas staff travel through to get there.

It is important to understand the difference between mere tolerance of an organisation's presence and programme and true acceptance. Sometimes people will accept an agency's presence only because they are in desperate need. At other times people may use aid as one source of support, but may not feel an active responsibility for the agency's wellbeing. Listening and responding to what people want, treating them with respect, acting transparently and being accountable may encourage a greater level of acceptance. This may even override the material dimension. An aid agency can find itself unable to provide an adequate level of assistance or periodically even any assistance at all, and yet remain accepted based on the quality of the relationship. That said, it is important not to create expectations that cannot be met. During the Indian Ocean tsunami response, for example, over-promising and under-delivering was a problem for a number of aid organisations.

If there is a high level of acceptance, members of the community may make suggestions as to how risk can be reduced. For example, health workers in Afghanistan are sometimes asked to sleep overnight in community members' houses rather than in the health post. In Somalia, community members have sometimes warned NGOs to leave the area ahead of a threat. In other cases, local people have helped recover stolen assets and provided information during

3 Security strategy

a kidnap situation. But do not overestimate the power of the local community. In other circumstances, communities will not be in a position to reduce security risks. They may be powerless to influence other actors, may overlook or misjudge new threats or calculate that it is in their long-term interest to associate with another, possibly armed, power-broker, rather than a temporary aid provider.

Acceptance may diminish over time as people's needs and expectations evolve. Once a situation has stabilised, new aspirations often arise. Over time, for example, Afghans started to define 'peace' in terms of 'electricity and jobs' rather than protection from physical harm.[1] The inability of aid agencies to meet such longer-term needs may lead to diminished interest and acceptance among populations.

Interacting with armed actors

Networking or negotiating with armed groups will often be unavoidable. Agencies working in an area where a certain group is in de facto control are likely to have to signal their presence to them and obtain assurances that their work is acceptable and that staff will not be harmed. However, proceed with caution when engaging armed actors – and prepare. Questions to consider include:

- What is the relationship between the armed group and the civilians the agency is trying to reach?
- What is the command structure, state of discipline, aims and objectives of the armed group?
- How will negotiations with this armed group affect relations with others (including the government)?

Understanding these dynamics and risks requires a proactive capacity to analyse them. It will often make sense to work with others (e.g. OCHA, another UN agency or a group of NGOs) to pool capacities and enable a common approach, or at a minimum ensure that differing approaches do not undermine others' efforts.[2]

Maintaining consistency in communications

For all stakeholders, communications need to be clear and consistent. An agency should know and be able to explain – in succinct, easy-to-understand language – who they are, why they are there, what they want to do and how they relate to others.

---

1 A. Donini et al., *Mapping the Security Environment: Understanding the Perceptions of Local Communities, Peace Support Operations, and Assistance Agencies* (Medford, MA: Feinstein International Famine Center, 2005), p. 8.
2 For more guidance on this topic, see M. Glaser, *Humanitarian Engagement with Non-state Actors: The Parameters of Negotiated Access*, HPN Network Paper 51 (London: ODI, June 2005).

Consistency should be both external and internal. Given that more people around the world now have access to global media, they can pick up information about an agency from the internet as well as global and local news. While certain communications may be adjusted slightly for different audiences, the overall message should be the same. This requires internal consistency, such that the website, a spokesperson at headquarters and a staff member talking to local media on the ground all say the same thing.

All staff, from senior managers to guards and drivers, need to be able to understand and communicate the goals and principles of the organisation. Indeed, junior staff members are more likely to have daily interactions with local government officials, armed actors at roadblocks and other members of the local population. One way to ensure that staff are able to communicate these messages is to develop a simple Question and Answer sheet.

Making formal agreements

Formal agreements, for instance with the government or with certain armed groups, are useful in that they provide official recognition and explicit agreement on specific issues. But they can also be problematic if they are valid for only a limited period of time, if they draw attention to areas where authorities may be inappropriately seeking to regulate or impede aid agencies' activities, or if they consume more staff time than they are worth.

Keeping the terms fairly general allows for flexibility, though it may also be counter-productive if it leaves the other party the scope to ignore their responsibilities. With regard to security, agreements should spell out detailed responsibilities, including the procedures to be followed if security problems do arise. But remember: written agreements do not have the same value in every social environment. For example, the word of honour of the right person might be more important. The obligation implied is likely to be more strictly observed if it is widely known that a respected person has given her or his word.

Conducting meetings and socialising

Messages are conveyed not only in meetings but also through the type of meeting that takes place. Who calls the meeting, who is invited, where it takes place, what the seating arrangements are: all are well-known aspects of diplomacy, and play a role in developing a certain type of relationship. Summoning local elders to the agency's office, for example, conveys a different message from going to see them in their own environment. People may come to the office to make demands that quickly reveal themselves to be unacceptable, but it may make tactical sense to spend more time with them than is needed to convey a response. It is important not to appear brusque or impolite. Slowing down, taking time to meet and converse with people, explaining, listening and generally showing basic politeness and respect can all be important in securing acceptance.

Socialising to develop a more relaxed and personal relationship is standard practice in diplomacy: government officials are invited to private dinners or parties at the residence of the agency representative, while agency staff may accept the hospitality of a tribal leader, who slaughters a goat or sheep in their honour. Building a relationship requires more than rare, brief, formal meetings. A formal agreement may turn into a mere piece of paper if there is no other contact to maintain the quality of the relationship. At the same time, socialising should not undermine the critical distance agencies need should real problems arise.

Negotiating and making public statements

Pay attention to the different interactional and negotiating styles of different social groups. National staff may be particularly beneficial as they will generally have a far deeper knowledge than expatriate staff. If they are from the same region they may also understand the vernacular language, be able to read non-verbal messages and be familiar with codes of social behaviour. Prepare for important meetings together in advance. What is known about the interlocutors? What positions and arguments are they expected to use? What will be the agency's position? What style and tactics will it adopt? In some contexts, it may be advisable that messages and decisions that are likely to displease an interlocutor come from an expatriate who is less susceptible to pressure, intimidation and possible retaliation than a national. Be clear in advance about respective roles in the negotiations.

Critical public statements are seldom received with gratitude. It is important to consider:

- The reasons for going public rather than delivering the message more discreetly.
- Whether to inform the recipient of the message in advance or deliver the message first before (also) going public.
- How to phrase the statement: what can be documented and substantiated if challenged, and is a less provocative phrasing possible?
- If possible, control the final version that goes into the public domain: for example, the content of a written press release is easier to keep under control than a press conference that allows questioning, or a live interview.

Beware also of 'leaked' statements: will a statement 'off the record' really be kept confidential? How confidential will statements remain which are made in an open forum such as an interagency coordination meeting? There may be any number of reasons why a statement might be leaked in a more or less distorted form.

3.2.2 Managing perceptions
The politics of the overall staff profile

Staff profile is important from a security point of view, for two reasons: it influences how the agency is perceived and therefore how people will relate to it, and the breadth of the informal contacts and information channels that the agency can establish and maintain.

In some conflict contexts it may be necessary to fill key positions with international staff, as it will be difficult to achieve the perception of neutrality and impartiality otherwise. In other instances it may be wise to steer clear of certain nationalities, for example, some NGOs would not put US, UK and other citizens with military deployments in Iraq into their programmes there. In an ethnically divided environment it might desirable to ensure that all major ethnic groups or clans are represented among the national staff. Elsewhere major divides can exist on the basis of the sympathies people have for one or another political party. Ending up with staff drawn entirely or largely from one political party is not a good idea, though this may not be apparent until a political crisis erupts, as was the case for some NGOs during political unrest in Kenya in 2007–2008. Another common divide is between people from urban and rural backgrounds. This can cause problems in places where the urban and rural environments constitute very different social worlds, and where city-dwellers can be as much outsiders as foreigners.

The ideal staff profile is a defendable mix of members of various groups. Where this is not possible, try to develop a balanced operational presence among different groups and, if possible, have mixed staff in the central field office in the capital city. A strategy of defendable mix for the sake of acceptance (for programmatic and security reasons) may override a policy of recruitment on the basis of skill and equal opportunity only. In other words, an agency may deliberately seek out, or give preference to, people from a certain category, even if they are not the best-qualified candidates. Anticipate that a mix of staff belonging to different groups, between which there are tensions or even open conflict, will import these tensions into the organisation. This is not something to avoid at all costs, but to manage constructively.

3 Security strategy

Appearance and behaviour

Appearance is important. Hairstyle, body decoration and manner of dress can carry important social and political meanings. This includes earrings, tattoos, make-up and style of eyeglasses and facial hair, as well as clothing and how much it covers or reveals. While inappropriate behaviour by itself does not necessarily translate into a threat, it could aggravate existing suspicions and tensions and provide fertile ground for those whose objective is to stir up animosity. Remember:

• The kind of behaviour that is considered appropriate or inappropriate in a particular social/cultural environment, and its possible connotations with status, gender and age. For example, in certain social environments certain categories of men are expected to show highly assertive behaviour. Other social environments emphasise the need for composure and self-control.
• Many social environments have implicit norms about the consumption of stimulants such as alcohol. Even when this is not frowned upon, its acceptance tends to be limited to particular places, times and occasions. The acceptance of alcohol consumption should not be confused with the acceptance of drunkenness, especially in public. Consuming alcohol with others can be an important ritual, but drinkers will be expected to be able to hold their drink (and of course the risk of saying or doing something inappropriate increases as self-control diminishes).
• The public expression of anger or irritation is always resented, and can be provocative. Firmness in saying no will generally do no harm when it is combined with a correct and polite attitude. But arrogance, real or perceived, tends to create resentment.
• Aloofness (keeping at a distance, in the car, in the office, with many barriers and gate-keepers) might also be perceived badly, but this has to be matched with organisational policies regarding travel and site security (see Chapters 8 and 9).

Gender dimensions

Many patriarchal societies articulate their moral and communal integrity in terms of the 'purity' of women, for which dress and behavioural codes provide a strong indicator. In times of conflict, when group identities are often redrawn or reaffirmed, such codes may apply even more strongly. The wearing of shorts, short skirts and open-necked blouses and sleeveless shirts can be seen as provocative and offensive. At one end of the spectrum the response may be disapproval. At the other end there may be sexual harassment or worse. Female staff should be mindful of these issues, though men too need to consider whether the way they dress evokes respect or is perceived as disrespectful.

It is also important to be sensitive to, and careful about, the social norms regulating the interaction of women and men outside the immediate family, as well as notions of public and private space. Many social environments have more restrictive codes about the public display of intimate behavior, such as holding hands, embracing and kissing. In Pakistan, for example, one NGO was warned that 'we are not happy that your male and female staff are housed in the same compound', so the NGO built a wall to separate men from women.

Cultural and religious considerations

In many contexts, cultural and religious norms will require special attention. In Sri Lanka, for example, it is considered disrespectful to use a Buddha image or statue as background to a photograph of someone. While such inappropriate behaviour by itself does not necessarily translate into a threat, it could aggravate existing suspicions and tensions. Faith-based organisations need to be particularly careful to manage their profile and consider additional security measures during periods of religious tension.

Programme activities

It is important to consider whether programmes enhance security or increase risk. One important question is whether the work is on a scale large enough to be meaningful for the people affected. Another element to consider is how programmes that are not strictly life-saving, including those that aim at broader social changes in society, may be perceived. This includes, for example, projects that support women's empowerment in conservative societies, or which do not meet the most urgent needs, such as a vaccination campaign in a highly food insecure area. Understanding these issues entails listening to people and reacting accordingly. Even if a programme has wide acceptance within a community, it may still aggravate other local stakeholders. This is true in virtually all sectors. For example, a food aid programme may anger local traders by cutting into their profits; providing free health services may draw patients away from paid-for service clinics, frustrating local health officials; recording protection threats against the population may anger those responsible for the violence.

Another consideration is the exit strategy. Often organisations run good programmes, but poorly executed exit strategies jeopardise the goodwill that had developed over the period of the programme. This means that they may face an uphill battle to gain acceptance if they return to offer assistance in response to another disaster.

3.2.3 Challenges to acceptance

In some operating environments, the pursuit of an acceptance approach can be especially challenging. These include:

- Deeply fragmented environments with a multitude of armed actors, and where command-and-control chains are unclear (e.g. eastern DRC, Darfur, Somalia and Afghanistan).
- Environments where armed actors accrue strategic benefits from chaos and instability (e.g. eastern DRC, Somalia, Afghanistan and Iraq).
- Environments with a profusion of international actors (military, political, humanitarian), where all foreigners are perceived to be 'amalgamated' (e.g. Afghanistan, Iraq and parts of Pakistan).
- Environments where the government or armed actors and sometimes even communities reject or are suspicious of those associated with the West or Western intervention, including aid agencies (e.g. Afghanistan, Iraq, parts of Pakistan, Burma, North Korea and Zimbabwe).
- Periods of major change in the arrangements of state and non-state armed actors (e.g. Iraq after the defeat of the Saddam Hussein regime in 2003).
- Urban environments with high crime rates (e.g. Port Moresby, Nairobi, Johannesburg and Haiti).
- Environments with local gangs or organised crime networks seeking to protect the spaces in which they operate (e.g. drug-traffickers in Colombia).

Challenging environments for acceptance

In some parts of the world, the general acceptance of (Western) aid agencies has become more problematic because they are now being seen as instruments of Western foreign policy or Western values. This has been the case most prominently in places where the 'war on terror' has played out (Iraq, Afghanistan, parts of Pakistan). But it can also be observed elsewhere: the Sri Lankan government has long harboured a deep suspicion of foreign aid agencies (including the UN) in relation to its conflict with the Tamil Tigers; the Burmese authorities were suspicious of the influence of foreign aid agencies following Cyclone Nargis; and the Mugabe government in Zimbabwe has periodically challenged the presence and programming of Western aid agencies. In Sudan, government suspicion towards and restrictions on international agencies increased following the International Criminal Court's indictment of President Omar al-Bashir in 2009.

How an agency is perceived may revolve around where it gets its funding. The suspicion that those who control the money wield all the power is becoming more widespread. This creates significant problems for the large majority of aid agencies that are at least partially reliant on government funding, particularly if that same government is a belligerent in a particular environment.

The acceptability of many international aid agencies has also been jeopardised by efforts by some Western governments to integrate their military and humanitarian strategies. In the lead-up to the invasion of Iraq in 2003, for example, senior US officials made statements portraying NGOs as instruments of foreign policy or 'force multipliers' and sources of intelligence. This prompted some Iraqi leaders to declare humanitarian agencies to be enemies of Islam.

Periods of rapid change

Analysing attacks in Iraq and Afghanistan, one aid agency concluded that, in both situations, it had failed to appreciate the implications of a rapid and profound change in the arrangement of actors. In both countries, the actors the agency had been dealing with moved very rapidly into opposition roles, while a multitude of new actors came onto the scene. In situations of profound change, the basis for an acceptance strategy may often disappear, at least temporarily, and contacts and relationships will need to be rebuilt. In the meantime, agencies are likely to face a period of heightened risk, possibly requiring a shift to stronger protection and possibly even deterrence approaches, or a much greater reliance on working with and through local actors. The scope of the aid effort may also be reduced.

Legal objections

In some contexts, both host governments and foreign donor governments may not want to see agencies negotiating access and acceptance with non-state or other armed groups. Host governments may frown upon or discourage such negotiations, while counter-terrorism legislation may impose penalties on agencies engaging with groups deemed to be terrorist actors, including the LTTE in Sri Lanka, Hizbollah in Lebanon, Hamas in Palestine, Al-Shabaab in Somalia, the Communist Party in Nepal and the Lord's Resistance Army in Uganda. Yet avoiding such groups may be very difficult if they have close ties with the local population and enjoy strong local support, or when they have control in a given area. This was the case during the wars in Lebanon and Gaza in 2006, when many NGOs, particularly those receiving funding from the US, struggled to deal with terrorism-related conditions.[3] Agencies that decide to accept funding with counter-terrorism clauses attached will need to see to it that all reasonable steps are taken to ensure compliance, including vetting new hires and maintaining strong financial tracking systems, without compromising the humanitarian mission. In the longer term, advocacy with

3 See K. Thorne, 'Terrorist Lists and Humanitarian Assistance', *Humanitarian Exchange*, no. 37, 2007.

donor governments may lead to greater clarity in what is still an ambiguous area of law.

Advocacy and speaking out

The pursuit and preservation of acceptance may require that agencies stay silent about humanitarian or human rights abuses. Speaking out may create security risks on the ground, or may lead to the agency's expulsion. This raises an obvious moral dilemma: an agency may feel compelled to speak out in the face of abuses, but doing so may well curtail assistance and make it impossible to act on abuses in the future. At what point and based on what criteria should an organisation decide that it does *not* want to prioritise acceptance above all other considerations? Although every situation will have to be judged on its merits, it will be helpful to develop a set of guidelines that can help frame the questions and weigh key considerations against one another. If a decision is made to speak out, security needs to be taken into account. A good organisational policy would be never to make any public statement about a particular situation without first having received the go-ahead from field-based colleagues.

3.2.4 Indicators of acceptance

There is no simple way of knowing how an agency is perceived and whether (and why) it is accepted, especially in more divided and fragmented settings. But it is important to try to gauge this, rather than simply assuming that acceptance has been achieved. It can be a positive sign of acceptance if local actors or groups:

- Actively cooperate with agency activities (e.g. local communities hosting a mobile clinic or helping with logistics), or armed groups let agency staff through checkpoints to reach programme areas.
- Warn that someone has been asking around about the agency or that a certain threat is likely.
- Help to secure the release of an abducted staff member or to recover stolen assets.
- Explain why they have a problem with the programme, its staff or a local sub-contractor.
- Acknowledge that they have a problem with the foreign policy of the agency's home government, but can distinguish between the agency and its home government.
- Identify a positive difference between the agency and other aid organisations.
- Apologise if members of a group do the agency harm.

If one agency suffers no violent incidents while others in the same operating environment do this might indicate acceptance, though it may just be a lucky chance – and it is best not to rely on this as an indicator. It is also worth bearing in mind that interlocutors may be lying, pretending to accept an agency's presence only for as long as this serves their interests. Other indicators include the frequency of meetings with key stakeholders and the level and nature of interaction with key actors. Try to gauge levels of acceptance (e.g. high, 'good enough', low) against the kind of objective criteria outlined above: relying on gut instinct is not enough. Assessments of acceptance could be integrated into local-level security audits or national security plans.

3.2.5 The practical implications of acceptance

Acceptance has practical implications, in terms of human resources, finances and administration.

Human resource requirements

An active acceptance approach requires staff with certain key competencies. These include:

- The ability to map out key actors and establish a wide network with stakeholders.
- A thorough understanding of the mission and values of the organisation.
- Strong diplomatic and negotiating skills.
- Fluency in the local language (one reason for involving national staff in such roles) and excellent communication skills.
- The ability to analyse changing political and security conditions.
- The ability to systematically use and update tools such as security audits and plans.

Many organisations have found that, to do acceptance well, it must ultimately be the responsibility of very senior staff. This requires these staff to have not only the requisite skills, but also sufficient time relative to their other responsibilities. In the ICRC, for instance, the Head of Delegation has the primary responsibility for establishing and maintaining acceptance, and is not expected to spend time on detailed programme and financial management. Within many NGOs, by contrast, senior managers are mainly responsible for day-to-day operational management, with external networking limited to the government authorities, donors and other aid agencies. Although this difference is in part explained by the nature of the ICRC's mandate to promote IHL, as well as perhaps differing overall resource levels, it also reflects the high priority the ICRC attaches to maintaining operational security in dangerous environments.

Examples of human resource needs for pursuing acceptance

ICRC had a team of between three and five full-time people dedicated to establishing relationships and external communications to regain acceptance in and around Iraq after the bombing of the agency's Baghdad headquarters in 2003.

A medical agency working for many years in the region deployed a staffer to tour several Middle Eastern countries and meet a wide array of political figures, social and religious leaders and business people to establish or deepen understanding of the agency and its work. This generated a wide network of contacts.

Financial and administrative implications

Acceptance is not cost-free. There are significant operational costs, including:

- Staff time, including hiring additional staff with security, outreach or media responsibilities.
- Training staff on how to communicate the organisation's mission and values, cross-cultural communication and diplomatic and negotiating skills.
- Additional travel (vehicles, fuel, staff time) is required to meet stakeholders.
- Translation of organisational materials or messages into locally appropriate formats and languages.
- Paying for the use of local radio and television, where necessary.
- Additional time required during the design phase of a programme (sometimes referred to as the 'Profile Management Plan'), which may lead to a reduction in impact relative to overall budget, making programmes appear more expensive.
- Procuring more expensive local goods, using less efficient local labour or less qualified local staff (see below).
- Developing a communication/outreach kit with flyers and documentation.

It might be worth identifying these costs upfront and discussing with donors how these might be met, especially as they are not necessarily part of budgeted security costs as traditionally defined.

Pursuing an acceptance approach may require adjustments to some standard administrative or legal regulations. For example:

- The rule book may say get three bids and go for the one that offers the best price-quality combination. But for the sake of acceptance, it might be better to spread contracts over different sectors of the local population, so that people feel that the benefits are shared fairly. Likewise, it may be a good idea to buy locally, even if a non-local provider offers better value for money.
- The agency may choose to ensure a balance of ethnic groups or use staff from the local area, even if this initially reduces overall quality and efficiency. This will require an adjustment to human resource practices.
- Many organisations have a policy of not offering transport to non-employees. It may, however, be difficult to justify not taking a sick child to hospital in an otherwise empty vehicle. Exceptions to a non-transport policy may be necessary, for moral reasons or to promote acceptance.

3.3 Protection

A protection approach tries to reduce vulnerability. It can do this in two ways, either by hardening the target or by increasing or reducing its visibility. A protection approach does not try to affect the threat (i.e. remove it). The risk is reduced only by working on the organisation's vulnerability.

3.3.1 Hardening the target

Hardening the target essentially relies on physical assets and procedures that either reduce the probability of a threat getting near to the target, or reduce the potential impact of violence on the target.

If offices and residences (and their occupants) are a potential target, physical protection can be added, such as perimeter walls, perhaps with barbed wire; creating a stand-off zone for vehicles; and installing metal gates and metal bars on the windows. Protective *procedures* include controlling visitors' access and undertaking spot checks and patrols. If armed attack is a threat when travelling, 'hard-skin' or armoured vehicles may be appropriate. Like body armour or blast film, these do not reduce the probability of a threat getting near the target, but can reduce the impact of bullets and blasts. The same holds for bomb shelters and sniper walls. For further discussion on specific threat management and mitigation measures, see Part 5.

A common tactic is to seek strength in numbers: driving in convoys, for instance, or arranging staff accommodation so that residences are grouped closely together. Strength in numbers can be very effective in many threat environments, but it will not stop a really determined attacker, and could be counter-productive. Driving in a convoy or grouping offices together may

3 Security strategy

present more targets to a would-be assailant intent on maximising the impact of a single attack. Likewise, while communications equipment such as radios and phones can be very effective, expensive equipment may also attract unwanted attention. Having a good communications system will also be of limited use unless a rapid intervention force is available at the other end. Light and sound (e.g. movement-sensitive floodlights or alarm bells outside a building) can give some advance warning of an attack, allowing staff to take evasive action (get into a safe room, slip out) or call for immediate assistance. Again, however, these devices will not necessarily stop an incident from occurring.

3.3.2 Low-profile/low-visibility programming

Low-visibility programming has become an increasingly common protective tactic among aid agencies. It involves removing organisational branding from office buildings, vehicles, residences and individual staff members. It can also involve the use of private cars or taxis, particularly vehicles that blend into the local context, limiting movement and removing tell-tale pieces of equipment, such as VHF radios or satphones and HF antennae. In certain very high-risk environments, anything that might link staff to an agency – memory sticks, agency identity documents, cell phones, computers – may be 'sanitised'. Staff likely to stand out from the local population may be redeployed. In Iraq, more radical steps have included staff using false names, working with no fixed operating address and not being told the identities of colleagues. Beneficiaries were purposefully not made aware of the source of their assistance.

Another tactic of a low-visibility approach is to use removable (e.g. magnetic) logos for vehicles, which can be removed in areas where visibility is discouraged. Knowing when to display a logo and when to take it off demands a very good, localised and dynamic risk assessment. One NGO working in the Occupied Palestinian Territories and Israel, for example, instructs staff to remove logos when working in refugee camps, where the risk of kidnapping is known to be high, while displaying the agency flag prominently when going through checkpoints or in areas where there is a risk of Israeli military incursion. Bear in mind that magnetic stickers can easily be stolen and used by others to impersonate the organisation.

A low-profile, low-visibility approach poses significant challenges. It can make programming more complicated, particularly in extreme cases, and can distance the organisation from sources of information that might otherwise enhance its security. It might also lead to suspicions and misperceptions of what the agency is doing, undermining acceptance. It is also a difficult approach to maintain if the organisation is seeking wider recognition of its work from the public or from donors. Agencies generally do not see a low-profile approach as a permanent way of operating; rather, it is viewed as exceptional and time-limited. It may also be adopted at the start of a programme, then gradually moderated as operations increase. This approach has been used in tribal areas in Pakistan, for instance.

3.4 Deterrence and armed protection

Deterrence means posing a counter-threat: essentially discouraging would-be attackers by instilling fear of the consequences they may face. In humanitarian operational security the term has for many become synonymous with the use of armed protection – the strongest form of deterrence used by aid agencies. There are other potential deterrents, however, and this section covers them briefly before going on to an in-depth examination of armed protection in humanitarian operations. The decision to adopt armed protection warrants extremely careful consideration. Even when a force is small, lightly armed and under orders to use its weapons only in self-defence, the potential use of firepower introduces a qualitative difference in security strategy. It also profoundly affects the image and perception of aid agencies in general.

3.4.1 Forms of deterrence other than armed force
Legal and diplomatic leverage
There are certain legal protections for aid workers under national and, to a limited extent, international law. Unfortunately, in most circumstances trying to get leverage with legal arguments will not be very effective. International aid agencies may get some backing from foreign donor governments, particularly in negotiating access or resolving administrative problems with host governments, but close interaction with donor governments can undermine the appearance of independence and neutrality. When liaising with or making requests of foreign or donor governments, it is important to reinforce the humanitarian principles of neutrality, independence and impartiality.

Suspension of operations or withdrawal
In the face of certain threats or after security incidents, agencies have at times temporarily suspended their aid programmes, or threatened to do so. The continuation or resumption of the programme is then made conditional upon the resolution or amelioration of the problem. Anecdotal evidence suggests that this tactic does not always work very well, and that agencies often resume their programmes despite no noticeable improvement, undermining their credibility and making similar threats in the future less plausible still.

The following are circumstances under which a suspension or threat of suspension may be effective:

- It is not perceived primarily as punishing civilians who are not linked to the causes of insecurity and are not in a position to improve security.
- An influential section of the population or local leadership can be mobilised on the agency's behalf.
- Agencies are prepared to maintain the suspension until the situation is satisfactorily resolved, and will not annul the decision too quickly because of internal agency or external pressure.
- Other agencies do not undercut the action by stepping in to fill the gap. A common front must be established before operations are suspended.

Unless the incident is very serious, a selective suspension (e.g. in a given location or for a given time period) or the gradual reintroduction of services may provide more room for manoeuvre. A total suspension tends to create a difficult all-or-nothing situation.

Another deterrence option is to forge an alliance with local strongmen. In the North Caucasus, for example, one agency rented offices and residences from a powerful local businessman. Without having to make explicit statements, it was clear that an attack on the agency would be an attack on him and his clan, constituting a sort of implicit deterrence strategy. This option needs to be approached cautiously as you may also become hostage to the protection of the power-broker.

3.4.2 Armed protection: the basic question

Armed protection and humanitarian action remain uneasy bedfellows. Although in reality virtually all aid agencies at one time or another have used some form of armed protection, discussions about it are highly sensitive. This section provides a more systematic framework for considering the matter. It is not intended as an argument for the use of armed protection. At every step in the line of reasoning it is possible to arrive at the conclusion that armed protection may not be an appropriate option. Before proceeding, however, bear in mind that considering armed protection at all may indicate that the threshold of acceptable risk has already been crossed, and the real decision should be to withdraw or stay out. If this threshold has not yet been reached, or if armed protection could perhaps reduce the risk to a more acceptable level, then three major areas come into play in thinking through the decision: principles, context and management.

Issues of principle and other considerations

The following questions need to be considered:

- Does the organisation object to the use of force in principle, regardless of the circumstances?
- Do the benefits of using armed protection in this context outweigh the risks?
- Are there serious concerns about how to manage armed protection, and can these concerns be overcome?

Some argue that armed protection is against the basic principles of humanitarian action. This position tends to be based on ethical or long-term operational considerations. The ethical argument holds that humanitarian action is never compatible with the use of force. From an ideological perspective, an agency may refuse armed protection because its use, as a matter of principle, contributes to the ongoing production and distribution of arms. A more conditional perspective might focus not so much on the production of arms per se but on their uncontrolled proliferation – i.e., the loss of a monopoly of violence by the authorities responsible for security and law and order.

The long-term operational consideration is that, whereas in a specific context armed protection might be justifiable, it erodes the overall image of humanitarian action worldwide and may therefore lead to increased insecurity elsewhere or in the future. According to this line of reasoning, resorting too quickly or too often to armed protection undermines global efforts to restore respect for international humanitarian law and independent humanitarian action.

There are also practical considerations. Armed escorts make aid work much less flexible in terms of movements, as permissions and escorts often have to be organised in advance. This should be considered in the programme design. Making movements more predictable may increase an agency's vulnerability to attack, particularly if escorts are not fully trustworthy.

While there is no disputing that consent and acceptance is the best way to obtain basic security, moral arguments may not be enough; even democratic, peaceful states need police and security forces to ensure respect for the law and for their citizens' basic rights. In some contexts the use of armed protection to facilitate the provision of aid may be a function of the state exercising its obligations under international humanitarian law. Arguments in favour of the use of armed protection hold that it can be acceptable as a last resort, and when people's survival would be at risk if humanitarian and other

3 Security strategy

assistance were curtailed (see, for instance, Inter-Agency Standing Committee and UN guidance).[4]

Another major consideration concerns who benefits from the armed protection: is it only the aid agency and its staff, or can the protection provide wider public benefits and enhance public security? Will the use of arms and armed guards – perhaps recruited locally – have a pacifying effect on the local situation, or will it ratchet up tensions? Is it contributing to the 'privatisation' of security, whereby those who are able to pay can buy security while others have to live in fear? Is it indirectly putting others at risk by making them soft targets in comparison? In extremely high-crime environments, armed escorts and guards may be widely used. For example, between the airport and the city of Lei in Papua New Guinea (a distance of 10–15km), aid workers travel in the purpose-built vehicles of a security company, escorted by armed guards. Although this may be unavoidable, it is important to consider what effect, if any, it has on the broader security environment.

Even if the use of armed protection is deemed necessary and legitimate, it may not be ethical or practical to pay for the service from private contractors, groups or individuals (as opposed to the protection of a state or internationally mandated police or military forces, which may be provided free of charge). Following experiences with protection rackets among Somali militia guards in the 1990s, some aid workers argued that aid agencies should never pay for armed protection. The reality is that most have done so.[5] In some countries the government security force is ineffective, and aid agencies have supported the state materially, for example with vehicles or paying for an escort service. In northern Kenya, for example, aid agencies pay the vehicle and fuel costs of armed police escorts.

Questions of context

If the threshold of acceptable risk has not been passed and armed protection is not excluded as a matter of principle, a set of further, context-specific questions should be posed. What are the threats and where do they come from? Is armed protection the only possible and the best answer? Does armed protection reduce or increase the risk?

---

4 IASC, *Civil–Military Guidelines and Reference for Complex Emergencies*, 7 March 2008; UN *Guidelines on the Use of Foreign Military and Civil Defence Assets in Disaster Relief*, November 2006 (Revised November 2007); *Guidelines on the Use of Military and Civil Defence Assets to Support United Nations Humanitarian Activities in Complex Emergencies* (MCDA Guidelines), March 2003 (Revised January 2006).
5 A. Stoddard, A. Harmer and V. DiDomenico, *The Use of Private Security Providers and Services in Humanitarian Operations*, HPG Report 27 (London: ODI, 2008). See Annex 4 for a detailed discussion on private security providers.

It should be noted that in some places, for example in Latin America, the use of armed protection is dictated by prevailing local security practices. NGOs use armed guards because 'everyone else does', and it is simply what is done. In such cases, moving away from the practice may require a wider interagency dialogue and joint action.

The nature and origin of the threats

What/who is armed protection supposed to protect you from? Where do the threats come from and why? The question of armed protection often arises when there is a risk of targeted assassination of aid personnel, kidnapping, armed robbery or ambush and robbery or destruction of aid convoys. Some important distinctions can be made between threats related to site security and to movement security, and between threats specifically to the aid agency (its personnel and assets) and more generally to affected populations. Deeper analysis should give some idea as to who is posing the threat, and why.

Threats or incidents may occur because the agency is not perceived as neutral in its operations. Armed protection may increase that perception. One approach might be to aim for a more balanced and 'neutral' political positioning, increased dissemination about the agency and how it operates and more active efforts to seek consent and acceptance. If this is impossible, alternatives to armed protection may still be available. If new four-wheel-drive vehicles are the attraction, use second-hand two-wheel-drive ones. Some agencies in Darfur have used donkey carts to transport goods in order to minimise the risk of carjacking. If international agency convoys and warehouses are a target because they are outside the 'social system', use local traders and merchants who are 'within the system'. If internationals are the only target of kidnapping, national staff could run the programme – assuming that they are not at equal or greater risk, and that risk is being transferred responsibly.

Even where armed protection seems justified, it may not provide a reasonable deterrent, or may increase the risk. For example, if burglars suspect that a resident has a firearm, they may turn violent if surprised in the act. If road bandits see an armed convoy they may shoot before looting it. If armed protection is provided by government forces or a particular faction, the agency may become a legitimate target in the eyes of the armed opposition. There is also the risk of accidents from 'friendly fire' or mishandled or malfunctioning weapons.

While armed protection may be the decision of the individual agency, its use also has implications for others; indeed, a sound operating premise is that people do not differentiate between different aid agencies or even between NGOs and the UN. One agency with armed protection will influence the

3 Security strategy

Maintaining the distinction between the agency and its armed protection

A basic rule in maintaining a perceptual distinction between the agency and the armed forces protecting it is for armed men protecting convoys to travel in separate vehicles. Weapons should not be brought into aid agency premises or vehicles, and aid workers should not dress in clothes that resemble those of armed forces. Aid agencies will not use the assets of security forces (e.g. trucks, armoured vehicles, helicopters) and security forces will not use aid agency assets. If this is absolutely unavoidable, then the asset has to be repainted and re-marked to reveal only its current user. Armed guards may also be excluded from the agency's compound, although this might make them less effective in case of an attack. If the threat is targeted kidnapping or assassination, armed bodyguards will have to exercise 'close protection'. Whether these steps will actually help to maintain a perceptual distinction and allow the agency to retain some part of its civilian and non-combatant image will depend on the specific local context.

image and perception of all humanitarian agencies, and therefore potentially affect everybody's acceptance and relationships. This is a topic that merits structured interagency reflection and discussion. A common policy position is much to be preferred over discord.

In dangerous environments agencies tend to think about measures that will enhance their own security. It may be helpful to consider whether and how security could be improved more generally. For example, armed guards in a refugee camp might be deployed in a way that protects not only agency staff, but also refugee women at risk of sexual assault when collecting water and firewood. A system might be developed whereby the armed guards of several individual agencies patrol the neighbourhood and therefore increase the security of all. Where a UN peace operation is present and has a mandate to protect civilians, troops may be deployed to areas that are dangerous for both aid workers and the local population. In the response to the earthquake in Haiti in January 2010, for instance, the US and UN provided armed protection during the early phase of food distributions.

It is also important to consider who is providing the armed protection. Sources include the national army, the national police, an armed resistance group, UN military peacekeepers and UN police, local militia, private security companies and armed guards on the agency's payroll. In some circumstances, an agency not opposed in principle to the use of force may find that none of the potential providers is acceptable and effective, leaving the agency to choose between operating without armed protection or withdrawing. Questions to think about when considering a provider include:

- What is the political position of the provider in a given conflict – in other words, will the agency be seen as taking sides if it associates itself with a particular actor?
- What is the provider's public image and reputation? If, for example, the national army or police is broadly perceived as an instrument of repression and exploitation, or if an armed faction has a reputation for brutality against civilians, using their 'protection' may damage the agency's public image.
- How important for the provider is the extension of protection to an aid agency compared with its other objectives? The provider may have another agenda (for instance engaging the enemy or capturing a criminal) that in critical moments may override concern for, even jeopardise, agency security.
- How professional is the provider? Are guards well trained, reasonably compensated, provided with functioning equipment, well instructed, supervised and disciplined? Low-paid, poorly trained personnel may be more of a liability than a help.
- How much management control does the agency need or want? National security forces, rebel groups and UN police and peacekeepers, for example, will retain their own chain of command. Hired militia, private security companies or guards on the agency payroll might be more closely managed by the agency. Having more direct authority over the providers of armed protection allows for greater control, but also makes the agency directly accountable for their behaviour and actions.

Questions of management

Key management questions to consider include:

- Are the in-house policies, procedures and management competence necessary for handling this relationship available?
- What are the necessary contractual stipulations?
- Who maintains command and control, and who has authority and responsibility for what?

Internal management questions might include:

- Who in the aid agency makes the decision/approves the use of armed protection?

- What knowledge and experience will managers need?
- How are tenders drawn up and bids assessed from local private security providers (see Annex 4)?
- What inquiries can be made concerning the professionalism and integrity of a potential service provider?
- Can the criteria for selecting guards be checked?
- Who in the country office has day-to-day responsibility for the management of the guards, and does that person have the necessary competence and confidence to do this?

Contractual stipulations include:

- Guard selection criteria, such as age, health, literacy, no use of alcohol or drugs and no other employment (at least to the extent that sleep is adequate).
- Essential requirements of supervisors and minimum standards in supervision.
- Minimum standards for recruitment and further in-service training, including basic training items such as local law and the power of arrest, fire and explosives, log-keeping, office evacuation, vehicle and body search procedures, package and mail search and first aid.
- If the service provided includes a rapid response unit to back up escorts or guards in case of a serious threat or incident, then all other agreements need to be applicable to these personnel and their actions. Check who makes up the force and whether agreed instructions are transmitted clearly to all.
- The need for armed protection is not constant and contracts may be ended suddenly. Spell out clear criteria and procedures for the early ending of contracts or agreements. Shorter-term, renewable contracts give more flexibility, but may be more expensive.
- There are legal rules governing liability and compensation in case of an exchange of fire leading to injury or death, though in some situations customary law will apply. Who is responsible should a guard, assailant or bystander be injured or killed in an exchange of fire? Can the agency's liability be restricted to actions that fall strictly within the agreed terms, or only when carried out following orders?
- Remuneration needs to be carefully considered. Guards often work long and unsociable hours and do a potentially dangerous job. Too low a salary may lead to low standards of performance.

A further crucial question concerns command and control: who are the guards answerable to, who has the authority of command, who is in charge of their discipline? Where external security forces provide armed protection, what is the relative authority of their commander versus that of the agency manager?

Who, for example, determines the rules governing the use of deadly force, and who ensures that guards have fully understood them? The basic rule is likely to be that force can only be used to protect life when clearly threatened, and as long as the threat persists. In other words, lethal force can only be used in defence and not, for example, to shoot a burglar, even an armed one, who is fleeing and no longer constitutes an immediate threat. Still, what constitutes an immediate threat to life and wellbeing will have to be worked through in concrete terms, imagining different scenarios.

Rules of engagement will also need to be clarified for the protection of assets. While an agency's instinctive preference may be that no force should be used when only assets are at risk, is it acceptable to do nothing while a warehouse is emptied or all the food in a convoy is stolen by armed men, especially if there are people that really need and are dependent on those supplies? The use of a firearm would not be authorised to prevent the theft of a wallet or mobile phone, but what of more valuable assets, like vehicles and computers? Draw a line, and make very clear where that line is. Another important point is to agree procedures and approaches. It is advisable to determine or to discuss and agree on procedures for a number of possible scenarios, for example what to do when a visitor refuses to be body-searched or insists on bringing in their own armed guards, and how far to go in the pursuit of fleeing robbers or attackers. Remember too that command and control works both ways: if an agency puts itself under the protection of an armed actor, it will be expected to abide by their rules. Suddenly leaving a convoy, speeding ahead or driving off will not be accepted by the escort provider.

In a multinational peacekeeping force, different national armies tend to have different traditions and cultures, including with regard to command and control, rules of engagement, and what is considered appropriate or excessive use of force. Detailed in-depth consultation with field-level commanders may be required to ensure a common understanding. Similarly, the national army may deploy changing contingents of troops to provide protection. Different commanders will have different views, entailing a detailed written agreement with a senior commander. Monitor this to make sure that replacements are fully briefed.

As regards weaponry and other equipment, agreement will have to be reached on:

- Who provides the weapons (normally the provider of the personnel).
- What type of weaponry the guards will use (e.g., pistols, single shotguns or machine guns).
- Who is responsible for providing the ammunition and for checking that the weapons are well maintained and properly registered.

- Who is responsible for the provision of additional equipment, such as rainproof clothing, flashlights and decent boots.
- Armed guards do not normally come with vehicles. Decisions will have to be made about if and when they can use agency vehicles.

Policy guidance

Organisations should have a policy on the use of armed protection. Important points to include will be:

- A clarification of the agency's position regarding the use of armed force in principle.
- The conditions that could justify the use of armed protection, for instance during the evacuation or relocation of staff in periods of extreme insecurity. This should include references to the level of humanitarian need to which the organisation is responding and the risk posed to its personnel and assets. Clarify that this is the option of last resort – all alternatives have been considered and no appropriate or adequate alternative for those circumstances has been found.
- The key considerations and risks (legal, reputational and physical), both for the agency concerned and for others, when choosing among potential providers, and how they are to be evaluated.
- The terms that need to be agreed between the agency and the provider.
- The organisational procedure for decision-making and periodic review.
- The obligation to accompany the use of armed protection with increased communication efforts to explain its rationale.

Do not confuse policy on armed protection with policy on private security companies, even though private security companies often are the providers. An organisation might use private security companies for other purposes (e.g. risk assessments and security audits) and it is by no means the case that armed protection in all operations around the globe will only be provided by private companies.

One possible policy

Under the policy of one agency, armed protection can be considered when:

- large numbers of lives are at risk;
- the threat is related to widespread banditry, not political;
- the provider is acceptable; and
- the deterrent can be effective.

Chapter 4
Evacuation, hibernation, remote management programming and return

Although never an appealing scenario, circumstances will sometimes demand that an agency withdraw or severely restrict its programming presence in an area due to high levels of insecurity. This chapter discusses the main operational responses and modalities within these so-called limited access settings. There are four basic scenarios to consider: evacuation or relocation, hibernation, remote management programming and return.

Evacuation or relocation refer to the physical withdrawal of staff (and/or their families) and assets from an insecure environment. Evacuation usually refers to movement across an international border, while relocation refers to movement within the country.[1] This can be precipitated by a renewed outbreak of conflict, increasing unrest, targeting of aid agencies by armed groups or a natural disaster. An evacuation can also be forced in the case of expulsion by the government. Hibernation involves stopping staff movement and programmes at a field base or staying behind in one or more concentration sites. This may be because evacuation is impossible or too dangerous, or it is thought that the situation may improve in the near future. Remote management programming is where an international organisation has had to significantly alter normal ways of working due to insecurity. Remote management is sometimes used to refer to any type of operation carried out from a distance (even out of choice), but this GPR uses the term to refer exclusively to a reactive, unplanned position due to deteriorating security conditions. Return covers the process whereby an organisation (or a certain type of staff, such as international staff) returns to an area from which it had previously evacuated or relocated, and resumes normal working.

4.1 Evacuation and relocation

4.1.1 Some common assumptions
It is important to be aware of four common but often misleading assumptions regarding evacuation and relocation.

---

1 Depending on geography, a small number of staff may be temporarily moved across a national border, so it should not be assumed that evacuation is necessarily more serious or complete than relocation; in many cases the terms are used interchangeably.

1. The deterioration will be gradual

Evacuation is conceived as the ultimate step in a gradual reduction of exposure – from suspension of movements of certain types of staff, to suspension of operations, to partial withdrawal of staff from a site, to total withdrawal and the closure of activities. Bear in mind, however, that events can overtake plans. Planning through security phases, although useful, can give the impression of a linear progression, when this may not always be the case (see Chapter 2 on 'Risk assessment').

2. Evacuation will go according to plan

While planning is always valuable, it is important to remember that:

- staff often do not refer to the plan in a sudden and acute crisis;
- important elements may have been overlooked and not planned for;
- things often do not go according to plan because of external actors and factors; and
- evacuation can be forced, for example when an agency is expelled by the government authorities. This requires a different kind of planning (see Section 4.1.4 below).

3. Evacuation will be possible

In many situations, evacuation routes are blocked, the logistical capacity for evacuation is insufficient, or it simply becomes too dangerous to try to evacuate and staff have to stay put and weather the crisis. Too many security plans only consider evacuation, neglect the relocation option and fail to consider hibernation.

4. Return will be possible

Evacuated staff may not be able to return quickly, and the agency may find itself withdrawn from the context or doing remote management programming for weeks, months or even years.

4.1.2 The decision to withdraw

Deciding to stay or go

Relocation and especially evacuation are difficult decisions – not just from a programmatic but also from an ethical point of view. The humanitarian imperative and the need to ensure the security of staff do not go easily together. If the mission involves the provision of services then it may be tempting to stay if this can still be done in a meaningful way and standards can be maintained. Staying may show solidarity with an endangered population and may maintain a monitoring or witnessing presence.

Other factors that may influence the decision to stay or go include:

- Internal agency procedures that require approval from headquarters before returning, which can reduce incentives for a quick or temporary withdrawal.
- Pressure to implement a project for fear of losing donor funds in the future.
- Individual staff in the field do not perceive the increased risks or feel that they are justified in staying for reasons of programme impact or even their own job security.
- A worry that withdrawing repeatedly or too quickly will undermine acceptance.

The temptation will be to postpone the decision until the last moment, when the situation has become so clear that there is no room for hesitation. This is a high-risk strategy, as events may change rapidly and withdrawal may become impossible. Getting out *before* something happens usually makes re-engagement easier than if evacuation is forced following a serious security incident. Good practice involves setting triggers or indicators for withdrawal before the situation becomes critical (see Chapter 2 for more advice on how to decide whether to stay or go). Be sure too to consider the possibility of temporary, preventative withdrawal, for example removing staff from certain locations in the run-up to possibly explosive political events, such as a contentious election or the announcement of election results.

Decision-making authority

It needs to be clear not only under what conditions an agency will evacuate or relocate, but also who has the ultimate authority to make that decision.

- Is it international HQ or the country director? What happens in the case of divergent opinions?
- Can a programme or office manager in a provincial base take the decision to relocate staff without prior approval from the agency representative in the capital?
- If the most senior manager in the field location has already withdrawn, who has the authority to order the withdrawal of more or all remaining staff?
- Is it clear to all staff that the decisions taken by management are mandatory?

See Chapter 5 on 'Incident reporting and critical incident management' for advice on how to put in place a team to manage an evacuation or relocation.

Interagency considerations

Evacuations in moments of serious crisis usually require interagency collaboration, which may be complicated by different appreciations of the risk (see Chapter 2 on 'Risk assessment'). The fact that some agencies evacuate while others do not may actually change the risk and increase the vulnerability of those remaining. There may no longer be a critical mass of agencies present, which may encourage looting, theft and attack. If an agency is reliant on the UN or a foreign government for support, for example to mobilise helicopters, planes, a convoy or a ship, how does this fit into its decision-making?

The politics of evacuation and relocation

The presence of the UN, NGOs and diplomatic missions can imply that the security situation is tolerable and that the local and national authorities are in sufficient control to maintain security for international actors. An evacuation will obviously send the opposite signal, something that political actors – whether the national or local authorities, a foreign government or an armed rebel group – may be keen to avoid. Keep this in mind when considering any advice from political actors. The question of whether the local authorities (or armed groups controlling the area) should be informed before exiting should be decided on a case-by-case basis. Failure to do so may cause upset and complicate relations when the agency returns; if informed, the authorities may try to put pressure on the agency to dissuade it from leaving.

4.1.3 Planning for and managing the withdrawal of staff

Establishing policy

Staff policy with regard to relocation and evacuation needs to be documented and communicated clearly to all in advance. As far as possible, the rights and responsibilities of employers and employees should be laid down in employment contracts or in the security policy. Explicit guidance should be in place that, in times of heightened security risk, non-essential staff will be relocated or evacuated from the area. It should be clear who is considered essential and non-essential staff, and how this determination will be made when the time comes (see below).

For international staff, it should be clearly articulated that refusal to withdraw from an area is considered as resignation and leads to immediate termination of the contract. Equally clear should be the right of an individual to request to be withdrawn from a risky area on the grounds of a profound feeling of insecurity. Note that this can entail significant financial expenditure, so this should be agreed at a senior management level. In the case of evacuation facilitated by an embassy (e.g. of a European or North American country), know in advance which staff would be eligible, and whether they would choose this option over an agency-facilitated evacuation. For national staff, it should be clear what their and their dependents' entitlements are in relation to relocation (within the country) and evacuation (internationally). These entitlements will depend on where their contractual base is, and if they are likely to be directly targeted (see below).

Partial withdrawals: reductions in non-essential or high-risk staff

Consider a partial withdrawal of staff. Moving just part of the team will decrease the security burden. In times of rising tension, and as part of the procedure associated with a specific security phase, non-essential staff should be relocated. The purpose of this pre-emptive measure is to reduce overall vulnerability by reducing the number of people at risk, thereby making a crisis relocation or evacuation more manageable.

Non-essential staff will usually include any staff not vital to the continuation of the programme. Assess how likely it is that certain programme components, or any programme at all, could be maintained. Consider staff who may be less senior, but who play a critical function in emergency settings (e.g. logistics or communications specialists). Consider too withdrawing staff who face particularly high risk, regardless of whether they are 'essential'. Certain nationalities or ethnic or religious groups may be a potential target. Likewise, there may be situations where women are at higher risk.

An individual staff member may find it psychologically difficult to deal with rising insecurity, or may perceive him or herself to be at high risk. This could include a staff member in a key operational position. He or she should probably be withdrawn, as maintaining such people in a deteriorating situation may eventually cause more problems than their earlier departure.

Considerations for nationally recruited staff

The sudden evacuation or relocation of international counterparts can leave national staff upset and angry. There may be resentment that the agency appears to be treating international staff with more concern, belying claims to equality of care for all staff, or national staff may not be aware until very late on what the limits of the agency's responsibilities towards them actually are. None of this is necessary: as part of the security management planning process, national staff should be clear about what they can and cannot expect, so that they can start making their own arrangements for their security and that of their dependants.

Most organisations believe that their duty of care for national staff does not generally include providing evacuation across international borders, since national staff remain first and foremost citizens of the country affected by the crisis. Even if an organisation did want to evacuate its national staff, there are no simple solutions to the gap between what an agency wants to do and what it can in practice do in view of the financial, legal and practical constraints it is under. That said, there are international legal instruments and national procedures to provide asylum to people with genuine fears of persecution. The UN, for example, is prepared to consider the evacuation of nationally recruited staff if their lives become endangered as a consequence of their employment. Similarly, an employee of an international NGO could be subject to persecution for his or her connection to the agency. This issue becomes more complex when a broader category of people is threatened. In the 1994 genocide in Rwanda, many Tutsi and moderate Hutu staff of international agencies were killed; international staff, though at far less risk, were evacuated. In the period after 2003, Christians in Iraq were targeted, especially those working for international NGOs.

National staff members may be working at an operational base in a different part of the country from their district of origin, in unfamiliar physical and social territory and without their normal support mechanisms. Relocated national staff can therefore be at higher risk. If the relocation was a consequence of employment, the agency should take responsibility for moving these staff and their families to their location of origin or recruitment, or to another safe area if that would also not be safe.

It would be wrong to assume that all national staff want to leave. A number may want to stay, to protect their dependants and assets, raising the question of what help, if any, they should be given. Support might include providing mobile phones, prepaid calling cards, access to agency buildings for themselves and their family or letters of employment or reference. In many circumstances, the most practical help will be financial. Discuss beforehand whether national staff prefer local or another currency or a mix of both. The calculation of a lump sum for staff who are not formally being made redundant but who will cease work because of security risks can be phrased in terms of ongoing payment during annual leave or extraordinary leave, severance pay or extra payment in lieu of notice. Depending on means, salary scales and the cost of living, something in the order of two to three months' salary will provide staff and their dependants with some financial reserves. Alternatively, everyone may be given the same lump sum regardless of salary scales. In order to effect these payments it may be necessary to bring in large sums of cash, which is itself a risk (see Chapter 11 on cash security). In high-risk environments, this money may be kept in reserve in a safe.

Domestic staff, contractors and consultants

Are domestic staff on the agency payroll logged as staff, or are they contracted by individuals (mostly international staff)? What responsibility can and will the agency take? Other people may be hired as contractors or consultants, for example drivers, builders or local analysts. In general these people will expect the agency to take responsibility for their security, so clarify when they sign their employment contract what they can and cannot expect.

Local partner organisations

Agencies working closely with a local organisation in a contracting or partnership relationship will need to clarify, at the stage of signing a contract or memorandum of understanding, what they consider their responsibilities to be, and what local organisations can realistically expect from them. This may include training on security management and involving partners in the development of shared security guidelines.

4.1.4 Preparing for a government expulsion: a special case

In some contexts, it may make sense to prepare for a potential forced removal in the form of government expulsion. This may be the case where similar agencies have recently been expelled, or where there is reason to believe that the agency may be targeted by an unfriendly host government. Many of the preparations will be similar to an evacuation due to security risks. However, consider the following:

- Will the agency try to appeal against the decision, and if so through what means (judicial, direct discussions with the authorities, advocacy or lobbying as part of a consortium, media campaigns, discussions with donors or embassies)?
- What steps have been taken to protect potentially sensitive, confidential or personal information from being inadvertently disclosed (see below)?
- Is the expulsion going to put national staff (or other remaining staff) at specific risk?
- Can steps be taken to prevent staff (especially remaining national staff) from being harassed or threatened by government authorities?
- Will national staff be paid salaries or severance pay, should this be required by the government, and for how long?
- Can the risk that assets will be permanently seized be minimised?
- What role might any government donors to programmes be able to play in overturning the decision or appealing to the host government for more lenient treatment?
- What will be the media reaction (locally and internationally) and how will it be dealt with?

4.1.5 Planning and carrying out an evacuation or relocation
Practicing for evacuation or relocation

The evacuation/relocation plan should be regularly reviewed and discussed with staff, especially if it is becoming increasingly likely that a withdrawal will be necessary. This can be carried out through simulation exercises[2] or a simple team meeting to review policies, procedures and plans. In the height of a crisis, individual staff members may be tempted to take all sorts of unplanned steps and go to places other than the planned assembly points. The effect is likely to increase confusion, delay the evacuation and heighten the risk for everybody. No individual initiatives that deviate from the plan should be taken without prior authorisation by the head of the crisis management team.

Logistics and route planning

Key issues to consider are:

- Which routes and means of transport are most feasible under different scenarios?
- Which is more likely to reduce risk, moving in high profile with logos, flags and HF mobile radio antennae prominent, or low profile with all of these removed?
- How much transport is available, for how many people? What kind of assets or personal effects can be taken?
- Who provides the transport (if not the agency itself then arrangements will have to be made with another organisation). Discuss in advance capacity, procedural requirements and the limits of the agency's responsibility and liability. This requires a thorough understanding of the policies of the organisation or the transport agent. Find out under what circumstances a private charter plane (or a Medevac flight) will not come to pick up staff, despite pre-agreements.

Many evacuations and relocations depend upon collaboration between different organisations. Do not draw up a plan in isolation. While it is usually safer to travel in a vehicle convoy with other NGOs, this also means less control over how the evacuation is carried out. Address with other agencies beforehand, if possible, how these issues will be handled.

In certain relocation or evacuation scenarios staff may have to drive or even walk a long distance. In others they will need to make their way from the assembly points to a port or airport. Ensure detailed route planning in advance, using, or sketching, maps. This will probably involve exploring

2 Any drills of this nature should be done discreetly, so that concerns are not raised among others that an evacuation is imminent or that there is a threat that others are unaware of.

alternative routes if the preferred one is blocked or considered too dangerous. Think too about the requirements of different routes and the potential impact of different climatic conditions. It may, for example, not be possible to drive all the way to the border, so staff may have to walk a long distance, even for several days. Be prepared, with supplies and walking equipment.

To prepare for an air evacuation, GPS coordinates, global satellite imaging (e.g. Google Earth) and details of the physical condition of airstrips should be held electronically at headquarters or with private flight charters in advance to speed up possible airlift options.

In high-risk areas where evacuation is likely or has happened already, more advanced preparations can be pursued. For example, prior to their evacuation to Jordan and Kuwait in 2003, many international organisations working in Iraq had already set up an office in these countries.

Preparation of assembly points

Identify sites where those who will be relocated or evacuated will gather before evacuation. The assembly point needs to be accessible, secure, large enough to accommodate many people and several vehicles and have reliable communications and emergency stocks (including medical supplies and fuel) to take along in the evacuation, or so that it can develop into a hibernation point if evacuation proves impossible. In some cases, the GPS coordinates as well as maps highlighting assembly points may be shared in advance (or even agreed jointly) with other agencies or the national authorities.

Individual preparations

The agency headquarters and the central logistics provider need accurate and regularly updated information on how many staff (and dependants) qualify for international evacuation. Special requirements should be indicated, for example of a medical nature or if there are infants. If it is likely that international evacuation will be to a neighbouring country, contact the authorities there or a relevant embassy, and explore the possibility of maintaining valid visas for that country for all those qualifying for evacuation. All those eligible should ideally be given cash advances or one or more credit cards to cover initial expenses until the agency's cash flow has been re-established.

During a relocation or evacuation, qualifying individuals are typically allowed only one piece of luggage or luggage of a maximum weight (usually 5–10kg). In times of high tension, staff should always keep an 'evacuation bag' and vital documents ready. Individuals should take care of their own passports; they should not be kept in the office safe.

Key organisational records and information

Certain essential information is needed in order to report to donors after the evacuation and to return properly informed to the operational base when the danger period has passed. This will include inventories of assets, accounts, bills paid since the last financial report, payroll details, contracts and outstanding liabilities, memoranda of understanding and registration and tax correspondence with the national authorities. For more on protecting sensitive information, see Chapter 7 on 'Managing communications security'.

Stocks, assets and liabilities

Clarify in advance which assets are to be taken, which left behind, and what will be done with the remaining stock. Keep track of outstanding financial obligations, for example to landlords, suppliers, contractors, staff and owners of rented vehicles, and consider clearing these prior to exit. If this is not possible, take up-to-date records for later reference.

4.1.6 After the evacuation or relocation

A number of immediate, practical steps need to be taken after a relocation or evacuation:

1. At the first opportunity, contact headquarters and provide a detailed update on staff, security, finance and expected imminent movement plans.
2. If the evacuation was international, contact officials in the country of arrival (if this has not been done by HQ or prior to arrival), as well as relevant embassies and the local authorities if the stay is likely to be prolonged.
3. Establish or re-establish contact and communications with those staff left behind (see below).
4. In the case of an international evacuation, consider who can usefully stay in the region (if in a neighbouring country) and who should go home (on annual leave or end of contract).
5. Organise medium-term accommodation (office and living) and access to finance.
6. Prepare a report for headquarters and donors, with detailed updates on personnel, assets, stock and finance and outstanding liabilities at the point of evacuation.
7. Debrief evacuated staff and provide psychological support, as evacuation is likely to give rise to a variety of difficult feelings, including emotional exhaustion and a sense of failure, anger and guilt towards those left behind.

Planning for programme continuation

National staff can be asked to continue the programme. It is imperative that this situation is planned for and communicated in detail in advance. Pay attention to the following areas:

- The allocation of tasks and responsibilities. Key areas include financial management, administration, security, internal and external communications, personnel management, logistics and programme activities and reporting.
- The limits of responsibility. It should be very clear that staff wellbeing comes first and that staff should not put themselves at risk trying to protect agency assets.
- The limits of authority. Can staff purchase or sell assets, hire and fire personnel or take disciplinary action, enter into new contracts, liaise with the authorities or decide on changes in the programme, for instance? What do staff need prior authorisation for, and what should they do if communications are interrupted for a prolonged period?
- The new arrangements may also affect others, including other agencies, relevant embassies, the local authorities and the bank. How widely and publicly the new arrangements are communicated will depend on the context and the size and visibility of the ongoing programme. National staff may be more vulnerable to pressure, intimidation and threats, in which case discretion might be more advisable.
- A protocol of communications with agency representatives.
- A timeline for when these arrangements will be reviewed and revised.

Bear in mind that the relocation or evacuation may last much longer than originally planned, and may evolve into remote programming; see below for additional guidance.

4.2 Hibernation

4.2.1 Hibernation scenarios

Hibernation in a danger zone can be voluntary or forced. Voluntary hibernation can be a good option when staying is safer than moving, or when time is needed to evaluate the ability to move (but bear in mind that hibernation can also put staff at risk: just because an agency and its assets have not been targeted in previous crises does not mean that they are forever secure). Forced hibernation can result from a rapid unfolding of events that could not be anticipated, or can be imposed if withdrawal becomes impossible (e.g. the scheduled plane does not arrive). Forced hibernation could mean that staff are confined to the same building for hours, days or even weeks on end.

Evacuation, hibernation

4

4.2.2 Preparing for hibernation

Identify and equip more than one retreat or hibernation facility, if possible. Long-term physical requirements include:

- food, water and essential medicine (including a post-exposure prophylaxis or PEP kit (see Chapter 12 on sexual aggression));
- facilities for sleeping, washing and using the toilet, and air circulation;
- fuel and equipment for cooking; and
- lighting, such as candles, flashlights and hurricane lanterns.

Long-term psychological requirements should also be taken into account; where possible, try to provide books and games, additional means to contact the outside world (radio, TV, telephones) and space for daily physical exercise.

Ensuring some means of communication with the outside world is crucial. This can be done through some combination of radio, mobile phones, satellite phones or internet access. It will require an ongoing power supply, such as a rechargeable battery. Keep in mind that generators can be noisy and can attract looters. In the event of looting, one of the most precious items to preserve is the means of communication. Try to hide a radio and aerial or satphone where it cannot be found, even if the whole site is being stripped down to the door frames.

Consider setting up safe rooms or bunkers if bombing is a possible risk. A safe room has no external doors or windows. Seek advice from qualified technical experts, as safe rooms and bunkers can be dangerous if not constructed to proper standards. This guidance should cover all practical considerations such as communications (keep in mind that a satellite phone requires a cable connection to an external antenna), access to power/generators and bathroom facilities.

4.3 Remote management programming

4.3.1 What is remote management programming?

Remote management programming, as practiced by most agencies, is normally a reactive rather than a planned position, due to poor or deteriorating security conditions or other restrictions in the operating environment. It can include:

- Withdrawing international staff or other categories of staff, in particular those seen to be at especially high risk from the programming location.
- Altering management structures to give more responsibility to national and or local staff who remain present.

- Forming new operational arrangements with local partners, including local NGOs, Community Based Organisations and local authorities.

Different terms are used to describe different types of remote management programming. 'Remote control', 'remote control management' or 'distance management' can refer to situations where the same management structure remains in place, i.e. with international staff retaining full decision-making authority. In this GPR, remote management programming is used as a generic term to refer to all arrangements as described above. Some also use the term 'limited access programming', but this refers to a much broader range of challenges than simply security, including government restrictions and physical remoteness. Remote management programming refers to an operational adaptation caused *specifically* by insecurity.

Remote management programming is not a new phenomenon. During the Cold War, solidarity agencies provided aid directly to resistance movements (in Eritrea, Ethiopia and Afghanistan in the 1980s), without much oversight by international staff. In the late 1990s, a serious deterioration in the security situation forced aid agencies to relocate their operational bases and international staff from Chechnya to Ingushetia and then to North Ossetia. In late 2003 and 2004, many agencies relocated their international staff from parts of Iraq to Amman in Jordan. Deteriorating security conditions later necessitated the use of remote programming in Afghanistan, Pakistan and Somalia. Remote management programming has also been used at different times in northern Uganda, Gaza, Sri Lanka, Colombia and in Darfur, Sudan.

The approach is becoming more common not only because of increasing risks to aid workers (including international staff), but also because of rapid advances in transport and especially communications technology. Cellular phones, satellite phones and the internet have made it easier than ever to maintain regular contact with national staff or partners based in the field and to monitor programmes. One international NGO working via partner organisations in Iraq recently closed its office in Amman and now manages these partners from Lebanon and the UK.

4.3.2 The challenges of remote management programming

As it is often a last-resort and *ad hoc* adaptation, remote management programming usually presents serious challenges. These can include:

- Ethical problems of risk transfer, specifically if the staff members or local partners taking over programme responsibilities are being asked to assume higher levels of risk in the process. The money they stand to gain may make it next to impossible to refuse the opportunity.

- Difficulties in assessing changing security risks, and the environment generally, as staff and partners in situ may become less attuned to subtle shifts.
- Communications and logistical difficulties involved in supporting staff in situ.
- Security implications of getting money or supplies to staff and partners.
- Over-reliance on a few staff in high-stress environments, leading to burn-out.
- Difficulty in ensuring proper programme oversight, affecting quality and accountability.
- Difficulty in sustaining interagency coordination in the location, as the staff and partners who take over programme responsibilities typically were not involved in coordination activities previously.
- It can undermine perceptions of neutrality and independence if the partner organisation is unable to maintain humanitarian principles. It can also undermine acceptance due to declining programme quality or increasing corruption (although greater local ownership may well increase acceptance).
- Difficulties in meeting donor requirements for monitoring and reporting.
- A heightened focus on security management, so that it no longer becomes a means to an end, but an end in itself.

The possibility that remote programming is simply transferring risk to national staff or local partner organisations deserves special mention. Security risks may be seen as too high for international staff, but this does not necessarily mean that national or local staff are any more secure. In Chechnya in the late 1990s, Iraq since 2003, Afghanistan since about 2004 and south-central Somalia and Puntland, both international and national staff have been at risk of kidnapping or targeted assassination, albeit to varying degrees. It is important to carry out risk assessments for remaining staff based on the specific conditions in the area, rather than simply assuming that local staff will automatically be at lower risk. In some cases, the lack of international staff presence may itself put national staff at greater risk.

Across the community of aid agencies, the general lack of contingency planning and strategic preparation for remote management scenarios greatly exacerbates the challenges involved. Moreover, the dearth of agency guidelines and procedures on the subject seems particularly problematic given how widely the practice is used in insecure settings.

4.3.3 Security management during remote programming

Remote programming also raises a new set of financial, safety and contractual considerations, entailing a new analysis of benefits and risks. Bear in mind that continuing with programmes under remote management may be riskier than shutting down altogether, and that there may be risks associated with closing a programme that has been managed remotely if doing so antagonises the staff affected.

If it is possible to continue operating under a remote programming approach, changes will be called for in management structure, style and approach. Management procedures may become more complex and onerous, with frequent check-ins or oral reports on financial, programmatic or personnel matters. New ways of monitoring programmes may have to be developed, such as taking photos of project outputs (e.g. water sources or schools constructed), with GPS coordinates attached. Some techniques may increase the security of staff, such as using third parties to monitor outputs or using local radio to advertise beneficiary entitlements. The programme aim or approach itself may have to be adapted to explicitly give more responsibility to national staff.

Making the switch

There can be a tendency for remote programming to creep in more-or-less unnoticed. As security conditions deteriorate, an organisation may not realise that it is gradually shifting towards a remote programming approach. Visits by staff to field locations may become fewer, but with the expectation that this situation is only temporary. Because remote programming has wide implications for security management (and other areas), it is important that senior managers do as much as they can to plan for and establish the new mode of programming in advance of a de facto remote management situation being established.

It may help to establish criteria in advance for when a change of working style must occur, and what this will mean for the team, partners and local authorities. Triggers could include the number of postponed management visits, the number of security incidents of a certain type or the number of trips rescheduled due to security risks. At some point, the uncertainty of an ambiguous situation may be so disruptive as to merit taking a different approach. One of the most important responsibilities is of course staff security: who is in charge, and what level of authority do they have? Formally switching to remote programming – and delineating what this means, for whom – clarifies expectations and responsibilities, including in security management.

Insecurity and increasing limitations on the way programmes are carried out can sometimes be recognised in advance. One international NGO working in Ethiopia, for example, designed a nutrition programme from the beginning with a partner organisation based in the region, since it knew that international staff would not be welcome there. Supplies were pre-positioned in anticipation of an emergency response, and staff from the local organisation were trained in the appropriate interventions.

Risk assessments

Even if national staff (or local partner organisations) are indeed at lower risk than international staff, security conditions can change rapidly, making it important to find a way to monitor the changing situation and stop programming if risks for remaining national staff become unacceptable. It is worth keeping in mind that national staff may be less likely than internationals to conclude that the overall risk level has become intolerable. International staff must be able to challenge the information coming from the field, and must have a way to crosscheck information. This can be done through a network of local contacts (i.e. traders, local authorities) who can be reached by phone, and by sharing information and analysis with other agencies operating in the area.

Training and resources

It may be possible to provide national staff with knowledge and skills training, including in security management. National staff in Iraq and Somalia, for instance, have travelled to Amman, Somaliland and Nairobi to participate in training on the mandate and mission of their organisation, humanitarian principles and security management. In Somalia, an international NGO operating exclusively with national staff brought several dozen staff members and partners to Hargeisa to review its security plan.

When working with national partner organisations, it will be necessary to consider whether they may need additional resources or training in security management. Although the same duty of care does not usually apply, an international agency may wish to fund hardware inputs (radios, vehicles, site protection) or skills training for a local organisation, should they request it. It should not be assumed that all national NGOs are able to keep themselves safe by means of acceptance only.

Practices identified in recent research as contributing to successful remote management programming include:[3]

---

3 Abby Stoddard, Adele Harmer and Jean S. Renouf, *Once Removed: Lessons and Challenges in Remote Management of Humanitarian Operations for Insecure Areas* (New York: Humanitarian Outcomes, 2010).

- Including the remote management scenario in contingency planning exercises; considering in advance potential local partners, management and monitoring structures and exit and transition strategies.
- Establishing clear procedures and instructions for staff and partners on communications, and reporting on activities and progress.
- Bringing local personnel or partner representatives out of the area on a regular basis for management, coordination and discussions.
- Performing spot checks and surprise visits and audits, as feasible.
- Crosschecking and verifying monitoring information with other organisations and field contacts. Establishing and maintaining a local network of information providers, intermediaries and facilitators within the local community.

4.4 Return

4.4.1 Deciding to return

The key question here is finding out whether it is safe enough to return or to increase staff presence, and who in the agency will take responsibility for the decision to conduct an exploratory mission and subsequently to return evacuated and relocated staff. In the absence of a fairly radical change on the ground (e.g. the leader of a rebel group is defeated and the armed movement rapidly collapses, allowing the government to restore its control over the whole territory), the return may also be gradual and phased. First may come a few short exploratory missions to reassess the situation, then possibly a more permanent presence of essential staff in one operational base, followed by the gradual return of more staff and associated personnel to more operational bases. This was the case with several large organisations returning to Iraq and Afghanistan.

Key information for assessing the security situation for an exploratory mission includes:

- The actual situation on the ground (security, military, political).
- Possible changes in the next 3–6 months, and their security implications.
- The status of logistics (airports, roads), communications and services (banks) following the crisis.
- The whereabouts and status of staff not evacuated.
- The status of property, assets and stocks left behind.
- The movements of local people.
- The availability of essential provisions, especially food, water and fuel.
- The image of the organisation on the ground, and whether and how perceptions can be managed.

4 Evacuation, hibernation

- The level of direct targeting of foreign elements, including aid workers.
- Organisational capability to manage security in the current context.
- An analysis of overall risks and benefits.

4.4.2 Managing a return

The return of international or other previously departed staff is likely to create a sensitive situation, certainly for local and national staff and counterparts, who have probably become used to greater autonomy and derive pride and confidence in having managed on their own. It will be important to make clear that staff are not returning because the organisation is concerned with how programmes have been managed in their absence. Meetings between field (often national) and senior (often international) staff at 'security neutral' locations (e.g. Somaliland for programmes in south-central Somalia with head offices in Nairobi) are also a way of maintaining coordination and relationships between staff from both locations. Generally, giving remaining staff greater initiative should be seen as a positive side-effect of remote programming. Higher levels of decision-making taking place at the field level should not necessarily be changed after the physical return of senior or other international staff.

Chapter 5
Incident reporting and critical incident management

5.1 The importance of incident reporting and monitoring

It is vitally important to report security incidents, including threats and near-misses, for three main reasons:

- To alert the field office and headquarters, so that they are aware and, if necessary, can provide help.
- To alert people in other organisations – and where appropriate the local authorities and population – so that they can take precautionary action.
- To allow for tracking and trend analysis of incidents to inform security risk assessments and decision-making.

Incident reporting can greatly assist security managers in understanding the operational context and predicting the kind of incidents that may be likely in the future. A reliable overview of reportable incidents around the world, worked through a database, allows for greater security analysis at the country, regional and global levels. Many larger aid organisations now have internal incident reporting systems, some of them accessible online. Having such a system can help to avoid confusion about types and classifications of incidents and to ensure that staff provide the crucial information required. These details can reveal geographical concentrations of incidents, provide insight into the types of incidents taking place and show whether the overall number of incidents is increasing or decreasing. This kind of information can in turn help in deciding where to allocate limited security resources (human and financial), for example what type of safety and security training to focus on.

Centralising the incident reports of all the agencies operating in the same environment, for instance through a security cooperation platform such as ANSO in Afghanistan, can also be of significant benefit. This can allow for a more objective incident pattern analysis and help to determine trends if the data are analysed over time. This is one of the functions for which an interagency security platform (see Chapter 1) can be extremely useful. Managerial guidance is required to ensure that people correctly understand what they are expected to report and how – and what the information can be used for.

Incident reporting

5.1.1 What counts as a 'reportable incident'?

A security incident is anything that causes harm to staff or associated people, or loss of or damage to assets. A 'near-incident' is something that almost caused such harm, damage or loss. A threatening action can be written, verbal or a physical gesture, as long as it credibly signifies the intent of an actor to cause harm. It is important to include even minor incidents, and to report near-incidents. If in doubt, report it. Reporting should also include incidents or near-incidents affecting other entities involved in the programme, including partner organisations and contractors. It may also be useful to include in the reporting requirements any incident in which a staff member has caused harm to a third party, or loss or damage to the property or assets of a third party.

5.1.2 The incident report

It is important to alert colleagues and associates of an incident as soon as possible after it happens, even if all information has not yet been obtained. A fuller incident report, however, is usually written up after the incident and the incident response – although for protracted situations (e.g. a kidnapping) a report may be produced before the incident is over. Incident reports are kept at field level and shared with headquarters, and could be shared with an interagency field platform, if one exists.

An organisation may have a standard incident report form, and may even have it available online for easy access. Whatever format is used, the important thing is that all the key information is provided. The incident report will focus on the basic questions: what happened, who did it, to whom, when and where. It is important to verify all of this information. It may or may not be relevant to add something about the 'why' and 'why this organisation' (this can be deleted in the incident report shared with other agencies). Was the organisation specifically targeted, and if so why? Be sure to indicate the degree of confidence in the answer. Sometimes it is obvious because the perpetrators said so, but in other instances this may just be speculation.

Common problems with incident reports include:

- Not knowing the identity of the perpetrators or their motives until much later, or in some cases never knowing at all. It is important to indicate the degree of confidence about statements, and to change internal organisational records if new details emerge.
- There is a natural reluctance to acknowledge that acts or omissions by the agency or some of its personnel have contributed to an incident taking place.
- Classification difficulties, for instance distinguishing between theft, burglary and armed robbery, and between abduction and kidnapping. How

these different categories are defined should be clear to all sharing the reporting system.

Key information in the incident report

- Incident type, e.g. kidnap, death, serious assault, theft.
- Who was involved?
- When did the incident occur?
- Where (as precisely as possible) did the incident occur?
- How many casualties occurred as a result and how serious are they?
- What emergency response action has been undertaken so far? Is additional response requested? If so, what?
- How many perpetrators were there, what did they do and where are they now?
- Is the situation ongoing?

It is important not to let confusion or disagreement over classifications and terminologies get in the way of instituting a system for incident reporting. If staff members are not able to consistently apply classifications, if there are language barriers or if staff find the process daunting and off-putting, do whatever is necessary to ensure that the information gets logged. Some organisations and security platforms centralise the classification of incidents, so staff can simply relay the information they have as quickly as possible, and security coordinators then follow up with them to answer questions as needed and do the classification and formal entry centrally.

5.2 Critical incident management

A critical incident is a security incident severe enough that it leads to a situation with the potential to cause significant disruption to operations or even discontinue them.[1]

5.2.1 Preparedness: establishing critical incident management structures
In order to respond to a critical incident an organisation should develop both a critical incident management process and a critical incident management team (CIMT). The critical incident management team should establish hierarchical responsibilities and draw a clear distinction between the roles played at the country office level, the regional office and global headquarters. Everyone needs to understand where they fit in. For some incidents, a CIMT may operate

5 Incident reporting

---

1 The definition is drawn from IFRC, *Stay Safe: The International Federation's Guide for Security Managers* (Geneva: IFRC, 2007).

only at field level, but there needs to be a clear understanding of when to bring in the regional and headquarters levels as necessary. Serious or prolonged incidents (an assassination, bomb attack, kidnapping, hostage situation or forced hibernation) or major changes such as a relocation or evacuation will typically require a dedicated CIMT.

Critical incident management is challenging and requires particular skills. A range of competencies and expertise will be required, some of which may have to be found outside the organisation. It makes sense to identify major potential human resource needs in advance, for example for psychologists or negotiation specialists. Some organisations draw on former staff members, who know the organisation and whose competencies and experience are recognised and trusted. Ensure that financial resources are available, and invest in advance in preparedness training, including simulation exercises.

Individuals within the CIMT (and their substitutes in case of absence) should be identified in advance (a clear Organigram Chart should be developed, with defined responsibilities and a contact list). A CIMT should be small and include representatives of a number of core functions, including the Country Director, the security focal point, logistics, HR, communications and legal advice. Alternatively, or in addition, a Critical Incident Manager (CIM) may be appointed. The CIM should have the authority to commit the appropriate personnel, equipment, finances and other resources to ensure an effective and timely response.

The first step in dealing with a critical incident should always be deciding whether immediate action is required to preserve life or to ensure safety. Verifiable information must be established outlining the details of the incident. This will be part of the initial reporting. Additional information or changes must be advised as they occur. Always have an incident reporting system in place to enable both the recording and analysis of incidents. The critical incident log must be initiated immediately after the incident is reported. This is to record the chronology of events, log phone calls, record notes of meetings and ensure that all documents are recorded and filed.

5.2.2 The role of the Critical Incident Management Team

On receiving an incident report, the CIMT must decide:

- Whether programme activities should be suspended or personnel withdrawn to a more secure location.
- If additional support personnel should be deployed to assist.

- What information should be circulated internally and externally, and any limitations or confidentiality issues.
- The end-state objective (injured person evacuated, body repatriated, kidnapped staff member released).

The CIMT will also need to consider medical and security issues, logistical support and surge capacity, legal issues and communications and media issues. There may be injured people who require immediate or long-term care. If lives were lost, family members will need to be informed and measures taken to provide for funeral, burial and other expenses. Security may still be a concern if individuals not caught up in the actual incident are still at risk, and logistical support may be needed to organise search and rescue or recovery missions, medical evacuations or the repatriation or return of the bodies of the dead to their families. Depending on the situation, specialised staff may be dispatched to the affected field office, for instance to provide search and rescue capacity, medical or forensic help and psychological and counselling support. The regional office and international headquarters may also require such expertise.

5.2.3 Evacuation and relocation

If the situation calls for the relocation or evacuation of staff, the CIMT will need to manage and monitor:

- Situational developments via a network of contacts, the telecoms system and local and international media.
- Logistics arrangements and security.
- The assembly and organised movement of all staff to be withdrawn.
- The assets to be taken along.
- Financial and administrative matters.
- Securing essential, confidential and sensitive documentation.
- Internal communications with headquarters and field staff.
- External communications with other agencies, the national authorities and relevant embassies.
- Public relations (communications with local people, the local and international press), including media messages (see Chapter 7 on 'Managing communications security' for more on dealing with the media).
- The attempted continuation of the programme.
- Internal coordination and monitoring of the various tasks being implemented.

In the case of an interagency exit operation, establish a central coordinating point. For more details on planning and carrying out an evacuation see Chapter 4.

5.2.4 Communications

At the country level

Many people and organisations may have to be informed very quickly at a time of crisis. Rather than have one person try to do this, establish a reliable communications tree or network in which each 'node' has responsibility for passing on information to three or four other nodes. An easy way to do this is to use the organigram of the mission. This needs to be updated regularly at preset intervals so that names and phone numbers are accurate. It should also be clarified in advance whether phone calls, SMS or radio will be used. A warden system, if in place, can be integrated into this. In times of emergency, national communications networks are prone to failure or overload: if possible, ensure that the organisation has alternative means of communications independent of the national infrastructure.

If the incident calls into question the continuation of programme activities and possibly even the organisation's continued presence in a given environment, it will be necessary to communicate with affected communities, the general public and key donors.

Between the country and regional/headquarters offices

Reliable, dedicated, round-the-clock and possibly secure communications will be needed between the field office affected and the CIMT in a regional office and at international HQ. Anticipate a temporary loss of communications, and prepare accordingly. Also anticipate the need for translation if the regional or headquarters team does not speak the local language. Communicate with other staff in the offices most directly affected, as well as with the rest of the organisation. For a serious incident, the Board of Directors will have to be kept informed and may be consulted on critical decisions.

It may be necessary to communicate with the local, national and international media – and be prepared when they contact you. Consider posting a statement on the organisation's website and intranet, and what information to include. Be very clear about what information is to remain confidential, who is included in the information circle and how confidentiality will be protected.

Families, neighbours and other agencies

You will have to communicate with the families of staff affected by the incident. Expect families to take initiatives themselves, especially if the incident lasts for a long time. You will also have to communicate with the families of non-employees caught up in an incident. If the agency's office has come under attack, for example, speak to the neighbours, whose sense of insecurity has probably been heightened. The primary focus must be dealing with the agency's own staff, but it will normally always be necessary to alert other aid agencies about a major security incident, so that they can take precautionary measures.

5.2.5 Relations with the authorities

Agreement and collaboration with the host government may be needed for the rapid processing of visa applications for crisis support or other surge staff. Depending on the nature of the incident, both the host government and the governments of affected staff may mobilise their own experts in response. This can create a difficult situation in terms of responsibility and duty of care. If another entity takes the lead, argue for what you consider to be the best interest of the victim – hopefully in alignment with the victim's family. It may be possible to pre-empt this by asking relevant government officials what actions they would expect to take in the event of a particular incident.

5.2.6 Administrative, legal and financial considerations

Some situations will require legal advice. This advice may pertain to terms of contracts, employee benefits, insurance questions, legal rights under applicable labour laws, legal representation with a host or home government, or dealing with legal challenges and claims for damages.

Managing a critical incident, particularly a prolonged one, also requires administrative support and specialised human resources. There may be other urgent expenses for travel, equipment or external services, and affected staff may be temporarily unable to work because of physical injury or psychological stress. To ensure some business continuity, it may be necessary to bring in temporary replacements. In short, expect to require extra cash because of unplanned and non-budgeted expenditures. Some but not all of these expenditures will be covered by the agency's insurance (see Annex 5).

People directly affected by an incident (including eye-witnesses) will need appropriate psychological and grief or trauma counselling support. Such support may also be offered to other staff members, and to victims' relatives.

5.3 Post-incident management

5.3.1 Debriefing and after-action review

Everyone, staff or not, who was directly involved in the management of the incident should have the opportunity for a debriefing. This may also include staff who were close to the situation but not directly involved in its management. Any incident or near-incident affecting the organisation, its programmes, its partners or its contractors merits analysis, and an after-action review should be standard practice. For serious incidents, consider a more thorough and ideally

Incident reporting

5

independent evaluation of why the incident occurred, how it was managed and why it had the impact it did. Key questions include:

- Were security measures in place?
- Were security measures in place but not properly communicated to staff?
- Were security measures in place and communicated but not understood?
- Were security measures in place but not followed?
- Were security measures in place and followed, but inappropriate to the threat?
- Were warning signs of a specific impending threat not observed, or observed but ignored?
- Were there no warning signs and was the incident not foreseeable?
- Was the risk of a specific threat occurring accurately assessed as low, and appropriate security measures were in place, but the incident occurred anyway?
- Was a CIMT not pre-identified, or pre-identified but not prepared?

Any serious incident affecting another organisation also merits attention and analysis. That analysis may not necessarily conclude that the organisation is at heightened risk. There may be various reasons why what happened to another organisation is unlikely to happen to yours. The ability to conduct a reasonable analysis of an incident affecting another organisation will of course depend on how much reliable information can be obtained.

5.3.2 Review the threshold of acceptable risk

Any serious incident, whether it affects your organisation or not, should trigger a review of the organisation's threshold of acceptable risk. Does this incident or near-incident signal that the initial analysis was flawed? Does it signal that the organisation has crossed the threshold of acceptable risk? What are the practical consequences? Can security measures be strengthened to reduce the risk? Should there be changes to the operational security strategy, and will these changes be effective? Should staff be relocated away from areas of high risk? If adjustments or changes are required, staff need to be assigned to ensure that these changes are implemented, and a timeframe established. This may require new or additional training.

5.3.3 Renew informed consent

This is also an appropriate moment to share with all staff the new assessment of the security situation and of the nature and level of risk, as well as the likely effectiveness of the organisation's security measures. Staff should be given the opportunity to decide whether they are prepared to continue working with the organisation in these circumstances.

Section 3
People in security management

Chapter 6
People in security management

This chapter discusses the role of people – the individuals and teams who comprise an agency's staff – in security management. The chapter starts by describing the role of the field-level security manager or security focal point, including elements of the job description and the benefits of employing international or national staff for this role. Next, the chapter addresses the kinds of personal skills and team competencies required for good security management.

The third section looks at the different types of threats faced by different kinds of staff: international, national and local, as well as men and women, and the gender elements of security management. This section also looks at staff as a potential source of some security problems, and how to mitigate this. The fourth section looks at issues that are typically dealt with by a human resource unit within an organisation, as they relate to security: staff composition, recruitment, insurance and access to training specifically on security. The final section deals with how to manage stress.

6.1 Field-level security managers

In high-risk environments, security management usually merits at least one full-time dedicated staff member. This person manages day-to-day security-related work, while the primary responsibility for security typically remains with the Country Director. The UN has been using field security officers for some time, and in recent years international NGOs have also begun to create such posts. It is wise to set indicators for changes in the security environment that create or remove the need for a full-time security officer. Officers may only be responsible for a certain high-risk area within a wider operational context. In low-risk environments, some tasks related to security can be delegated to the logistician or an office manager.

There are three areas to consider when appointing a security manager or focal point:

- What will be their job description?
- What skills are required, and hence what background and experience are desirable?
- Should an international or a national be appointed?

6.1.1 The job description

The job description for a field-level security manager could include the following:

- Conduct ongoing risk analysis of the operating environment, including sending out security alerts to staff and associated personnel.
- Help to develop risk mitigation strategies, including standard operating procedures, guidelines and contingency plans (including crisis response and relocation and evacuation).
- Brief incoming personnel and ensure personnel are kept up to date on changing security conditions.
- Maintain an incident reporting system.
- Advise on technical protection and communications matters, such as site selection and protection, as well as the functioning and good use of communications equipment.
- Oversee adherence to procedures and plans.
- Manage security-related staff such as guards, radio operators and national security focal points.
- Provide training and mentoring of colleagues to develop security-related competencies.
- Provide advice on budgeting for operational security expenditures.
- Be involved in incident response and crisis management and subsequent reviews and evaluations.
- Liaise with and exchange information with other aid organisations and with the authorities.

Performing all of these tasks would be a tall order, all the more so if security managers are expected to be on call 24 hours a day, seven days a week. Field-level security focal points are often overworked and highly stressed. Mitigating measures need to be considered, such as establishing a duty roster so that one person is not always the first to be called, and minor issues can be dealt with by someone else. Nor can the security manager have sole responsibility for security management: a team approach is essential, with security made a topic, preferably the first item, on the agenda of all management meetings. Security issues should also be discussed within teams. The emphasis should be on mainstreaming security as part of the management process.

6.1.2 Knowledge and skills

Security skills can be broadly categorised as 'soft' and 'hard'. Hard skills are more technical, and relate to the nature and functioning of special assets, such as radio equipment, alarm systems, blast film, body armour and blast walls. These skills are often associated with a background in the security forces, such as the military, police or intelligence services, where individuals may have developed knowledge of weapons, military tactics, police operations or counter-terrorism. Hard skills may also include investigative skills, meaning the ability to impartially investigate an incident and then provide solid recommendations, and threat and risk analysis.

Soft skills relate to the ability to work with a multicultural team, mentoring and training skills, relationship-building, good communications and planning and budgeting experience. They also include an ability to develop and maintain networks in the community (particularly for information on possible security threats), as well as the ability to understand and analyse often very different cultural, social and political environments (and the violent conflicts being fought out in them).

The skills required may depend on the broader skill patterns in the team: perhaps the logistician and construction engineer can bring some of the harder skills, leaving the security manager to focus more on the softer side of the job. It may also depend on the context in which the agency is operating: in an environment with active combat and military units (perhaps irregulars and insurgents), such as in northern Sri Lanka in 2008, more hard skills and military-related knowledge may be required. In an environment characterised by tribal and local militia, where everyone is effectively an irregular, such as parts of the Somali regions and the DRC, someone with more soft skills may be called for. High-crime contexts may need a full spectrum of skills, which a single individual is unlikely to be able to offer.

6.1.3 International or national security focal points?

A key decision is whether a security focal point should be an international or a national staff position. Although one should be cautious about generalising too much, each tends to bring different skills and competencies to the job. Some of these are summarised in the table below. It is usually best to have a security team comprising both internationals and nationals, perhaps starting an operation with a senior international staff member as the security focal point, with a national staff member taking over the role eventually.

Turnover of international staff can be high, and they are not always very familiar with the context. National staff have often been engaged in aid work in their own society for many years, and some may also have worked for the same organisation for some time. For national staff, there is however a concern about danger habituation: because they live and work in a high-risk environment, their perception of threats and risks may well be different, and behaviour which they regard as safe may not be so for international staff.

People in security management

6

Table 10: Strengths/weaknesses of international and national staff as security focal points

International staff	National staff
• May have a broader understanding of the organisation, and its values, culture, policies and procedures. • Better understanding of donor and project management and reporting requirements. • Likely to be more objective in analysing the risk environment. • Likely to be perceived as more impartial by parties to a conflict. • Less susceptible to pressure from local actors. • In a better position to impose discipline on national and international staff. • In a better position to liaise with international staff in other organisations. • May have more experience producing written reports.	• Better knowledge of the social, cultural and political environment. • Knows the history that shapes the perceptions and attitudes of local people. • Speaks local languages. • Has local network which can provide information and access. • In a better position to liaise with national staff in other organisations.
• Does not have the same understanding of the social, cultural and political environment. • Not familiar with the history that shapes the perceptions and attitudes of local people. • Does not usually have access to local media or local networks of information and access. • More likely to engage in inappropriate and insensitive behaviour.	• Has become habituated to living in a high-risk environment, has become less risk-conscious and may not identify risk to international staff. • Belongs to a sector of the society and therefore may not be objective, or may not be perceived as such. • May not be able to resist pressure from other actors in society. • May not have been given the opportunity to develop project management skills. • May not be able to impose discipline on international staff. • May be more motivated by the economic opportunity of the job (though the same may be true for some international staff).

In Nairobi, for instance, national staff may feel comfortable riding in *matatu* taxis, whereas international staff may be banned from using them.

International staff may be better able than national staff to address security issues impartially, or at least to be perceived as doing so. This can include ethno-political conflicts where there is clear animosity between staff of different backgrounds (for example in Sri Lanka, between Tamils and Sinhalese). Here, an international staffer could address security management issues in a way that was commensurate with the risk and not based on ethnic mistrust. In other contexts, an international staff member may be seen as more impartial by a military force that is a party to a conflict (for example in discussions with the Sudanese government in Darfur or the Israeli military in the OPT).

6.2 Personal competence

6.2.1 Guidelines for behavioural self-discipline
The following behavioural guidelines for individual staff members are part of good security practice.

Maintain constant situational awareness
Remain aware of the broader context you are working in, and how you might be perceived. Keep your eyes and ears open, listen to people's opinions and be aware of local perceptions through the local press and through listening to and talking with colleagues and local people. In your actual location, maintain terrain awareness: know where you are, scan the environment for potential threats and for where you might find help or cover, or in what direction evasive action might be taken. Err on the side of caution – if in doubt, stay out or get out. Trust your gut instincts and do not allow yourself to be swayed by others.

Remain security-conscious
Follow the agency's security guidelines and procedures, and accept that, in violent environments, insecurity and danger will impose constraints on personal freedom. Understand that risk-taking behaviour can put colleagues at risk and affect the image of the organisation. Feel responsible for security and act when security measures are neglected on the road, around the office or during and after working hours. When you see or hear something that may have security implications, report it even if you are uncertain whether it is important. Remember that nobody is helped by you getting yourself injured or killed.

Maintain a low profile
Do not make obvious displays of wealth or foreign status and keep personal opinions about social and cultural issues to yourself. A quiet and unassuming individual is less likely to attract unwanted attention.

Maintain contact and communications
Always let someone know where you are going, and when you expect to be back. Always travel with a means of communication and a list of key contacts to hand.

People in security management

Move with self-confidence and determination

You should not appear arrogant, but also not uncertain or lost, which could be perceived as a sign of weakness or vulnerability. Walk as if you know where you are and where you are going even if you have lost your way, and show self-confidence and appear composed in your body posture, facial expression and eye movements.

Be tactful and diplomatic

Avoid getting into disputes with local people and displaying anger or arrogance. Avoid arguments about sensitive cultural or political issues with people you do not know well. Refrain from making disapproving or derogatory comments about local customs and habits. Always be respectful. In programme matters, take time to listen to people's concerns, priorities and complaints. Don't make promises you can't keep or leave disputes unresolved.

6.2.2 Defusing anger and hostility

Different cultures and social sub-cultures have different codes with regard to displays of anger and hostility. International staff members generally come with their own such code, from their home country. It is advisable to discuss this informally with colleagues and to consider potential implications. In Indonesia, for example, as in many other South-east Asian cultures, there is a strong emphasis on formal politeness, respect for elders and superiors and self-control, and expressions of irritation or anger are disapproved of. International staff unfamiliar with the culture may not realise when they are provoking anger or hostility if they do not notice cultural signs and expressions. National staff, on the other hand, may have difficulty responding appropriately if suddenly confronted by an expression of anger. Both may have to learn to adjust their habits.

From an immediate security point of view it is useful to learn how to defuse anger and hostility in yourself as well as in persons facing you. Sometimes tense and potentially threatening situations are partially open to influence, depending on how one behaves; the ability to maintain self-control and a clear mind is therefore an important part of self-protection. There are two simultaneous challenges: controlling one's own reactions and defusing hostility in another person. Guidelines for defusing hostile situations include:

- Be aware of your facial expression and body language: 90% of communication is non-verbal. Stand at an angle to the angry person rather than facing them full-on.
- Keep your voice calm.

- Listen without interrupting, as interrupting will only increase anger (when the angry person starts repeating themselves, learn how to paraphrase what the person is saying so as to signal that you are listening and have got the message).
- Become a curious listener and ask for clarification and information in order to understand what really upset the other person or caused their hostility. Do not contradict or correct an angry person before they have finished venting their anger.
- Focus on the issue and not on the person: do not confront the other personally and avoid openly judging them; do not respond to provocative judgements about yourself or your organisation.
- Maintain your own dignity, but allow the angry person to save face too.

It is a situational judgement whether or not you should try to control anger and defuse hostility. Doing so is most likely to be effective with somebody who is hostile and angry but not at the point of preparing to cause harm. If somebody becomes very threatening either disengage or comply without delay or verbal resistance. If the main message of the angry person is to express objection to your presence, then say that you have got the message and leave.

6.2.3 Incident and crisis survival techniques

Confrontations and acute danger cause shock, fear and terror. This can be overwhelming and can lead to behaviour that increases rather than reduces risk. With some preparation, however, people can learn to increase their ability to survive in dangerous situations. The purpose of prior exposure to threatening situations through training and in simulations and role-plays is to reduce the element of surprise and help staff members to retain mental control, enabling them to react in a manner that will not exacerbate the danger to themselves. The key elements of mental control are:

- don't panic;
- act or react quickly, but with situational awareness;
- don't show anger or fear to your attackers;
- retain your dignity; and
- preserve your life.

It may be impossible to avoid or restrain the aggression against you, and you may be overwhelmed by force. This can happen, for example, in the case of sexual assault, detention or kidnapping. Under such circumstances the emphasis will shift from behavioural to mental survival techniques. These are discussed in the relevant chapters.

People in security management 6

6.3 Team competence

6.3.1 Why teams?

Effective teams are an important factor in risk reduction and incident and crisis survival. Good teamwork means that:

- Everybody is security conscious and contributes information.
- Everybody helps in maintaining a high level of security awareness.
- Team members support each other in coping with stress and fear.
- At the time of an incident those caught up in it can concentrate on the attackers and the do's and don'ts, knowing that the others present are also reacting competently.
- Crisis management is smooth, efficient and competent because team members know their roles and tasks.
- Team members know the hierarchy and also each other's strengths and weaknesses, and can switch roles as the situation requires.

6.3.2 What makes for an effective team?

The elements that make for effective teams are the same in the aid world as anywhere else, namely:

- A clear identity and shared mission and purpose.
- Clear roles.
- Overlapping responsibility and authority (no authority without responsibility; no responsibilities without authority).
- Clarity about how decisions are made and what decision-making processes apply when (consensual when the circumstances and issues allow; consultative, but not necessarily so, when decisions need to be made; centralised with regard to mandatory rules and orders and in times of crisis management).
- Good information sharing.
- High awareness of the value and importance of teamwork.
- Constructive personal approaches and relationships.
- Effective conflict management approaches.

A team has a horizontal ethos: everybody in it has equal value, though they have different roles and responsibilities. At the same time, teams operate within organisations with a line-management structure, and not everyone has an equal say within the team. Different aid organisations tend to have different emphases, but in practice all organisations need to combine both of these aspects of teamworking.

Principles of leadership and management style

- Authority is allocated, leadership is gained.
- A leader is respectful and is respected.
- The respect of team members comes from the perception of the leader as:
  - responsible, competent and skilled;
  - making their case based on arguments rather than on authority;
  - aware of their own weaknesses and willing to ask for and listen to advice;
  - fair, just and even-handed, and ready to change a decision if more information or better arguments are presented;
  - allowing everyone a valued space and place in the team;
  - addressing the professional problem rather than judging the individual;
  - consultative when possible, decisive when it matters; and
  - accountable for their decisions.
- Different members of a team can demonstrate leadership in their own field of competence.

6.3.3 Teams and leadership

The key elements that help to bind everyone together are leadership and management style. It is important not simply to be aware of these concepts, but to understand what they mean in practice. The box above spells out the principles that might inform a management style. Leaders encourage teamwork, but not to the point that the management line and the allocation of responsibility and authority becomes blurred. Ultimately, organisations exist to fulfil certain functions and specific objectives. While teams are an important and vital means to that end they are still only a means. Managers should encourage and foster good relations with everybody, but not to the point of shying away from problems with professional responsibility, performance and discipline. Effective teamwork and staff morale can be seriously undermined by allowing a non-performing staff member to get away with it for too long.

Managers have a responsibility to stimulate effective teamwork by showing leadership, but this responsibility cannot solely be theirs; every staff member shares this responsibility – all the more so in unstable and dangerous situations. This is especially the case as staff turnover and many other pressing obligations make it impossible for a field manager to bear this responsibility solely and completely.

6.4 Differentiating threats and risks for different types of staff

This section examines the differing security circumstances faced by different types of aid agency staff. National, local and international staff will face different threats and have different vulnerabilities, as will men and women, and may perceive similar threats in markedly different ways. The various threats against different categories of staff and the resultant risk will depend on the context, as determined by a detailed security risk assessment (see Chapter 2). Staff can themselves be a source of security threat; this is also discussed below.

6.4.1 International, national and local staff

Aid agency staffing has evolved significantly over the past 15–20 years. In many international aid agencies, national staff make up 85–95% of their global workforce. For many, a large proportion of national staffers have been with the agency for five years or more, forming a substantial core of experience and institutional memory in their field settings.

International staff often include workers who started out as national staff and later took positions for their organisations in other countries, or members of a diaspora population returning to work in their home country. Some organisations also have an intermediate category of regionally recruited staff, i.e. people from neighbouring countries, such as Kenyans working in Sudan or Sierra Leoneans working in Liberia. Although not always giving rise to contractual differences, national staff may also be classified as local (i.e. working in their home environment) or relocated (i.e. working in a different part of their own country). Finally, third-country nationals are foreigners hired locally, who for legal and contractual purposes are treated as local staff.

Most organisations say that they regard national staff as equivalent to international staff in terms of duty of care. In practice, however, there are differences in what an organisation can and will be prepared to do for international and national staff at a time of crisis. It is still the case in many agencies that internationals are afforded the majority of organisational resources for security, be it training, more secure housing and means of transport or communications equipment. This, alongside the longstanding practice of evacuating international staff at a time of very high security risk, and the more recent spread of remote programming, may give rise to an implicit or explicit assumption that national staff are at less risk than their international colleagues. The facts do not support that assumption. The available statistics suggest that the long-term trend of attacks against national staff relative to their numbers in the field has been rising, and misplaced assumptions about their safety may be in part responsible.[1]

Simply being 'of the place' does not automatically imply lesser risk. In fact, national staff can face a range of threats that internationals do not:

- Because they are part of the wider population and share the same vulnerabilities.
- Because of their perceived social or political identity within their own society, where that society is deeply divided or at war with itself.
- Because their job with an international agency gives them enhanced status and visibility, and makes them look wealthy by local standards.
- Because they may handle assets or money or have influence on the recruitment of people or the awarding of local contracts.
- Because their job places them in dangerous situations and locations that they would not otherwise be in.
- Because their job with an international agency makes them a target for those wishing to specifically target that agency or an international agency in general.

This can generate all sorts of pressures and threats, such as:

- Resentment and accusations from conservative circles of society for failing to respect traditional customs and norms, by being a part of an organisation that demonstrates different, perhaps more liberal, values.
- Pressure to provide jobs or other benefits.
- Pressure to provide inside information about valuables and how and when to access them.
- Risk of being forcibly conscripted by armed groups or of being arrested by the authorities as being a suspected supporter of an opposition group.
- Coercion from government or other groups to provide information and intelligence about the agency.
- Accusations of helping a 'foreign occupier', as 'spies' or 'collaborators'.

6.4.2 Gender roles and security risks
One's sex is a biological given, but gender is a social and cultural construct that expresses itself in behaviour and relationships, which can complicate security management. For instance, to appear strong, a man may refuse to admit that he lacks certain skills (how to drive a four-wheel-drive, for example) or may

1 For an analysis of the threats facing national aid workers, see the *Providing Aid in Insecure Environments* report of 2006 and update 2009 (Overseas Development Institute).

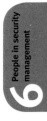

People in security management **6**

adopt a macho attitude or appearance that may provoke anger and contribute to the escalation of an already tense situation. In a dangerous situation, men may want to assume leadership and portray themselves as protectors of women. This can lead to team tensions which, in a delicate or dangerous situation, can increase risk. It may also lead to feelings of guilt and humiliation in the aftermath of security incidents involving female colleagues. Situations can more quickly escalate where men are concerned, simply because the aggressor expects them to be a potentially greater threat or more likely to put up resistance. This is why, for example, many airlines train their female cabin crews to deal with difficult passengers and even hijackers.

Women tend to be more aware of their particular vulnerabilities, especially to sexual aggression. Many agencies now seriously consider the special threats that female staff face in the field and incorporate this into their risk management process. It is important to remember, however, that men can also be victims of sexual assault, and that men and women may perceive the level of risk differently. Additionally, depending on the environment and the attitude of their male colleagues, female staff may have to work very hard to be taken seriously, and may have to assert their independence and freedom of choice in ways that their male colleagues do not, which may in turn complicate team coherence, or even spur risk-taking behaviour.

Gender and authority

Most international and certainly national security or risk management advisors (and security trainers) are male, although the number of women in the sector is gradually increasing. It is likely that women will feel reservations about reporting incidents regarding unwanted sexual advances, sexual harassment or sexual assault to a male colleague, who may be equally uncomfortable in taking the report. When the roles are reversed, male staff, depending on their attitude, may accuse female managers of being overly risk-averse, and may consequently be reluctant to accept their risk assessments and resulting security procedures. Conversely, female staff may contest the security measures taken by a male manager as patronising or sexist, especially if they impose restrictions on what are considered to be personal freedoms. Restrictions may be placed on women's choice of residence, for instance, or they may be obliged to move around accompanied at night, while men are not. In some contexts dress codes may be less tolerant for women than for men, and women may be advised not to socialise too publicly with men who are not members of their family. Restricting what are perceived as individual freedoms, especially after working hours and at weekends and on holidays, is always open to contestation. Discussing these issues openly and developing

> # Case study: challenges to the risk assessment of a female manager
>
> A female country representative in a high-risk country eventually resigned after the agency's HQ did not offer her tangible support when male colleagues refused to accept her security guidelines, regarding them as overly restrictive and excessive. HQ told her that security management was her responsibility but did not back up her authority. She felt that, with her authority challenged and undermined, she did not want to take responsibility if something happened, and so resigned.

an internal code of conduct for staff can go a long way to maintaining clarity about individual responsibilities and freedoms.

Gender and negotiation

Security guarantees have to be negotiated with governmental and non-governmental actors. Security problems may require negotiation for their resolution. It is likely that the interlocutors will react differently when negotiations on behalf of an agency are conducted by a woman rather than a man. In conservative societies interlocutors may be offended by having to discuss issues with a female. In some contexts, however, women may be considered less threatening to men than other men. It might therefore be a deliberate choice to appoint a woman as spokesperson. For similar reasons an organisation may choose female interpreters, though women may be seen as easier targets for aggressors wanting to show off their power, or who are insulted by having to talk to a woman.

6.4.3 Staff as a source of security problems

Staff members themselves can be a source of security problems.

Irresponsible staff

Staff who behave irresponsibly, incompetently or arrogantly can be a threat to themselves and to their colleagues. Irresponsible behaviour can include abusing alcohol or drugs (on or off the job); publicly voicing personal political views on the job; being dismissive about security procedures; being overconfident that they can handle any security situation because they have done so for many years; or taking a fatalistic approach to their wellbeing. The consequences of such behaviour affect more than the individual, putting at risk the reputation of the agency and the safety and security of other staff and agencies.

People in security management

Disgruntled staff

Disgruntled staff who feel they have been badly managed by their employer may feel less loyalty and may create security problems. Minimising these risks requires employment and personnel policies that are clear, consistent and transparent, including clear procedures for disciplinary action and for redundancies and dismissals. Being perceived as a fair and just employer will strengthen loyalty among staff. In sensitive situations or with regard to particular individuals, it may be a good idea to seek advice from trusted national colleagues on the best way to sanction or let go of national staff. The best course of action from a security point of view may not always be strictly in accordance with formal procedures.

Disloyal staff

National staff could be providing 'insider information' to criminals in exchange for a share of the goods or assets subsequently stolen from the agency on the basis of that information; or they may pass on real or false sensitive information to the authorities or non-state actors to compromise the agency's image and security procedures. Care in recruitment, transparency about the agency and its mission, staff supervision, internal checks and balances and security alertness will reduce the risk.

Corrupt or dishonest staff

Financial checks, stock control or incident analysis may suggest that an international or national staff member has been corrupt or dishonest. For example, they may be stealing money from the organisation or hiring relatives or friends in contravention of HR policies, thereby affecting the image of the organisation. This is a difficult situation that requires careful but also determined action. Care is required to avoid false accusations, and to forestall a violent reaction if a dishonest staff member becomes aware of being investigated and feels under threat. Action is nonetheless necessary to prevent a general atmosphere of pervasive mistrust. As long as there is suspicion but no clear evidence of wrongdoing, the investigation will have to be discreet. International staff should take the lead in these investigations, as national staff may be more vulnerable to retaliation. If there is enough evidence to justify dismissal, think through how this should best be handled.

Discipline

Any security strategy will be undermined if staff do not have the discipline to follow it. The challenge for the manager will be to demonstrate competence in security management and the soundness of the risk analysis, and involve the team in security planning and reviews, so that staff understand the logic rather than reacting to what they perceive as senseless administrative edicts. In higher-risk environments security procedures may have to be mandatory, and breaches made a disciplinary offence.

6.4.4 The private sphere

Another difficult area is the private sphere. During a security alert phase it may be easy to instruct international staff to behave carefully in their free time. At other times, however, it may be difficult to explain that, for example, heavy drinking in public, too many liaisons and indiscreet affairs or arrogant behaviour and improper dress are not acceptable ways to relieve stress and are not the sole concern of the individual involved, but affect the image of the agency and of international aid workers as a whole. Doing aid work does not require one to live like a saint, but it does require social and cultural sensitivity and does not offer a licence for total personal freedom and liberty. This is a difficult and sensitive issue, and has to be dealt with at the organisational level. Managers should lead by example and persuade by argument, and should not shy away from confronting staff whose behaviour is considered offensive and dangerous. Many international organisations have an internal code of conduct governing behaviour and attitudes, which new staff members have to sign. Such codes then have to be enforced.

For national staff the question is slightly different; as citizens, after all, they are entitled to behave as they wish within the bounds of the law of their country. National labour laws will also restrict what employers can demand from national staff outside working hours. This is clearly an area for discussion among and with national staff.

6.5 Human resources

6.5.1 Staff composition

As a general rule, staff composition should be broad-based and balanced, i.e. it should reflect the composition of the host society, either across a country or at the least at the local or individual office level, in terms of ethnic and religious composition, for instance, and across all levels of society. This is not to say that technical and professional criteria should not be the driving factor in recruitment at an individual level, but it does mean that other factors need to be considered as well, at least at an organisational level. Staff composition is a very important factor in how an agency is perceived, which in turn is critical for an agency's acceptance strategy. Diversity of staff in a socially diverse and politically fragmented environment is generally an asset. It supports claims of neutrality and impartiality, can help develop broad-based relationships

People in security management

6

and can give access to information and perspectives from diverse sources. The drawback is that it may import external tensions and conflict into the agency. This creates its own difficulties, but these are generally outweighed by the benefits. In addition, if the organisation is engaged in peacebuilding or conflict resolution in the wider community, it is essential to be able to promote such understanding first and foremost among its own staff.

There may be situations where a balanced staff profile is not possible or desirable, at least not at a higher (i.e. country) level. Where there are strong antagonisms between groups, some staff may not be trusted or feel secure in areas controlled by people of an opposing identity. This should not be assumed automatically, and sometimes an individual can be accepted even where their group as a whole is not looked upon favourably. For similar reasons, organisations should be careful when relocating staff, who may be viewed with jealousy or suspicion by their new host community. In this context it is generally useful to 'spread the wealth' by offering employment to qualified people as close to the host community as possible.

Similar considerations may also apply when recruiting international staff. Where a conflict has a regional or international dimension, it may be difficult for an international staff member from a certain country to overcome automatic and generalised suspicion and hostility. For example, an Ethiopian may have difficulty working in Somalia and an Indian national may not be the most suitable choice in certain parts of Pakistan. The same may also apply with regard to religion: it may be more prudent to recruit Muslims to work in some predominantly Muslim societies, or Hindus in areas affected by Hindu fundamentalist agitation. For long periods only Tamil staff could work safely in the Vanni area of northern Sri Lanka. After the US invasion of Iraq in 2003, international organisations that retained their predominantly Sunni staff had difficulties interacting with the new, primarily Shia government. Not surprisingly, the government did not appreciate the fact that every national programme officer or translator was from the other religious group.

6.5.2 Recruitment

Failing to invest time in careful recruitment and subsequent staff monitoring can be costly, both in terms of job performance and security.

International staff

The criteria for recruiting international staff must involve more than just technical competencies. Tact and interpersonal skills, cultural sensitivity and a mature sense of responsibility and self-discipline are important contributory factors to security (and programme) management. Experience in the field is no guarantee of maturity: quantity does not guarantee quality. Additionally, while experience is desired, taking on a staffer still burnt out after a previous demanding posting is clearly not wise.

In some organisations, HQ assumes certain tasks for pre-mission preparedness and orientation, but inevitably the best learning takes place on the ground. Since in some places the record shows a heightened risk in the first three months of an assignment, it is imperative that intensive briefing is provided to newcomers upon arrival. This should include detailed contextual orientation and explanation of the logic behind the security measures in place.

National staff

Recruiting the right national staff is crucial but also difficult, especially when an agency is new to an environment and needs to respond urgently to an emergency. The first few national staff recruits will be important, since at least for a while these staff may acquire a strong influence in the agency's management, and in hiring additional staff. The following are principles of good practice in recruiting and contracting national staff.

First, be diligent in obtaining and following up references – professional and social. Technical job qualifications are a necessary but not sufficient criterion for recruitment. Professional references should always be consulted. It is also good practice to take up what might be called 'social references' – i.e. identifying other people in the community, preferably with standing and authority, who are prepared to vouch for the integrity of the applicant. In more traditional social environments these people can come to act as the guarantor of a staff member. Seeking out social references takes time and effort, but it may prevent the recruitment of people with known bad reputations or even criminal affiliations. It may also create stronger relationships within the surrounding social environment. One practice needs to be guarded against, whereby the national staff member recruited on the recommendation of another local person is subsequently forced to pay a percentage of their salary to the guarantor. Be aware that guarantors may challenge the aid agency over perceived poor personnel policies and practices.

Second, start with short-term contracts. If recruiting in a totally new environment or in a hurry, it may be wise to issue short-term contracts with no guarantee of renewed employment. At the same time, know and observe national labour legislation with regard to repeated renewals of short-term contracts.

6.5.3 Insurance

Medical insurance, including medical evacuation insurance, will not prevent disease or injury, but it does enable physical and financial access to medical care, which may prevent worse consequences. Life and disability insurance helps to mitigate the financial consequences of an incident. Many national staff do not have any such insurance, because it is not available or is too expensive. Where they do have some insurance, this often only covers some risks, and may be financially so low that it is inadequate in case of a serious affliction or injury. If national staff make up the bulk of the workforce, their insurance needs must be addressed (see Annex 5).

6.5.4 Access to safety and security training

Make special efforts to ensure that all staff have access to security training and learning opportunities. Although in the past decade the supply of safety and security training has increased, it has largely been made available to international staff. Given that national staffers make up the bulk of the workforce, and typically provide most continuity in a given operational environment, it is critically important to provide them with training. The translation of training materials into local languages, and the training of local trainers, may be too demanding and expensive for any one agency, and so may be another area for interagency collaboration and joint investment.

Training courses tend to remain one-off experiences: much of the information imparted is quickly forgotten without regular practice. Ongoing reference to safety and security issues in routine work, and of course especially in times of heightened risk, is essential – as are periodic drills. The active involvement of all staff in the management of the safety and security situation is a further critical element in developing competencies.

6.6 Stress and stress management

Stress and security are related in various ways:

- Living in a dangerous environment contributes to stress.
- When people are stressed, their professional effectiveness and situational judgement are affected and they may start behaving in ways that increase the risk to themselves and others.
- When people are directly affected by, or witness, an incident in which their own physical integrity or that of people around them is threatened or violated, they can come to experience acute stress disorders.

The management of stress is therefore a dimension of security management. Like security more generally, managing stress is both an individual and an organisational responsibility.

6.6.1 What is stress?

Stress is a natural reaction, and it can be positive and stimulating. Not all stress is debilitating. There are different types of stress, both healthy and unhealthy. Healthy stress helps people focus on the task or situation at hand, mobilises energy and prepares them for action. For example, having a deadline can cause someone to be stressed but can also help to get a task completed. In situations of tension or risk, people can also experience a rational fear, which is a functional reaction of justified alarm, and can give them the concentration they need to survive.

When stress occurs too often, however, or is too intense or lasts too long, it turns from positive to negative. All stress uses energy. A never-ending series of tight deadlines or continued exposure to high-risk situations can deplete energy reserves. Unhealthy or dysfunctional stress comes in two major forms: *cumulative* and *traumatic* stress. Less easily recognised or admitted and yet very much present among many professionals, including aid workers, is cumulative stress. This prolonged stress eventually leads to physical and emotional exhaustion or burn-out. Traumatic stress results from directly experiencing, or being otherwise closely exposed to, traumatic events or incidents that are life-threatening or deadly, and involve physical and emotional loss. Mental health experts further distinguish between *acute stress disorders*, which occur a few hours or days after the event, and *post-traumatic stress disorders*, which can occur several months or even years after an event.

6.6.2 Who is affected by stress?

Everybody is susceptible to stress, but every person will not necessarily be stressed by the same things or equally stressed in the same environment. Stress is the outcome of a combination of external demands (stressors), and of individual resources. Different individuals also manifest stress in different ways.

All field staff

All staff, both international and nationally recruited, are vulnerable to stress. National staff may have the advantage of being in an environment that they know intimately and may retain their social support networks. However, they are often not outsiders to the conflict, as expatriates are, and they may have been exposed to danger for months, if not years. They may find cultural

People in security management

6

differences in working style stressful, and may worry about job security and their financial and emotional responsibilities towards their wider family.

Field-level managers

A major unrecognised problem in field situations concerns who supports the manager. Personnel management is part of the responsibility of the field manager, who is therefore expected to be a pillar of stability, support and sound judgement at all times. Clearly this is not realistic, but certainly in more hierarchical organisations, it is not clear how the manager manages their own stress levels. A manager who takes the safety and security of his or her staff seriously is probably also going to experience this responsibility as stressful, especially in volatile and dangerous environments. Professional counsellors and mental health professionals can also become affected by the stress of ongoing exposure to the problems of those they are trying to help.

Security managers

Security managers are vulnerable to significant levels of stress for a variety of reasons: they too will feel a personal responsibility for the safety and security of their colleagues, and may feel an obligation to be constantly on call. Explicitly or not, they may blame themselves if someone followed their guidance and advice but was still affected by a serious incident. They may also be confronted with the sometimes gruesome impact of an incident (e.g. a major bomb explosion). They may have to deal with prolonged frustration stemming from insufficient commitment to security management within their organisation.

Managers in headquarters

Staff at headquarters, some of whom no doubt have many years of field experience, may bring cumulative stress and some of the living and working patterns of the field to the job at HQ. In times of tension and risk in the field they may feel unable to switch off. In addition, significant amounts of stress may be generated by workloads, internal rivalries, institutional politics and organisational crises at HQ level.

Family and loved ones

The separation and reduction in communication, different experiences, substance abuse (such as increased alcohol consumption) and perhaps a change in character or outlook on the world and on life resulting from intense experiences can all affect family relations and friendships. The proactive and retroactive management of stress therefore needs to involve the family.

Men and women are equally susceptible to stress

Women can experience heightened stress because of fears about gender-related violence. Uncertainty and lack of confidence in one's management abilities and position can equally affect men and women. Their responses however can be different. Some research suggests that women tend to respond differently to stress, seeking more social contact and support from others and intensifying a protecting and caring role, whereas men have greater difficulty admitting that they have reached the limit of what they can handle and are in need of a break.

6.6.3 Symptoms of negative stress

There is a wide range of possible symptoms of negative stress, and individuals differ in terms of the symptoms they exhibit.

- Common physical symptoms include continuing fatigue and a sense of exhaustion, yet these may very well go together with hyperactivity and overwork, or sleeping difficulties. Excessive, continuous sleep, often with slight flu-like symptoms, can occur after critical incidents or can be a sign of more general burn-out; other symptoms include headaches, backache or gastro-intestinal disturbances. Cold sweats, heightened blood pressure and heart rate, general trembling and nausea to the point of vomiting can all occur in situations of acute stress disorder.
- Behavioural symptoms include avoiding genuine social contact and relationships, substance abuse, notably caffeine, alcohol, cigarettes and perhaps drugs, a series of short and casual romantic relationships or unprotected sex, and dangerous driving and risk-taking in general.
- Work-related problems may include work-aholism, tardiness, absenteeism, lack of concentration and diminishing productivity or poor work performance.
- Emotionally, affected individuals may experience low morale, pessimism and cynicism, along with feelings of anxiety, guilt and depression. However, excitement and a feeling of power and invulnerability can equally be symptoms of excessive stress. Another expression of emotions can be over-identification with the target beneficiaries and excessive empathy, leading to a loss of perspective. Nightmares, flashbacks or intense emotions surrounding anything that evokes a critical incident, and therefore often a tendency to want to avoid and repress any thoughts or feelings about it, are among the symptoms of post-traumatic stress disorder.
- Relational symptoms of stress include distancing oneself from the beneficiaries of aid by intellectualising about or dehumanising them, or constantly making jokes about them (this is known as compassion fatigue,

People in security management

and will find expression in cynical comments); poor communication with colleagues and family; and withdrawal into oneself, irritability or a constant tendency to pick quarrels and be aggressive.

- Spiritual or philosophical repercussions include doubting one's value system or religious beliefs, questioning of major life areas (profession, employment, lifestyle), feelings of threat and victimisation, disillusionment and self-preoccupation.

6.6.4 Managing stress

Stress needs to be managed at multiple levels of the organisation. This section discusses how to do this, at a broad organisational level, at the field level and by individuals themselves. Lastly, it discusses the importance of understanding cultural differences in how stress is managed.

The organisational level

Whereas more aid agencies are beginning to pay attention to safety and security, and offer in-house or external stress counselling support, many still do not recognise staff stress as an organisational concern, despite the fact that far more staff experience stress than security threats, and stress affects performance, morale and motivation, eventually influencing the length of time a staff member is willing to remain in place. It therefore also affects staff turnover.

Organisations can help to manage stress by recognising it as an organisational responsibility, by talking about it and by developing general and situation-specific rest and relaxation policies. Stress levels and stress resistance should also be explicitly taken into account in recruitment and redeployment decisions. Organisations need to review what they expect of field-level managers in complex, volatile and highly constraining environments, and the practical support they offer them. Maintaining expectations that would hold for a stable environment is unrealistic and sets a manager up for failure.

Field management level

There are various things that the field manager can do to help manage stress among his or her staff.

A senior manager should spend time with a new staff member so that there has been a personal exchange. This is an opportunity to talk to the individual about security issues and to signal that stress will be a part of their experience, and that it is a normal phenomenon. It is also an opportunity to establish some personal rapport and to signal that managers are accessible if there is a problem. After an initial period of about three weeks it is good practice to organise another meeting to discuss how new staff are settling in, and what is going well and what appears more difficult, personally as well as professionally.

All field-level managers should receive basic management training. This will help to ensure that individuals are prepared for and have realistic expectations of their role, which can help to reduce stress. This training should cover the basic principles of staff management and could include an identification of their personality type and working style. On-the-job learning for field managers can also take place by discussing concerns in management team meetings and making explicit principles of good practice, including with regard to stress management.

Good management also means intervening sensitively and respectfully when a person is showing symptoms of excessive stress. Prepare carefully beforehand: this is not an easy task as the staff member is more likely than not to deny there is a problem, and may become defensive and even more upset. It may be necessary to extract an overstressed person from a difficult environment, for their own wellbeing and for the safety and security of the team as a whole. Managers should have the confidence to take that decision, after consultation with superiors. The approach should be firm but supportive, and should not stigmatise the person concerned.

Talking about stress in staff meetings and encouraging staff to recognise it may also be useful, though in some contexts this approach may not be culturally appropriate.

A buddy system is a common technique among civil defence rescue workers, fire fighters and ambulance staff. It consists of two colleagues who get along fairly well making an advance agreement that they will watch each other for symptoms of stress and give feedback. It is not unlikely that buddy pairs organise themselves among international and national staff separately. Nationals and internationals may spend more off-work time in their own group than with each other, and there may be language challenges. Still, a buddy system that pairs a national with an international staff member – if they feel comfortable enough with each other – could be a valuable learning experience for both.

Policy and practical adjustments may also be required in highly stressful situations, for instance on rest and relaxation and family contacts, for national staff as well as internationals. This may have short-term resource implications but it will yield long-term benefits if staff stay longer in an assignment or

People in security management

with the organisation, and risk is managed better by everyone. Practical adjustments may include trying to improve living conditions, or rearranging the configuration of a team if an individual is not fitting in well. If work demands are unrealistic, discuss this and establish priorities.

Prior to a stressful or distressing action in the field, such as driving through a dangerous area, recovering the dead from under the rubble of houses following an earthquake or bringing in the first supplies to a group of acutely malnourished people, the team leader may hold a short pre-departure briefing in which the fact that the action involves exposure to stressful factors is acknowledged. Upon return to base the team can again sit together for a short 'defusing' exercise – a review of the day's experience, the activities undertaken and the emotional reactions of each team member.

When a staff member shows symptoms of acute distress after experiencing or witnessing a critical incident, and is therefore vulnerable to post-traumatic stress disorders, emotional first aid may be needed. Key here is the ability to listen with empathy to the emotional impact on the survivor. Emphasise that the distress experienced is a perfectly normal and healthy reaction, that there is nothing wrong with the person and that, with time and rest, they will regain their physical and psychological equilibrium. Exploring deeper personal and emotional issues brought up by the incident should probably be left to an experienced professional counsellor.

Critical incident briefing and follow-up requires special training and preparation. It is best undertaken by someone who understands the context but who also stands outside of it. Do everything possible to create a protective and supportive environment for the person concerned while waiting for the specialist to arrive: create a place where they feel safe, have access to communications with loved ones and are physically comfortable. Be aware that the survivor may deny the depth of their distress and oppose the calling in of a specialist: make it clear that at that moment the person involved may not be the best judge of their own state of mind and that it is better to get specialist care.

Helping the stressed-out manager

In volatile environments, expectations of field-level managers tend to be unrealistic – both in terms of the volume of tasks and the level of skill with which they need to be performed. The level of responsibility can be a significant source of stress, especially when it does not stop at night, or on weekends or holidays. All staff need to feel that their managers are strong, solid and reliable and a source of stability. A senior manager who shows signs of severe stress, or who continues in post although burned out, is likely to demoralise his or her staff. The following tactics can help senior field managers to cope with stress.

- Acknowledge your own limitations, to yourself and to your staff. Admitting that you too are not immune to stress does not need to undermine your authority if you are managing according to principles and arguments that are defendable. Invite everybody to take their share of responsibility.
- Develop a good relationship with your own manager, be that at regional or HQ level. Ask them to come and experience at close hand the realities you are facing, and ask them to protect you from unnecessary pressures from HQ.
- Delegate or share tasks with a deputy representative, an office manager, a senior programme officer or a security focal point. This will be a great help if the people in these positions have experience and ability and are not themselves on a steep learning curve. Insist on appointing a high-quality person when the post needs to be filled.
- Try to create a senior management team around you that shares responsibility, although you remain the ultimate decision-maker.
- Find a sounding board or possibly a buddy in one of your peers from another agency.
- Manage your stress levels the same way you recommend that your staff manage theirs.

Individual level

Each individual staff member has a responsibility to manage their own stress level. Factors that play a role here are personal characteristics, expectations, lifestyle and knowing one's limits.

A number of personal characteristics help in resisting the negative impact of stress, namely a positive self-image or self-esteem; realistic self-confidence; a vision of a moral order or a personal philosophy; the intellectual ability to see a situation in its various dimensions and not just through the filter of one's own emotions; a good physical constitution; the ability to be constructive and see the positive elements in a situation; and – above all – a healthy sense of humour. All of these give emotional strength and resilience. Accept that there are things you can't do anything about, and try to focus on areas that you can influence.

Sleep well and eat healthily, and control the use of substances such as caffeine, cigarettes and alcohol, which give a superficial sense of relaxation but add to the stress on body and nerves. Create a 'nest', a space you can call your own where you have a stronger sense of privacy and relaxation. Do

People in security management

6

regular physical exercise, especially if confined to a compound or office due to security restrictions. Staying in touch with close friends and relatives is important and nowadays has become much easier and cheaper with mobile and internet phones. Seek out colleagues or friends, and try to talk about things other than work. Use free time for relaxation. Laughter is a great tonic, and has not only mental but also positive physical effects.

Know your own limits and the limits to your self-sufficiency. In other words, acknowledge that you don't have unlimited reserves and that, when you reach the limit, it is wise to call on others for help and support. Distress does not disappear because you keep it bottled up. It is a perfectly normal human reaction from which nobody is immune, so talk about it and ask for help when you feel you need it. You are unlikely to know your acute stress reactions to a life-threatening event until you experience it, but you can certainly show mindfulness in watching yourself on a daily basis and learning to recognise the factors that cause you stress and your symptoms. Over the years stress may accumulate. Make it clear to the organisation when you need an assignment in a less stressful environment; end a long-term contract in advance if you feel you have reached your limit, or take a longer break between stressful assignments. If there is no other option, change jobs.

Cultural and situational experiences of stress and stress management

Notions of stress and coping with stress tend to reflect Western ideas about mental health. It should not be assumed that these ideas will be valid or easily understood across cultures. For example, there are cultures where managers are expected to exercise authority and not be supportive and attentive to personal distress. In some cultures it is rare to speak openly about emotions, and admitting to levels of stress which are no longer manageable would constitute a loss of face. In many societies, people are much more likely to cope with stress through social rituals than through individual means such as counselling.

National staff may have a very different reaction and approach in dealing with what international staff might deem a traumatic event. It may be very difficult to demarcate a critical event for national staff who have been living in a violent environment for years, if not decades. In such situations, debriefings and the notion of post-traumatic stress might seem odd to national staff. Because national staff live in the environment, their experiences with violence might be expressed in social and political as well as psychological terms, and effective long-term coping may have significant dimensions of justice, reconciliation and compensation that go beyond what an organisation might first seek to deliver in terms of post-traumatic support.

It is advisable to try to understand how stress is conceived of in the particular context. Actively seek advice and insights from national colleagues. For example:

- Is there a concept of stress and trauma in the culture; how do people experience it, identify it and describe it?
- How has it been dealt with traditionally and historically, and who would deal with it?
- What is the nature of stress and trauma today, and how has it changed from before?
- What coping strategies are currently being pursued and why, and how effective are they?
- What resources can be used to address current needs?

The nature of the response may be more important than its speed.

Section 4
Communications security

Chapter 7
Managing communications security

7.1 Telecommunications[1]

7.1.1 Telecoms and security

Communications technology has expanded considerably in recent years, providing humanitarian agencies with higher-quality and less expensive ways to exchange and manage information. Mobile phone networks are increasingly found even in remote areas, reducing agencies' traditional reliance on radios. Satellite phones, used in areas without mobile phone coverage or where service has been disrupted or is unreliable, have become lighter and less expensive. Internet access is also becoming more widely available even in remote areas, thanks to satellite technology. Voice Over Internet Phone (VOIP) technology (such as Skype) has reduced the cost of long-distance phone calls, making it easier to keep in contact with headquarters or regional offices. Global Positioning System (GPS) receivers can help determine one's location in remote areas and to communicate with other actors about the precise location of a village, distribution site or landmark.

This chapter reviews some key managerial aspects of telecoms from a safety, and especially security, point of view. From a security perspective the first question will be not only establishing effective communications in a given context, but also how to maintain communications in a crisis. This is an internal and an interagency question. It is important not to assume that communications technology will in itself make an agency safer. If well used, it can be invaluable. Should staff disappear, colleagues may be able to monitor their movements and find out their last known location using software that tracks personnel using their cellular or satellite phones. Means of communication can reduce exposure by enabling a user to take appropriate security actions based on alerts and advance warning via SMS text messages, so that preventive action can be taken. In some contexts, however, the use of telecoms assets can increase risk. In highly insecure environments, some communications devices (such as radios and satellite phones) are very expensive and can attract criminals and armed groups looking to steal them. Technology like GPS devices, satellite phones or digital cameras can

---

1 This GPR is not a technical manual. However, it provides pointers to indicate where technical competence is vital. Radio operating hardware requires technical expertise to install and maintain. Detailed good practice on telecoms equipment installation and maintenance is available on the ICT Humanitarian Emergency Platform, www.wfp.org/ict-emergency.

provoke suspicion. In Somalia, for example, some NGOs found that using GPS devices was not worth the security risk because of accusations that they were assisting military actors by providing them with the locations of rebel groups. In contexts where there is a high likelihood of crime stemming from the possession of such items, staff should be instructed to use equipment with discretion.

7.1.2 Choosing communications equipment

Different communications systems have advantages and disadvantages. These are described in detail below. Some general considerations are discussed first.

Legal compliance

Ensure that communications equipment complies with national laws and regulations. Usually, communications networks require licence agreements with the host government. In some countries, specific types of communications equipment are prohibited.

Performance

Consider local/national/regional/international coverage. What distances does the telecoms system cover, and how well does it do so? This is especially relevant for radios (HF/VHF; see below) and mobile phones. A standard target is that coverage is available 90% of the time over 90% of the area. Different types of equipment also have different lifespans. The average lifespan of a base station radio can be more than five years, of a mobile radio two or more years (typically the life of the vehicle it's in), of a handheld radio battery about 18 months if used every day. Sturdier, heavy-duty commercial equipment will obviously last longer than non-commercial, 'amateur' kit.

Network compatibility is also a consideration. Are telecoms compatible with existing public facilities or those of other agencies? Interagency networks (e.g. HF, VHF, UHF and satellite communications) are available in most emergencies and can offer practical advantages in terms of operations and security, but this requires the systems to be in line with established standards. In places where the Emergency Telecommunications Cluster (ETC) is established, the lead service provider agency, WFP, should be able to give information regarding standard equipment.

Internet or mobile phone networks may become busy or overloaded, which could slow performance or block messages altogether. In emergencies the local infrastructure has usually been damaged or disabled, and mobile phone and internet services may not be available. In addition, certain kinds of mobile

phones, radios and satellite phones may not receive distress calls or security notices when the system is busy transmitting data. This can constitute a risk.

Cost

Project budgets should include estimated costs for telecommunications equipment, since these can vary widely according to region and the needs of the programme. The costs of communications equipment can often be justified by security needs. Do not forget to include the cost of training staff on how to use equipment, as well as start-up and operating costs. Satellite phones, for example, are reliable but relatively expensive to run; HF radio communications are less reliable but free once the investment has been made.

Operational requirements

Communications requirements will depend on the type of programmes or projects the agency is running. The requirements of a large-scale food aid operation with a trucking fleet and several distribution points will not be the same as those for a small, community-based psycho-social counselling service or a family tracing programme. Take into consideration the number of project areas, the distance between them (including the topography), the type of project activities, the number of personnel envisaged in each project area and the facilities already available. Also consider programmatic scenario changes: what might future needs be as programmes expand or adapt? Anticipate programme developments with staff changes, different office and base scenarios and changing travel needs.

Vulnerability

In times of crisis, certain communications equipment may get overloaded and therefore no longer perform effectively, or may deliberately be shut down. When there is a major security incident or a natural disaster (e.g. an earthquake), networks can quickly become overloaded. In other cases, the authorities may shut down networks for personal calls to reserve them for the emergency services. Mobile phone networks can also be shut down for security reasons, for instance in the event of a coup. In some contexts, mobile phones, satellite phones and handheld radios have been modified to become triggers for improvised explosive devices (IEDs). In such contexts, the network may be shut down after an explosion.

The most robust systems are likely to be HF and VHF radios, satellite phones and internet-based communications. Remember, however, that it is possible to scramble radio channels and to disrupt internet access. A combination of several means of communication is likely to be the safest and most reliable option, especially when travelling. The advantage of systems such as HF/VHF radios and, to a large degree, satellite phones is that they are under the agency's control and are independent of public facilities, which can suffer from technical failures or come under political control. Relying fully on public facilities for international communications can mean getting cut off in times of crisis. Similarly, mobile telephones and VHF networks that rely on repeaters for range/coverage are very vulnerable. In times of crisis the repeaters can easily be put out of action. Telephone landlines can become inoperative if telephone exchanges are damaged or destroyed. Are spare parts available, along with the expertise to make repairs if something goes wrong? Can the organisation bring in outside resources? Are power supplies robust?

Interagency coordination

In many high-risk operational areas, the ETC provides telecoms services to the entire humanitarian community, including NGOs. Consider contacting the local ETC working group, or the service provider of the ETC, WFP, for information on what services are available in your area of operations. The United Nations has established a policy on Minimum Operating Security Standards (MOSS), which in some high-security situations requires the implementation of a communications system that is independent of the local infrastructure. In regions where the Saving Lives Together approach is being used (see Annex 3), there may be opportunities for NGOs to take part in the UN Radio System. In some regions, specific NGO frequencies have been designated.

Administrative permissions, licensing and ownership

Each country is sovereign in internal communications matters and will exercise control to a larger or smaller degree, in the first place through licensing. Normally permission to use radio equipment is granted by the national post and telecommunications office. In times of conflict, however, other governmental authorities, such as the Ministry of Defence, can take overriding authority. Where there is no functioning government a lead agency, usually the UN, can become the controlling authority. Before purchasing and importing equipment, be clear about: permission to operate (operating licence); allocated frequency; call-sign; and import licence. If active, the ETC can be a useful resource here. The local WFP information and communications technology (ICT) officer, or WFP headquarters at ictemergency@wfp.org, can be contacted for information and advice on communications arrangements.

The authority granting operating licences usually also allocates frequencies. Note that its remit will typically be for in-country communications; for international radio communications the authorities in other countries may have to be contacted. The authority may allocate an individual call-sign, and will levy a licence fee. Issues likely to be raised in the application process include:

- What equipment is going to be used, including details of manufacture, technical specifications, model numbers and the height of the aerial above the ground.
- The number of base and mobile stations and their locations.
- What functions the equipment will have (e.g. voice only or fax/data transmission too).
- Hours of operation.
- The languages to be used in the communications.
- Whether communications are encoded or not.
- Frequencies.

An operating licence may be a precondition for an import licence. Inquire in advance about import duties and import and customs clearance procedures. Failure to observe these procedures may mean that equipment is held up at entry points.

Telecoms equipment is a valuable asset. Establish at the beginning of a project whether these assets will be disposed of at its conclusion. Some countries make a point at the importation stage (especially where an agency has asked for tax relief for 'aid' material) of insisting that project assets are gifted to the host government once the project has ended.

7.1.3 Types of equipment
High Frequency (HF) radios
The advantages of HF radios are:

- short- to extremely long-range communication without a relay station;
- less affected by topographical variation;
- high degree of independence;
- easy to network, with multiple stations sharing the frequency;
- messages can be sent simultaneously to multiple destinations;
- monitoring is simple;
- well-adapted for use in vehicles;
- adaptable to changing operational conditions;
- relatively cheap to purchase; no call charges;
- relatively easy to diversify functions of the network (voice, fax, GPS tracking, SITOR or PACTOR data transmission);
- possible to integrate with other networks (phone/email); and
- requires limited maintenance.

The disadvantages are:

- not secure – anybody can listen in;

- requires registration and licensing in most countries;
- transmission strength varies during the day depending on solar activity;
- 'skip zone': no reception between maximum extent of direct wave (ground wave) and longer radius starting with the closest reflections from the ionosphere;
- staff have to be trained in order to take full advantage of the network;
- need for additional compatible equipment to allow communication with UN partners; and
- technical expertise needed for installation, and HF can interfere with other electronic equipment if not installed correctly.

A radio set should have the following capabilities.

- Remote diagnostics: one unit can interrogate another to get details on operational factors such as power output, signal strength and battery voltage. This allows for diagnosis of potential impediments by a technician who does not have to be physically present at the unit.
- Emergency call: distress signals are automatically sent out to a number of pre-programmed stations, prioritising the urgency of the call for the receiver.
- A GPS connected to a personal computer with tracking software installed can interrogate a GPS connected to a mobile unit without the occupants of the vehicle being aware that this is happening. Vehicle movements can thus be monitored.

The most commonly used brands of HF radios are Codan and Barrett.

Very High Frequency (VHF) radios
The advantages of VHF radios are:

- fairly inexpensive;
- user-friendly;
- sturdily built: can be dropped, withstands rain, etc.;
- well-positioned repeaters can increase area coverage; and
- 24-hour contact if users are monitoring the VHF.

Disadvantages are:

- limited battery life (need for spare batteries/ongoing recharge);
- inappropriately placed repeaters greatly limit the utility of the network;
- hand-held units are frequently lost or stolen;
- repeaters are very vulnerable to intentional damage; and

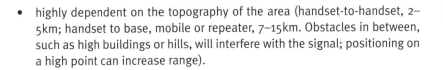
- highly dependent on the topography of the area (handset-to-handset, 2–5km; handset to base, mobile or repeater, 7–15km. Obstacles in between, such as high buildings or hills, will interfere with the signal; positioning on a high point can increase range).

The most commonly used brand is Motorola.

7.1.4 Installing radio systems

Technical expertise is needed to install radio equipment properly, and to train users in correct handling. Agencies can work cost-effectively by sharing this expertise. Again, contact WFP or the local ICT working group to find out what resources can be shared.

Locating the base station

The base station needs to be close enough to the agency office to be easily accessible, but far enough away that noise from the radio room does not disturb office activity and there is no interference from office equipment such as computers and photocopiers, or from satphones. A convenient link to the power supply is needed, as well as easy access to the outside for cables. In a high-risk area, where 24-hour radio monitoring is envisaged, think about radio operators' comfort. For safety reasons all equipment should be supplied from one isolation switch. This can make the whole station safe in case of malfunction or fire.

Choosing and setting up the aerial

Take into account antenna characteristics such as polarisation, bandwidth, effective height and impedance, and be sure to select the right type of antenna (dipole, vertical, inverted V, broadband). Generally, aerials function best when installed in open terrain and as high up as possible, e.g. on the roof. Setting up the antenna correctly is crucial to the performance of the radio system.

Installing an HF radio unit in a car

The radio unit itself may consist of a separate control panel and main unit; the control panel must be fitted where it can be used easily, but the main unit can be mounted in the glove compartment or under or behind a seat. It is important that the radio is properly earthed and that no one steps on any part of the installation when entering or leaving the vehicle. A crucial factor is the location and mounting of the antenna. Faulty mounting is often the cause of equipment failure. The bracket holding the antenna should be bolted or welded to the car chassis to guarantee good earthing. The main part of the antenna needs to be clear of the vehicle framework. For safety and security purposes it is a good idea to remove the antenna when not in use. It can be stored in the vehicle. Transmitting with the engine switched off will quickly drain the battery, and should be avoided.

Power supply

No radio system works without power, with generators and batteries normally providing back-up. Common operational problems are poor maintenance and servicing of the generator, and poor storage and discharging/recharging of batteries.

Electricity

Given the dangers of working with electricity, all items of equipment must be separately earthed and terminated in suitable plugs and sockets. A surge protector can help prevent damage from voltage spikes. Check that fuses and circuit breakers are in good condition, of the right size and have not been overridden or bypassed. Always use double-insulated cable. Cables should not pose a tripping or overhead hazard.

Radiation

Antennae emit electromagnetic energy in the form of radiation, which can affect the human body. Do not use hand-held radios with damaged antennae or with the 'bobble' at the top of the antenna missing. Do not use hand-held radios too close to the face (18cm away is adequate). There is a particular hazard with satellite terminals, whose energy density is very high and also focused in one direction: while operating a satphone, observe the radiation hazard notice and position yourself as required, and ensure that nobody else walks past in the danger zone.

Lightning hazard

Remember that antennae can be a lightning hazard. Dangerous static voltage can build up and there is the risk of a lightning strike. Technical precautions can be taken to reduce the risk, including ensuring good grounding of all equipment.

Electric shock

If someone receives an electric shock, never hurry to touch or try to release them. The first step is to switch off the power. Only when that fails pull or push the victim clear, using non-conductive material such as dry rope, a dry stick or dry clothing. Obtain medical help as soon as possible.

Radio frequency burn

When fixing or removing the vehicle-mounted antenna, the car engine should be switched off to avoid receiving a radio frequency burn from an aerial during

transmission. These burns are particularly painful as they appear under the skin and can take a very long time to heal.

7.1.5 Mobile phones

Mobile phones are easy to use, relatively inexpensive and small and ubiquitous enough to be inconspicuous. Coverage has expanded to include even very remote parts of the world. Text messaging and emailing capabilities allow information to be sent and received discreetly (although text messages could be monitored). A new generation of phones also offers internet access. Many NGOs take an international mobile phone and replace the SIM card with a local one, reducing costs. If the intention is to use a corporate NGO phone while overseas, it will be important to ensure that it is unlocked. Some phones come locked, and the local service provider can unlock them to allow foreign SIM cards to be inserted. Where private mobile phone providers exist, there is typically no problem with licensing, although some countries require proof of identity and a local address before you can get a local SIM card.

Not surprisingly, mobile phones have become the dominant tool of communication for aid agencies in many operating environments. Partly for this reason, it is important to be aware of some specific vulnerabilities related to mobile phones:

- As with all telephone systems, users can usually only talk to one person at a time, unless a conference call has been set up beforehand. For this reason, mobile phones are sometimes not as effective as radios for the rapid dissemination of emergency or security information. Many cell phones now come with 'talk to talk' capability, allowing those on the same network to communicate (e.g. Blackberry messenger).
- Many intra- and interagency security networks rely on text messages which can very quickly circulate through a communication chain. While most text messages may arrive very quickly, occasionally there can be some quite lengthy delays. For important alerts, some agencies require text feedback to confirm receipt, and follow up with a phone call to those who have not replied. Network overload and network shutdown can be a problem.
- Mobile phones have battery limits. Where a mobile phone is a major security asset, it is likely to be kept on day and night, which means having a reliable electricity supply at hand and the time to charge the phone. Alternatively, carry a spare battery or a second phone.
- Talking and sending text messages on mobile phones is not fully secure. Like landlines, satellite phones and email, communications can be listened in to or intercepted. The fact that a mobile phone service provider

is a private rather than a state-run company is not a major obstacle to intercepting calls.
- Most mobile phones that are GPS-enabled can track users through a GSM system, whereby a satellite tracks the exact latitude and longitude of the phone. This may or may not be a positive benefit, depending on who is doing the tracking. Although this tracking capability is commercially available, NGOs have only recently begun to use it.

7.1.6 Satellite communications

Satellite technology connects users to orbiting satellites instead of land-based cell sites. It can be used for both voice and data connectivity. Satellite communications have extended the reach of communications much deeper into the field than was possible before, and new technologies are appearing all the time.

VSAT (Very Small Aperture Satellite) is a high-powered satellite communications device. A VSAT involves a relatively small satellite dish and antenna, and can supply internet connectivity to an entire neighbourhood. Advantages of VSAT are that it is compact and mobile, reliable when properly set up and fairly independent. Disadvantages are that it is relatively expensive, vulnerable to theft, it may require technical expertise to set up data services and it can become overloaded in times of crisis.

Some common providers of satellite communications used by aid organisations are Thuraya, Iridium and Inmarsat. These companies offer different types of voice and data communications. Thuraya provides handsets, mainly for voice connectivity through the Thuraya global satellite network. It is used mainly in Europe, Africa and the Middle East. Iridium offers similar services, mainly in the Pacific region. Using these two providers for data connectivity is also possible, but bandwidth is limited and it can be costly. Recently, Inmarsat has introduced BGAN (Broadband Global Area Network), which allows for more portable and cost-effective voice and internet access than was previously possible. BGAN can enable the rapid set-up of a temporary office anywhere in the world, with no technical expertise required.

7.1.7 Landline phones

Landlines are less frequently used as mobile phone services have become more common. Perennial problems with landlines can include long waits for installation and frequent service failures. That said, having a landline is probably not a bad idea. It is generally more cost-effective and provides another option should the mobile phone network or other telecoms become unavailable. Internet access via a landline phone is generally slower than other means.

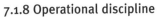
7.1.8 Operational discipline

The key principles of operational discipline in telecommunications are clarity, brevity and security.

Clarity and discipline in communication

The following guidelines are geared towards radio users, but many also apply to conversations by telephone.

Clarity and brevity are achieved through the use of procedure words (or 'prowords') and communication signals (such as 'over' or 'say again'). Clarity is also enhanced when:

- messages are prepared in advance;
- messages are presented point by point;
- users stop talking when they have nothing to add;
- users speak in short sentences, in plain language and standard 'broadcasting' language, rather than local dialects;
- users do not speak too quickly, especially when the recipient needs to write the message down; and
- they speak in a normal tone of voice (shouting will impair the quality of reception).

There are ways of imposing discipline, such as automatic identification of the caller through the use of ID codes in a VHF system, limiting the use of radios to authorised personnel and, in the worst case, withdrawing an operating licence for continued abuse.

Message logbooks are an essential element of good radio management. The basic components of the log include time of transmission, time of log in, source of the message or the transmission, the identity of the person filling in the log, and the person to whom the message is ultimately addressed, the key points of the message (verbatim for important ones), follow-up action to be taken by the radio operator or others and whether action has been taken or not, and equipment faults or problems. A good radio operator has sound technical knowledge and a very good ear, a clear voice, a clear and structured mind and clear handwriting, with the ability to concentrate and a strong sense of discipline. In recruiting, therefore, personality characteristics are as important as technical qualifications.

For security reasons it is advisable always to keep the radio on 'ON', except if immediate security conditions preclude doing so. Turned-off radios are not able to receive emergency calls or other security-related messages.

Distress and security calls

There is an internationally agreed radio protocol for emergencies (with many local variations). The caller seeks clearance on the channel by repeating three times 'MAYDAY MAYDAY MAYDAY' or 'PAN PAN PAN', usually followed by 'ALL STATIONS'. There is an absolute obligation to accept emergency calls and to interrupt ongoing conversations. A security message that does not indicate a threat to life or property (e.g. notice of civil disturbances in a town that therefore needs to be avoided) can be initiated by repeating 'SECURITY, SECURITY, SECURITY'.

The chart in the box below provides guidance on how to communicate by radio in an emergency. It can be attached to every radio, phone or other communication device, or pinned up in radio rooms and attached to phone trees. Practicing this sequence can help reduce errors in the event of an emergency.

Emergency calls must be responded to, i.e. reception must be confirmed and the identity of the receiving station given. All stations receiving the emergency call must confirm, even if other confirmations have already been heard. Normal radio communications should not be resumed until the emergency has been cancelled. It is normally the responsibility of the station issuing the emergency call to indicate the end of the emergency. Security messages do not require confirmation unless that protocol is established. They can be repeated at intervals to maximise the chances of everybody picking them up.

How to communicate in an emergency

Follow the format and sequence below:

1) **Who you are:** Bob Smith
2) **Your organisation:** NGO or agency
3) **Your location:** GPS location, or nearest major routes, towns, etc.
4) **Type of emergency:** mine accident, under fire, medical evacuation, etc.
5) **Number of people injured**
6) **Current negative activity:** Is it safe for a rescue now?
7) **Past negative activity**
8) **Next time of communication**
9) **How to contact the caller:** phone number, radio frequency, etc.
10) **Other information**

During times of crisis, decision-makers can be bombarded with so much inform-ation that it is impossible to differentiate fact from rumour. To be effective at these times it will be important to minimise communications to only those matters of direct importance. Again, this can be achieved through training and discipline.

7.1.9 Preparation, training and equipment maintenance

In recent years, knowledge about operating radios has declined due to increasing dependence on mobile phones. This suggests that current practice can be improved. A sensible approach would be for HQ to ensure basic training for all internationally recruited staff, with the country office providing training for nationally recruited staff and refreshers or context-specific training for international staff.[2] Written guidelines on the standard radio language and radio-operating procedures cannot substitute for practical training. As with all training, the first questions managers need to answer are who needs to be trained, for what (hardware care and operation; competence in communications) and to what level. Clearly, radio operators need training and refresher courses, as do any staff who will normally be using a radio (e.g. project managers at field bases, or every staff member with a VHF). Drivers of vehicles with a mobile unit might also need training, for instance in technical maintenance or radio operating procedures.

If a project vehicle travels for days on end in an environment where its radio is the only means of communication, at least one member of the team must be able to undertake basic radio maintenance and repairs. Ensure too that essential spare parts are available for the vehicle. If in the course of their work trained staff move away from the vehicle, the driver needs to know how to operate the radio or satellite phone in case of an accident or security incident.

7.2 Protecting communications equipment

Like all assets, communications equipment and computers are vulnerable to loss, theft or damage. Given the important role these assets play in security management and in the functioning of the overall programme, it is important to take steps to prevent this. Dirt and being dropped on the ground are the most common ways for communications equipment to be damaged or destroyed. Every phone and radio should have a protective, shock-absorbing cover. The cost of the cover is much cheaper than buying a new device.

In addition to the normal precautions against theft (see Chapter 9 on 'Site security'), additional measures can be taken in areas where the risk of theft

---

2 The ICT Humanitarian Emergency Platform provides some training to humanitarian organisations at both headquarters and field level. See http://ictemergency.wfp.org.

or sabotage is especially high. Equipment can be etched with the name of the organisation or an identification number in order to deter theft or to identify it if it is stolen. Computers can be fixed to desks with a locking security cable.

7.3 Information security

Information is critical to the success of the operations of any aid agency. With improving technologies, there are more and more ways to store, access and share information. With these technologies comes greater need to secure this information. There are two elements to this: protection against loss and protection against people with potentially hostile intentions. Information about individual staff, the activities of the organisation, intended beneficiaries and contacts can all be used against the organisation. In some cases, staff may say or write things that do not truly reflect the mission and aims of the organisation and are not meant to be shared externally. In other instances, information may simply be misconstrued or taken out of context.

Because the values of many aid organisations are based on openness and transparency, the question of how far to go in protecting information is a matter of some debate. Nonetheless, many types of documents should be protected. The box below lists some elements related to information security. These can be part of an organisation's overall security policy.

Elements of an information security policy

1) A definition of what constitutes 'sensitive information'.
2) Who is authorised to see sensitive information.
3) How sensitive information is to be:
   - Stored
   - Communicated
   - Transported
   - Un-sensitised
   - Destroyed.

7.3.1 Maintaining and protecting key records
Depending on the situation, key records may include:

- copies of the passports, including visas, of international staff;
- lists of international and national staff;
- individual health records, including blood groups;

- lists of next of kin or others to inform in case of an emergency;
- lists of agency ID cards and their details;
- inventories of assets;
- vehicle chassis and engine numbers, and copies of purchase/import documents;
- office equipment identification numbers and copies of purchase/import documents;
- radio equipment identification numbers and copies of purchase/import documents;
- lists of keys of houses and cars, how many duplicates exist and who has them;
- staff contracts, contracts with suppliers or service providers, lease agreements; and
- lists of telephone numbers (residences, offices, emergency contacts) and radio frequencies.

All of this information should be readily available at the field office and at headquarters, with up-to-date details of international staff on file with their respective embassies. Many organisations encourage employees to keep copies of their passports in a draft file or email in their personal internet email accounts (e.g. Gmail, Yahoo). These digital files can be accessed anywhere there is internet access.

Information about many human resource issues must be kept confidential. This includes information about medical or psychological conditions, salaries, performance appraisals and disciplinary actions. Keep track too of agency ID cards and make sure that they are handed in when staff leave the organisation, or international staff leave a field office. Whether international staff carry their passports on them depends on the situation. In principle avoid this; rather, provide them with an ID card with their details, in local languages as well, and photocopies of their passport. Passports are a valuable commodity and may be stolen. Only carry them when the local circumstances require it. Generally speaking staff should also carry a list of emergency contacts, including radio frequencies, the local authorities, the embassy and, unless this is seen as increasing suspicion and thereby risk, maps. Documents can be confiscated, so staff should memorise key numbers. Memory drills of key contacts and their details may be required. In very hostile situations, where somebody may be targeted simply for belonging to an international aid agency, it may be unwise for staff to carry anything that might identify them.

The key principle in protecting information is to have back-up copies and have the back-up copies *elsewhere*. This will protect against loss, but obviously not against theft. Back-up copies should be kept of vital individual documents, and all important programmatic and organisational documents. Key documents may have to be backed up both digitally and in hard copy. Basic elements of good practice in protecting hard-copy information include:

- Do not leave papers lying around printers or fax machines.
- Private information needs to be locked away and a copy stored elsewhere, ideally overseas.
- Potentially sensitive information in hard copy should also be locked away, and a copy stored elsewhere, ideally in headquarters.
- Do not put sensitive documents in a paper recycling bin or a rubbish bin. Shred them or burn them.

In some circumstances it may be necessary to destroy sensitive documents at short notice. Destroying files is difficult and time-consuming, so it might be wise to minimise the amount of documentation kept in the office, for instance by keeping records electronically, rather than in hard copy, and transferring records over two months old to offices overseas. A stricter way to secure information is to limit knowledge of sensitive matters and to restrict access to key documents to a limited number of people.

7.3.2 Cyber crime

Cyber crime, where criminals seek to profit from access to other people's information, is a booming business, and everyone using a computer connected to the internet is vulnerable.[3] In general, the major threats are the introduction of malware (or 'viruses'); the loss of confidentiality in communications or identity theft; and computers being taken over by hackers to send spam or other negative content, such as pornography. For the most part these threats will be best addressed by the information technology department. The main steps are introducing anti-virus and anti-spyware software, installing a firewall and maintaining robust passwords. Staff also need to be trained in how to use USB keys (memory sticks), as these can be a source of viruses. Staff should also be cautious when opening suspicious attachments, and should only use password-protected Wi-Fi (wireless internet) networks.

Intruders can quickly install spyware, such as keyboard stroke identification programmes (which reveal what is typed on a computer keyboard). Do not leave computers on and unattended. Set computers to lock down by themselves after a few minutes, to be opened again only with a robust

---

3 An excellent resource on this topic is *Security-in-a-box: Tools and Tactics for Your Digital Security* (http://security.ngoinabox.org), available in English, French, Spanish, Russian and Arabic.

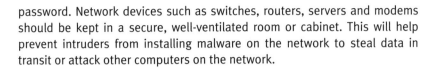

password. Network devices such as switches, routers, servers and modems should be kept in a secure, well-ventilated room or cabinet. This will help prevent intruders from installing malware on the network to steal data in transit or attack other computers on the network.

Email can be monitored with computers that scan traffic for certain key words, certain senders or certain recipients. Steps to make email traffic more secure include:

- Create an account under a name that is not related to your personal or professional life.
- Use a more secure email account (https: instead of http:).
- Use anonymity software to hide your chosen email service from someone monitoring your internet connection.
- Use a public key encryption on the content of emails. Outlook email, for example, allows one to add a digital signature that will authenticate the sender of the message. The use of encrypted emails can make you 'visible' and attract attention, however, and is illegal in some countries.

However secure the email system, remember that it is impossible to control what happens to a message once it arrives in the recipient's inbox.

As with hard-copy files, circumstances may require the deletion or destruction of sensitive files held on computer. Unfortunately, simply deleting a file does not mean the information is deleted, and a determined hacker can find a great deal of information on a hard drive. Securely deleting files requires special procedures or software. An information technology specialist will be able to advise on this. In very fraught circumstances, where rapid action is required, the fastest way of getting rid of electronic information is to physically damage or destroy the computer's hard drive. The same holds for USB sticks. With CDs or DVDs, it is best to cut them into pieces and scatter the bits in different locations. Alternatively, burn them.

Key places to think about when 'cleaning up':

- Temporary files and files in the Recycle bin.
- Files deleted but not 'wiped' on your computer or on an external storage device (e.g. memory sticks).
- Sensitive information on CDs and DVDs or stored on a local server.
- Sensitive names and contacts in mobile phone books, or constant companion cards.

- Sensitive photographs on camera memory cards and video footage on video cassettes.
- Hard-copy documents that have not been shredded.

7.3.3 Securing verbal communications

Phone calls from landlines, mobile phones and satellite phones are all automatically logged (number called, time, duration of call and sometimes location) by the billing department of the phone company. Skype to Skype (i.e. between computer terminals) conversations (both voice and VOIP SMS) are more private than conversations over a landline or a mobile phone, because Skype is secure and encrypts or otherwise scrambles information that is transmitted over the internet. It is certainly secure against casual snooping. Bear in mind, though, that Skype conversations are not totally private: malware on a computer may reveal information about Skype conversations conducted through that computer, someone might record the conversation at the other end and usernames and passwords may be stolen. Using Skype to speak to a landline or a mobile number means the conversation enters into the standard public telephone network and can be monitored there. Sending text messages or exchanging files over Skype is not necessarily more secure than email. Other 'safer' channels include public pay phones, or new pre-pay mobile phones, regularly changed.

In general, as soon as an exchange is not face-to-face, assume that it can be overheard. It is wise to express yourself in a moderate, factual and non-partisan way. If you are in a situation where you might be the target of criminal, terrorist or military acts, you may have to encode certain information that could give away your position or movements. There are various ways of doing this. Use code words to designate offices, people, routes and route points, vehicles and types of cargo, etc. This is popular but seldom well-managed, and therefore not very effective. It requires careful briefing and agreements in advance. Metaphorical expressions can be used to refer to politically sensitive events, for example 'The sky is overcast' can indicate that a particular place is under air or artillery attack. Ideally the code words or phrases are known by heart (rather than written down in a codebook). For politically sensitive events metaphorical expressions should allow for plausible denial. Change codes every so often because monitors will break them after a while. A code that is broken can constitute a major vulnerability. Note also that having too many code words may confuse staff.

A more sophisticated and difficult-to-crack version of this is to introduce a system with internally agreed temporal and spatial references. For example, 14.00 hours can be taken as the internal reference time (TEMPUS) and any communication about time is subsequently expressed as 'TEMPUS plus 3' or 'TEMPUS minus 6.45'. Spatial locations can also be disguised, for example by always adding 50km to the real distance, hence 'I am 75km from the target' really means 25km away. Use a language that those who might be listening in are unlikely to understand. This only works, of course, if both ends of the line understand each other.

7.4 Dealing with the media

In recent years, many aid agencies have expanded their outreach to the media. This is done mainly to raise awareness about a crisis, to push advocacy messages and to increase an agency's visibility and profile, which can in turn help with fundraising. Engaging with the media may also have security implications. A poorly worded, inaccurate or inflammatory statement can put staff in direct danger and may even result in expulsion from a country. At times, a media department based in headquarters and programme staff based in the field will have conflicting goals. What raises an agency's profile internationally may not help build trust with communities and local authorities in the field. A clear system must be in place for engaging with the media. For example:

- Who will be responsible for initiating contacts with the media? Who will draft press releases? Working with the media requires special skills that may only be found in headquarters or in regional offices. On the other hand, media staff can lack local knowledge and may not be able to nuance information in ways that are politically sensitive. It can be helpful to work collaboratively on press releases, but this requires extra effort (and reliable telecommunications) and these roles need to be clarified ahead of any crisis. Ultimately, the views of the country director and their team must be respected, whatever the possible media priorities of headquarters. In most cases, the decision to engage the media should be made by the country director.
- Who signs off on the final version of a press release? Many organisations have found that, for security reasons, it makes sense for the head of the agency in-country to have ultimate authority over all media messages. Other regional and headquarters staff may also need to be involved, depending on the importance and global profile of the crisis. For organisations that work in a confederation, it will be important to set ground rules for which organisation can initiate or must sign off press statements, since it should be assumed that local actors will not distinguish between, say, 'Save the World UK' and 'Save the World Belgium'. In some circumstances an inter-agency forum will want to put out a statement together. Such processes

often take considerable time to negotiate and agree content, and in some cases only a very watered down statement can be agreed.

- Which staff are authorised to conduct interviews? Media professionals will often want to speak with people who are close to the action, but these staff are not always properly trained to handle the media. Identify qualified individuals ahead of time, and perhaps offer training to key staff in how to conduct interviews. It may be a good idea to limit this to the country representative only.
- There are many different overall approaches to working with the media; decide which approach is best before a major crisis hits, if possible. For instance, an agency may have long-running programmes in Pakistan. It will want to have plans in place for how it will work with the media in various scenarios, such as a major natural disaster, an increase in terrorism directed at foreign aid agencies or a spike in localised violence not directed at foreign entities. Prepared statements and press releases are useful, so that when an emergency occurs, or a crisis reaches a critical moment, the media can be engaged rapidly. There is little point engaging with the media on an issue that happened a week ago.

7.4.1 Deciding to engage

In some situations, the role of international agencies may be so contentious that drawing further attention to it by working with the media would be counter-productive. In this case, develop a good defensive strategy, either refusing to comment, limiting remarks to basic factual information or clarifying misinformation by issuing short reactive statements. Such an approach would be used in a kidnapping crisis (see Chapter 14). However, do not assume that adopting a low-profile security strategy in terms of physical movements (unmarked vehicles, unsigned office buildings etc.) automatically dictates a low-profile media strategy. Some agencies have found that they are not doing enough to explain their role and promote their principles. Consider reaching out to respected local, national or international media as a way to influence opinion-makers and local communities.

7.4.2 Defining goals and shaping the message

Why engage with the media? What defines success? Some media department staff may see success in terms of how many 'hits', or how much coverage, the organisation (or crisis) receives. This may be useful for raising the organisation's profile or helping solicit funds from the public for an emergency appeal. But does it make operations safer? Could it even make them less safe, if messages are not properly framed? For example, if a staff member makes exaggerated claims in an interview about the number of people affected by a drought, the government, which might wish to downplay the crisis, could

become angered. If the goal of media work is largely to advance advocacy goals, carefully balance this against security concerns. For example, a press release blaming a particular rebel group for violence against civilians could anger that group and put teams in the field at risk. Messages that reinforce neutrality and independence might promote staff security. It might be helpful to prepare a list of possible questions and answers (a Q&A) before an interview with a view to keeping messages focused squarely on the people in need, how the organisation is helping and the general changes that need to happen so that people can become safer.

7.4.3 Choosing the medium

If the main goal of a media strategy is to raise an agency's international profile, fundraise or advocate with international actors (foreign governments, donors, the UN, etc.), the target is likely to be the large international or region-specific media, or perhaps publications in the country where the organisation is based and where it has active constituents. But if the aim is also to increase staff safety by promoting a better understanding of the agency's mission and goals, in-country mediums such as national, local and even non-traditional media (such as internet blogs and community theatre) are very important and require considerable outreach at the country level. Clarifying goals will make it easier to choose the most appropriate medium. Define the audience, and then identify the publications they read, the TV channels they watch and the radio stations they listen to. Keep in mind that a good local media strategy will always be in addition to, and not in place of, a good outreach strategy to local authorities, the community and those actors that could be a source of threat. Local staff will be in a much better position to determine the reliability and professionalism of local journalists, both of which can vary widely.

7.4.4 Setting ground rules for engagement

Working with the media, even granting a simple interview, requires practice and expertise. It is easy to get thrown off guard by a provocative question and say something regrettable. A full examination of media techniques is outside the scope of this GPR. However, some tips for maintaining good staff security include:

- Be careful when attributing blame for a crisis. In many complex political emergencies, it will not be possible to say unequivocally who is responsible. It is important to agree in advance an institutional response for the media. Be careful when relaying information. Make sure it has been verified by a reliable source; if it has not, say so clearly. Spreading inaccurate rumours could inflame tensions.

- When giving background information to journalists off the record, make sure that the journalist is professional and objective, and agree between you what off the record means. Verify how the information source will be presented. Some common forms of light disguise in media reports, such as 'a senior UN source' or 'aid agencies operating in the conflict zone', may not be very effective. There may be only a few such agencies, and it might be obvious to others who the senior source was.
- Not all issues require media attention and it might be appropriate to discuss possible concerns with the local or national authorities in advance, to see whether problems might be resolved through other means.

Section 5
Managing specific threats and risk situations

Chapter 8
Travel and movement security

8.1 Security on arrival

8.1.1 Pre-departure and on-arrival briefing

Contextual knowledge and situational awareness about the operating environment is critical to reducing risks. This applies to staff, colleagues and visitors. Organisations should ensure that procedures are in place to fully inform staff and visitors of the general context and specific security considerations for their country, region and area of operation. Wherever possible, this information should be provided before a person arrives in the country of operations, and followed up immediately on arrival.

Pre-deployment preparations are a joint or shared responsibility between employer and employee. The organisation's management has a responsibility to ensure the traveller has access to the necessary information and training. The traveller has a responsibility to ensure that they are adequately informed and prepared. Critical elements to go through prior to travelling include:

- Health risks and prevention.
- Risks of crime and violence.
- Natural disaster risks.
- Accident risks (e.g. safety concerns about local airlines or boat or bus services).
- Essential telephone numbers (office, mobile phones of key staff, medical facilities, the police, key embassies).
- Ideally a map of the city with key locations (including office and hotel) clearly identified. If maps are not readily available, open sources such as Google Earth may provide sufficient geographical information.

Information that is not subject to rapid change can be made available in a pre-departure briefing note. When travelling, make sure you have essential phone numbers with you – and not only stored in your mobile phone: the battery may run out, or the phone might get stolen. A briefing on arrival completes the initial orientation.

8.1.2 Airports, ports, train stations and taxis

Airports, train stations and ports are often high-crime areas. New arrivals should where possible be met, preferably by someone they know. If not known, get the driver's name, licence plate number and mobile phone number in advance, or, if this is not possible, ask to see their identification document. If it is not possible to get a driver, then try to get a prepaid and officially registered taxi. Display confidence at all times: criminals will be on the lookout for lost and confused travellers.

It might be necessary to rely on taxis rather than the agency's vehicles while on mission. Taxis can be dangerous. In some cities there is a fair risk of being robbed or even assaulted. Local representatives should have a list of reliable taxi operators and their phone numbers, or should identify a reliable driver and car.

8.1.3 At the hotel

When checking into a hotel, do not simply accept the first room offered. Check its location and the access points (doors and windows) from a security point of view. If you are unhappy with the room that has been booked for you ask for another. If you can't get another one, consider changing hotel. Factors likely to increase vulnerability include:

- A room on the ground floor, especially one with a covered approach (e.g. from vegetation).
- A room on an upper floor close to a fire escape or service stairs that are accessible to an intruder; a room on a high upper level can make it more difficult to escape in case of fire.
- A room at the end of a long corridor away from the main movements of hotel personnel and guests, where suspicious noises from inside are less likely to attract attention.
- A room with a door that can easily be forced, and which has no security lock or chain; a room with a window that is easily forced, especially when at ground floor level.
- A room without good curtains that can conceal who is inside, and without a functioning telephone line to hotel security.
- A hotel without guards or one that is poorly guarded and a hotel without night-service at the reception desk to respond to an emergency call.
- Balance the need for privacy with the need for security: consider sharing a room with a colleague or at least getting adjacent rooms and returning to the hotel at the same time.

Do not admit into your room anyone you don't know well, for example somebody you met during the day, the taxi driver bringing up your luggage, or someone you haven't called, for example 'service staff' bringing food or drinks that you did not order.

8.2 Vehicles and security on the road

Road accidents, carjacking, banditry and other vehicle-based attacks are by far the most common causes of death and injury among aid workers.

8.2.1 Vehicle choice

Choice of vehicle can impact on safety and security. New four-wheel-drive passenger vehicles are very popular among aid agencies – but are also attractive to warlords and carjackers. In some high-crime contexts, agencies deliberately use small, unbranded cars, motorcycles or even donkey carts, all of which are less interesting to carjackers and thus lower the risk. More modest vehicles can also reduce local resentment against aid agencies, especially in transit or base towns where aid is not given directly to the population.

8.2.2 Vehicle safety

Vehicle safety partly depends on the vehicle being in good working order: water, oil and fuel levels checked, tyres in good condition, seat belts installed and used, essential equipment (jack, spare tyres, first aid kit etc.) present. Make sure that drivers check their vehicles daily, that vehicles are cross-checked before major journeys, that mechanics are good and that the logistics manager keeps a servicing and maintenance schedule. Car users should be taught how to do basic emergency repairs.

8.2.3 Safe driving

Safety on the road also depends on safe driving. This tends to be a major problem area for expatriates and local drivers alike. Driving conditions in emergency contexts usually carry a heightened risk: driving behaviour may be less disciplined, animals, cyclists and pushcarts may all share main roads with cars, pieces of road under repair may not be marked and roads may not be lit at night; rural tracks may be muddy, and mountain roads dangerous.

Safe driving requires mastery of the vehicle, the terrain and the traffic. Mastering the vehicle means, for instance, knowing how to operate a four-wheel-drive vehicle properly, knowing the capacities of the engine under various circumstances (acceleration, steep uphill climbs, etc.) and appreciating the stability of the vehicle on different surfaces. Mastering the terrain means being able to drive safely and competently on, for instance, sandy or icy tracks or on mountain roads, or being able to cross a river bed. Mastering the traffic means recognising that other road users may not obey traffic rules or may drive in undisciplined ways. An anticipatory or defensive driving style will be important. Knowing how to drive safely is particularly important for international staff. Staff who do not know how to drive (or who can only drive certain types of vehicles, such as automatic transmissions) should learn prior to deployment, and should be provided with opportunities to practice during their deployments.

Speed

Always respect the speed limits imposed by national laws whenever such laws exist. Speeding always increases the risk of road accidents and will not endear culprits to the locals. Some agencies have installed devices to monitor the speed at which their cars are driven. Only in exceptional circumstances, for example where sniper fire is a risk, can high speeds be justified.

Seat belts

Seat belts should always be worn. Only in circumstances where a quick exit from the car may be in order – for instance during an aerial attack or an armed robbery – should seat belts be dispensed with.

No-go zones and driving at night

Some agencies establish clear no-go zones in the cities or areas in which they work and also enforce a no-night-driving policy for any trips, professional or personal, outside of the city centre. This policy usually cannot be enforced for national staff, but it can raise awareness of the possible risks.

8.2.4 Drivers
Recruitment

The recruitment of drivers is a critical management issue for at least three reasons:

- Drivers need to be technically competent and safe.
- Travelling a lot, and being able to influence decisions at critical moments, means that drivers have an important role to play in security management.
- As they come into contact with large numbers of people, drivers informally represent the organisation and therefore affect the image that people form of it.

Drivers should have:

- A valid driving licence.
- Language skills (essential or desirable).
- Good eyesight (this should be tested).
- Driving experience and a good driving record.
- Technical competence in maintenance and repair (test this).

- Ability to drive in difficult terrain and in undisciplined traffic (test this too).
- Reliability. Establish the credentials of the individual and their possible networks. A social or character reference is a good means of establishing reliability.

In insecure environments other factors may also come into play, such as ethnic identity, age, temperament, analytical and observational skills and local knowledge of the area of operation.

Training, induction and supervision

Drivers need training and supervision. As they informally represent the organisation they need to be able to give a succinct but accurate picture of what it is and what it does. They also require security training, and regular meetings should be convened with the logistics manager and security manager.

Driving policy

Establish a driving policy for staff who are not drivers. Can other national and international staff drive vehicles? If so, under what conditions? This can involve introducing driving tests and training. This policy should clarify liabilities in case of an accident caused by a driver or by another member of staff. Also consider the necessary insurance arrangements for drivers and other staff who may drive.

8.2.5 Organisational policies on passengers and accidents

Passengers

Drivers and other staff travelling in vehicles should have a clear understanding of agency policy towards picking up passengers who are not employees of the organisation, and to accidents involving other people. In practice policies might need to be interpreted depending on the level of insecurity, which might mean that the organisation defines some strict rules on certain issues, while being more flexible on others. Rules could prohibit the carrying of weapons in agency vehicles (stickers with the symbol of a gun with a line through it can be affixed to the windows to remind everyone of this rule); no cargo other than that of the agency can be transported; vehicles cannot be driven by non-employees; and vehicles on mission should not be left unattended.

Guidelines may also be set out regarding passenger policy. These can be printed on a laminated card in the local language, for drivers to show that they are acting under orders. It is of course possible to insist that nobody other than identified aid agency employees can travel as passengers, but this may be untenable and self-defeating: in many situations a local may be taken along to act as a guide, or lifts may be given as a measure of reciprocal hospitality and in an attempt to build up good relations. Exceptions may also have to be made for sick or injured people in need of medical attention. A waiver of liability document in the car could exempt the agency should anything happen, though in some circumstances a signature on a piece of paper is likely to carry little weight. Discuss with community leaders in advance any concerns about liability and compensation in the event of an accident, and where available seek local legal advice.

Giving lifts to soldiers is another difficult issue. In general, avoid transporting anyone who is armed, in uniform or known to be affiliated with an armed group, especially in areas where several opposing parties are moving about. Again, however, an element of judgement may come into play, for example where:

- The agency may need temporary armed protection and it is impossible for a military escort to travel in a separate vehicle.
- A solider coerces a driver to provide transport, and resisting his orders would put passengers at risk (this should be reported as a security incident).
- A soldier is injured or ill and requires urgent medical attention (this should also be reported as a security incident, especially where it may compromise perceptions of neutrality).

Accidents

Guidelines should be set out on how to react in case of an accident, especially if it causes the injury or death of local people. In certain countries the advice might be to stop and help the victim; in others it might be not to stop, but to continue on to the nearest police post or agency office if bystanders are likely to attack the driver and their vehicle, whether or not the accident was their fault. If this is the case, the agency, perhaps with the local police, needs to come back and sort out the matter. Do not leave disputes unresolved.

8.2.6 Protective devices

Protection against theft

A number of devices help to protect vehicles from theft, including lockable fuel filler caps, lockable wheel nuts and steering locks. Windows and other detachable parts can be etched with the agency's name, to deter theft or aid in recovery. An electronic immobiliser may need some specialist input. A hidden fuel cut-off switch can prevent car thieves from getting very far; avoid instant fuel cut-off devices, as thieves may become angry or frustrated if they can't get the vehicle running.

Radios

Radios allow others to monitor vehicle movements and enable drivers to report problems and call for assistance. However, driving around with huge antennae attached to the car also defeats any attempts to keep a low profile and may mark the vehicle out as a worthwhile target for militias or criminals. Mobile phones are a more useful tool, perhaps with satphones as a back-up. Always switch the radio off before putting on, taking off or touching the aerial, to avoid radio frequency burn (see Chapter 7 on 'Managing communications security' for more details).

Vehicle tracking systems

A tracking system follows a vehicle and can indicate its location on maps stored in the control station computer. It can also be programmed to send a warning signal when the vehicle is approaching an exclusion zone. It can therefore have a preventive function by signalling to the vehicle's occupants that they are entering a high-risk area or crossing a border, for instance. Good maps with precise geographical coordinates are required. Locating a vehicle following a distress call is useful, but in itself says nothing about what the problem is and does not improve the capacity to respond. Tracking devices can be useful in high-crime contexts where carjacking is prevalent, to track and locate stolen vehicles.

Flashing lights

In areas where aerial attack is a risk, agencies have installed blue or orange flashing lights on the roofs of their vehicles to increase their visibility and make them easier to identify. However, if others copy the practice it loses its protective value. If this strategy is applied, consult and communicate with the parties to the conflict who are using aerial bombardment as a military action. In such instances, coordinated travel or travel advisory procedures should be considered. For example, in Lebanon in 2006 the Israeli Defense Force was advised of the movements of aid convoys to ensure that vehicles were not mistaken for military targets.

Essential documents

Keep a list of:

- The engine and chassis numbers of all vehicles (consider taking photos of vehicles to assist in identification if lost or stolen, and record identifying marks such as paint decals or colour schemes).
- Insurance policy documents and contact details.
- Vehicle owner details.
- Lease agreements.
- Fuel and maintenance procurement agreements.

8.2.7 Journey planning

Journey planning takes time, but this is no reason not to do it.

- Keep the journey plan confidential if there is a risk of targeted attack.
- Study the route and all possible problem points (natural, such as flooding and snowed-up passes, and man-made, such as checkpoints or good areas for ambushes).
- Estimate travel times rather than distances, and plan the journey so that you arrive well before nightfall or curfew hours. Build in time for local inquiries, e.g. about the risk of mines (see Chapter 15 on 'Combat-related threats and remnants of war'). Anticipate possible delays. You can then indicate estimated departure time, arrival time and return time.
- Emergency options: are there alternative routes, or fall-back places where you might get help or find sanctuary?
- Establish a monitoring system: radio call times, from where and at what intervals; who decides about deviations from the planned journey? Define code words or coded phrases if necessary (see Chapter 7).
- Inspect and prepare vehicles in advance: have they been serviced and are they ready? Do you have all the necessary equipment? Do drivers and passengers know how to use the equipment? Do you have all the necessary documentation for vehicles and passengers? Are copies of all key documents available at base?

Prior to departure it is useful to have a team briefing in which the journey plan is reviewed and discussed. A returning team should be debriefed on any changes in the route taken.

If venturing into unknown territory, take time to inquire about the landscape ahead: ask questions of local people, and stop regularly on the road. If a local guide is accompanying you, elicit details before setting out. Ask for details of the route ahead, useful reference points and road conditions, and work these through on a sketch map. Take notes on the route and draw maps for the benefit of those following after you. Keep track of distances using the mileage counter. If the security situation allows, consider using a GPS device to track the route.

8.2.8 Checkpoints

Aid agencies tend to focus on checkpoints as a critical moment in a journey. This is generally correct: armed men at a checkpoint can harass, intimidate and even threaten aid workers. The situation can spin out of control because they are tense or drunk, or because they find offence in what you represent, carry, say or do. Staff interaction with those at the checkpoint will influence how the agency is perceived and how other aid personnel trying to pass through afterwards will be dealt with. Be aware of and try to adhere to any common practices among aid agencies in dealing with checkpoints, for example refusing to pay illegal 'taxes' or bribes.

Rapid assessment

Not all checkpoints are equally critical. A key skill to develop is rapid assessment of the type of checkpoint: where it is located, who is manning it and what their mood appears to be. Checkpoints at crossroads, bridges, mountain passes and town entrances and exits are to be expected, and are likely to have been set up for the general monitoring of all passers-by. Checkpoints in the middle of a forest or on a mountain road away from habitation may exist for a more ominous purpose. Checkpoints manned by regular army and police forces may be less problematic than ones manned by irregulars.

When approaching a checkpoint, signal clearly that you have no harmful intent:

- Inform base before approaching the checkpoint and resume contact when you have passed it, but consider turning off the radio if you feel that it might attract unwelcome attention while passing through the checkpoint.
- Slow down.
- Wind the window down.
- After dark turn on the light inside the car cabin so that all passengers are clearly visible.
- Stop the car a few yards from the barrier, but always keep the engine running unless ordered otherwise. If there is more than one vehicle, the next one should keep its distance.
- Take off sunglasses so that people can see your face and eyes.
- Avoid any brusque movements in the car, and keep your hands clearly visible.

A spokesperson should be identified beforehand. Drivers often play a lead role either because they talk the team through the checkpoint or because they also act as translator. They should have a clear understanding of when to switch role from spokesperson to translator.

Any team member could potentially be interrogated. It is therefore necessary for everyone to know what cargo the vehicle is carrying, and to have the same story about what their organisation does and what the purpose of the journey is. Passengers should also have identification in the local language other than their passports, and passports should not be handed over if it can be avoided.

If asked to go inside a guardroom, try to avoid leaving the vehicle unattended. If one of the vehicle occupants is considered vulnerable or at risk, accompany that person if they are called away from the vehicle for interrogation or to have their documents inspected.

8.2.9 Convoys

Convoys can take various forms depending on their composition and what they are transporting; the numbers and types of vehicles, and the type of cargo, will determine the convoy's length and speed. A large convoy may reduce risk through strength in numbers, but it also moves more slowly; it can portray an image of power and wealth, but this might stir up resentment, and it might be mistaken from afar for an army column on the move. Smaller convoys may be more vulnerable to ambush but are perhaps easier to negotiate through checkpoints and less likely to come under aerial attack.

Convoys need to be managed, and should have a leader. When different agencies participate in a convoy, or when they join a convoy under armed protection from national army troops or international peacekeepers, there is often reluctance to accept leadership. This can affect discipline. It is not acceptable to join a convoy for one's own security and then try to change the rules or break convoy discipline.

Planning the journey

Draw up a journey plan and establish an assembly point and assembly time well before departure. Obtain precise details of all vehicles expected, along with the passengers and cargo. Assemble all the documentation that will be required.

Constituting the convoy

How the line of vehicles in the convoy is ordered will depend on the number and types of vehicle there are (trucks, buses, four-wheel-drive passenger vehicles, a water tanker, an ambulance, an armoured personnel carrier) and what cargo and assets they are carrying, as well as the types of threats and problems anticipated (a vehicle getting stuck in the mud during a river crossing, heavy trucks unable to climb a snowy road, a road block by irregulars, mines, physical aggression, etc.).

In the light of these possible scenarios, consider how to line up the convoy. If man-made problems are anticipated, think about having a scouting vehicle ahead of the convoy. This needs to be able to maintain radio contact; it should probably carry the deputy convoy leader, rather than the leader him/herself. Consider too whether the local guide will go with the scouting vehicle or stay with the main convoy. The convoy leader will be in front, but there should also be someone at the rear of the convoy with experience and decision-making authority. Decide whether to maintain radio or other communication between the front and the rear of the convoy; perhaps establish a signal code using car horns and headlights. Armed escorts should be in separate vehicles. If the escorts do not have their own transport, you may provide a vehicle, but all agency identification marks should be removed. Ideally, an armed escort should be split over more than one point in the convoy. Finally, buses or other passenger vehicles should be in the middle, with medical supplies and food, water and blankets. Ensure sufficient vehicles so that, if one breaks down, the convoy can continue.

Pre-departure checks

Prior to departure the convoy leader must ensure that all vehicles have been checked:

- Are the vehicles suitable for the journey (e.g. are trucks small and light enough to negotiate all the bridges and tunnels along the route?).
- Do they all have enough fuel and spare tyres?
- Can they handle difficult terrain?
- Is all the necessary documentation ready?

It is very important for the convoy leader to know the details of the cargoes carried, and convoy leaders must have the right to inspect the cargoes of constituent vehicles prior to departure.

Communicate the convoy rules

All drivers in the convoy need to know who the convoy leader and deputy leader are, and everyone must be familiar with the convoy rules. General movement rules should include the speed of the convoy (it will travel at the speed of the slowest vehicle), minimum and maximum distances between vehicles, lights on for easier visual contact, regulations on radio use or mobile phone communications within the convoy and between the convoy leader and the monitoring office and agreed stopping and resting points.

General scenario rules include establishing how the convoy will act when approaching a checkpoint, what it will do if one vehicle experiences problems at a checkpoint while the others get clearance and what will happen if a vehicle breaks down but cannot immediately be repaired. There have been instances of truck drivers being killed when their vehicle broke down and they stayed behind.

Distance-keeping

Keeping the right distance between convoy vehicles can be difficult. Vehicles should never be so far apart that visual contact is lost; at the same time, they should not be so close together that they get caught in the same incident (an ambush, a roadside bomb, slipping into each other on an icy road, damage from a mine explosion). Appropriate distance varies according to the terrain and the weather and security conditions, and may have to be adjusted over the course of the journey.

If you are not travelling in convoy it is generally good practice to try to keep a significant distance between your vehicle and any security force convoys or even single security-force vehicles. Military actors and their vehicles may be the target of a roadside bomb (an IED). Slow down and let them get ahead of you if they come too close. If you happen to be in the vicinity of an explosion, avoid, at least initially, your natural impulse to go closer and investigate or assist. The best advice is to stop, get out of your vehicle and take cover on the ground or at the side of the road to avoid any possible crossfire.[1]

8.3 Road travel: incident preparedness and incident response

This section focuses on armed robbery on the road and carjacking. Other types of threat are dealt with elsewhere in Part 5.

8.3.1 Threat analysis and preparedness

Carjackers will want to steal the vehicle. Armed robbers may only want valuables, although they could use the car to make good their escape.

A good incident pattern analysis can identify high-risk zones. It can also suggest high-risk times, for example that carjackers seize vehicles when their owners get into them to leave in the morning, or when they return home in the evening. Under such circumstances, closely watch your surroundings before getting into and out of your car. Alternatively, carjackings may occur at a stopping point – a red traffic light, for instance. In this case, trying never to be the front car waiting at a red signal will reduce the risk. More commonly, carjackers and armed robbers may follow their target in another car, then suddenly overtake and force the vehicle to stop. If a victim's regular route is known and the attack has been planned, the attackers may be lying in wait, and may suddenly block the route by parking their vehicle in front of the targeted car. Another technique is for the robbers to deliberately fake an accident by bumping into a vehicle to make it stop and force the driver out. If this happens, do not stop immediately but signal to the other car to follow you and try to reach a well-lit, busy area. Constantly monitor whether another

1 Drawn from David Lloyd Roberts, *Staying Alive: Safety and Security Guidelines for Humanitarian Volunteers in Conflict Areas* (Geneva: ICRC, 2006).

vehicle is following you. If you think you are being followed, head back to the office. Call ahead to alert the guards and the security officer.

Door locks and seatbelts

Whether drivers lock the car doors when driving or not is again a contextual decision. Where thieves generally operate without weapons (e.g. snatching a bag from the passenger seat while a car is waiting at a traffic light) or with knives, locking the doors offers protection and gains seconds in which to accelerate out of danger. However, if an incident pattern analysis reveals that armed robbers are likely to shoot if they encounter any obstacle that frustrates their attempt, it may be safer not to lock the doors.

8.3.2 If an incident happens

Trying to escape

Specialised security training teaches drivers how to throw their vehicle into rapid reverse, to hit a vehicle trying to push them off the road or to crash through another vehicle blocking the way. Unless you consider yourself an expert this is not advisable. You are likely to provoke gunfire or crash your car. Always assume that attackers are armed and that they will shoot if you try to escape. That said, if your threat analysis indicates that people are often shot and killed in the course of a carjacking you may decide to try evasive action.

Types of attackers

Armed robbers can be of two types: inexperienced and opportunistic, often adolescents, or experienced robbers. The experienced robber is likely to practice techniques of intimidation and submission: they may force you to face the car, go down on your knees or put your hands behind your head, and they may put a gun to your head. You may be hit hard on the head or neck to signal that you should not try to resist; what you do not know is how likely they are to pull the trigger if they think you are resisting. Experienced robbers may also practice ambush techniques, blocking you in front and behind to prevent you escaping. An attempt to reverse or accelerate out of the ambush may have been anticipated and may be met with gunshots. The inexperienced robber can be more dangerous: they may be far more nervous, pepped up with drugs or alcohol and not in control of their weapon or themselves; a weapon can go off very easily and almost unintentionally.

In general, any robber will be watchful for anything that signals resistance, and nervous about delays. Remember:

- No vehicle or amount of money is worth your life.
- Never put your life at risk by resisting an armed robbery.

- Keep your hands visible, and make no sudden moves.
- Avoid displays of anger, rudeness or aggression.
- Give up the vehicle and valuables as instructed.

If instructed to leave the vehicle, do not attempt to take anything with you (for example a personal bag). Comply swiftly with the attackers' orders, but do not initiate any action, such as getting out of the car or handing over wallets or car keys, unless instructed to do so.

Danger moments

Spontaneous movements may prompt a reaction from your attackers. Never grab for the door handle, release the seat belt or touch the handbrake, for example, without alerting the attackers to what you are doing: they may think you are reaching for a weapon. Keep your hands visible, and say or signal what you intend to do before making any movement. Leave the car door open when you are out of it. Surrender personal items on demand. Don't show resistance, fear or anger.

Negotiating

There may be circumstances when you could try to negotiate – for instance so that you can keep your passport or the radio, so that you are allowed to first make a distress call or so that you can keep a supply of water and food (when ambushed in a remote area a long way from help). This again is a situational judgement: in general, avoid negotiating when the attackers are very nervous, visibly anxious to get away as quickly as possible or highly aggressive.

8.4 Travel by aircraft and boat

Aid agencies use commercial airlines and boat services, and they may also charter them. Smaller commercial airlines can spring up and disappear very quickly. Not all of them meet international aviation safety standards. Some national carriers do not meet those standards either. Entities like the European Commission maintain a list of airlines that are banned from the European Union because of safety concerns. Consider avoiding such airlines.

There can also be significant problems with commercial boats running between or within countries, especially if they operate in areas where the weather is frequently bad. If official safety standards are not enforced vessels may be overcrowded, with insufficient lifeboats or lifejackets for all passengers, inadequate fire-fighting equipment and cargo unevenly stowed, increasing the risk of capsizing in heavy seas. If possible, avoid using such vessels. If you must use them, bring your own lifejacket, and stay on deck throughout the journey so you can get off the boat quickly if a situation turns bad.

When chartering planes, helicopters or boats, determine clearly the safety and security standards you want to see in place – and check that they are.

- The safety of the vessel (aircraft or boat). Is there a maintenance record? If it is a seagoing vessel does it have spare engine parts, a second engine and a spare battery? Does the navigational and communications equipment work properly? Are there lifejackets, distress rockets, torches, functioning fire extinguishers and spare oars for lifeboats? Is there enough fuel, with spare capacity beyond the estimated journey requirements? Is the weight of the cargo within safety parameters, and is the cargo evenly stowed?
- The qualifications of the pilot/captain – and crew. Is the pilot/captain licensed? Do crew members have proper mechanics skills? Do they speak the right languages?
- Moving safely in a potentially hostile environment. What is the weather forecast? Is the pilot/captain using proper maps or charts, and do they know about current security conditions – what information can you provide them? Is prior clearance from the authorities necessary? Is the security situation at the planned landing strip or port of destination confirmed? What will you do if there is no additional fuel available at the landing strip or security clearance cannot be obtained? How is the aircraft/helicopter/boat identifiable (colour, logos)? Are you confident that the vessel is not also engaged in smuggling (e.g. of arms or minerals) and might be perceived as doing so while operating under contract for you?

8.5 A checklist for staff preparation

Travellers and new arrivals
- Consult your managers and ensure that you receive your pre-departure briefing. Do your own research as well; have essential phone numbers with you and obtain guidance on reliable means of local transport if you're not going to be met at the airport.
- Ensure that you receive an in-depth safety and security briefing on arrival.

Drivers and field staff: key skills and equipment
- map reading and use of compass;
- mastery of the vehicle, terrain and traffic;
- a 'get yourself home' basic car repair kit;
- instructions on driving and convoy discipline;
- key messages about the agency and its mission; and
- simulation training: under aerial attack, in a mined area, armed robbery on the road, checkpoints, journey planning, venturing into unknown territory.

Logistics managers: key skills
- knowledge of advanced vehicle repair;
- driver training skills or clear criteria to identify a good driver-trainer;
- competence in installing and using protective devices;
- management of the vehicle pool and maintenance and repair scheduling;
- simulations on journey planning;
- simulations on convoy constitution; and
- security management.

Field managers
- ensure that pre-departure and on-arrival briefing notes are provided;
- set driver recruitment criteria;
- set driver policy and disciplinary policy (who is allowed to drive what and when);
- set passenger and accident policy (procedures and guidelines); and
- simulations on convoy constitution.

Chapter 9
Site security

Site protection can deter or stop intrusion, delay attack and mitigate the effects of an incident in the immediate vicinity.[1] 'Site' here refers to the real estate that the agency uses on a regular basis, notably offices, residences and warehouses. The focus of this chapter is on office and residential protection. It is also necessary, however, to consider site security for staff spending time in programme settings, for example residing in refugee camps or in a medical facility or school building. It is also necessary to consider site security for project delivery sites, for example distribution sites in camps and also for general distributions that may be held outside of a camp setting. In addition to primary facilities and international staff residences, protection measures may also be needed around the homes of national staff.

9.1 Site selection

Site protection starts with site selection. For safety and security purposes, potential locations will need to meet special criteria beyond space, aesthetics and price considerations.

9.1.1 Key considerations in site selection
Physical criteria
Physical criteria for the location and the building include:

- If there is a risk of extreme weather conditions and related natural disasters such as floods or landslides, determine if the building is in a potentially vulnerable location, and whether the structure is robust enough to withstand the elements.
- Avoid areas that offer many possibilities for concealed approaches and escapes, for example areas with dense bush or a dry river bed, with narrow, dark alleyways, with factory grounds, storage spaces and warehouses that are largely abandoned at night, or containing damaged and destroyed buildings.
- The actual building or flat constitutes the inner perimeter. If a flat is part of a block, or a building set within a compound or a larger gated area, this constitutes an outer perimeter. A double perimeter is generally preferable to a single perimeter.

---

1 The risks change dramatically in situations of insurgency and war, where additional measures are required. These are considered in Chapter 15 ('Combat-related threats and remnants of war').

- Consider how easy it would be to get out of the building or the immediate area in the event of fire: are there different exit routes, and can the local fire brigade get close enough to the building?

The wider area

When considering a particular district, check an area of at least 1.5km radius thoroughly, to get a better feel for it. Questions to ask local residents and authorities include:

- What sort of neighbourhood is it? Are most people local residents, or do large numbers of workers come into the area daily? Do large numbers of travellers pass through the area? The less local the population, the easier it will be for outsiders to enter the area unobtrusively.
- What local authority and rescue services are there in the area? Where is the nearest fire station? Where are the police posts? Where do the influential local leaders live? Find out if there is a police patrol, and where the more regularly patrolled areas are.
- What type of access control measures are used by those in the local area? Are there guards outside homes? Are homes heavily fortified?

Possible vulnerabilities

Consider too the potential vulnerabilities of the neighbourhood.

- Are there military installations, police premises or government buildings? Are there important socioeconomic or religious targets (the temple of a religious minority, the headquarters of a militant trade union, the office of an opposition newspaper, a radio station etc.)?
- In the event of political unrest, demonstrations are likely to focus on government buildings. However, if foreign intervention is resented demonstrations may target diplomatic buildings; a university area may be susceptible to student unrest, and marketplaces can be targets for terror attacks. A neighbourhood where a minority group lives could be vulnerable to mob attacks.
- Crime levels can be high in wealthy as well as poor areas. Whatever the level of affluence of the chosen area, try not to project the appearance of wealth.

In a high-crime environment, it may be advisable to choose a site close to a police station (but bear in mind that police stations may be targeted in an insurgency or during social or political unrest). While security conditions may require it, locating offices or residences in a relatively wealthy area, in a diplomatic enclave or in a gated community will project a certain image and will influence how the agency is perceived.

Single or multi-tenant occupancy

The advantage of multiple tenants is that the presence of other people offers additional awareness and protection. Some of the advantages of strength in numbers can be gained if several agencies occupy sites close together. UN agencies increasingly group their offices in a single location, both for security reasons and reasons of cost, and some NGOs have followed suit. There are obvious advantages to co-location: the cost of security and guarding services can be shared and more people will be around to provide informal surveillance and to offer help in an emergency. But there are also risks. Grouped sites tend to become gated communities separated from the wider social environment, and the concentration of possible targets means that an attack will have a much higher impact if successful. Ensure that acceptance strategies and image considerations are shared with co-tenants. Single-tenant sites may be more fully under the agency's control.

It is often advisable to rent office space or a flat on a lower floor, but above the ground floor (the ground floor is more vulnerable to intruders and higher floors may be unreachable with emergency equipment and difficult to escape from, for instance in case of fire). Additionally, if the roof is accessible, perhaps from a neighbouring building, taking the flat just under the roof could be risky. Whether choosing a block of flats increases or decreases risk depends very much on the stability and social cohesion of its resident population. If this is high, there is probably a good implicit neighbourhood watch scheme. If it is low there may be a general lack of interest in the security of neighbours and strangers may have easy access to the building.

Gender considerations

In some circumstances it may be culturally unacceptable or simply unsafe for female colleagues – national or international – to live alone, and it may be necessary to find shared living arrangements that work for female colleagues and that do not clash with social norms. Consider having separate quarters for male and female staff. (For more details see the section on gender considerations in risk assessment in Chapter 2.)

The landlord

Try to find out as much as possible about the landlord: their occupation, social background, possible role in the local community, political affiliation and so on. Where possible, try to avoid renting from a person involved in suspicious dealings, someone who is politically prominent or someone who is a leader (or close family member) of a party to a conflict. In some contexts the landlord's clan affiliation will also be important. The tribal tradition that a host is duty-bound to protect his guests may come into play if a landlord sees

Case example: a secure site in Ossetia

For reasons of security an aid agency decides to relocate from Ingushetia to North Ossetia. When looking for a secure site it notices that the international staff of another agency are housed in flats (it is the agency's policy for staff to find their own accommodation). The agency is wary of the dark entrances and alleyways around the flats and decides to look for a compound where offices and residences can be combined, vehicles parked and telecoms set up. The logistician (a man) finds what looks like the ideal place in terms of access and space. Female staff, however, raise concerns about the neighbourhood. Upon inquiry the agency learns that there is indeed criminal activity in the area. In the end, a local, who had already been acting as an adviser to another agency, finds a compound on the outskirts of the city. The building has the necessary physical security requirements; the area is relatively affluent, with many guard dogs and high security awareness.

his tenants as guests. In other places the fact that the landlord belongs to a minority group could constitute a risk factor.

In practice, it will be necessary to balance various considerations. The perfect choice will seldom exist. Weigh up the pros and cons of every site from a security point of view, in the light of how the agency will be perceived, its security strategy and contingency planning. Once a site has been chosen identify its weaknesses and address them. What are the physical strengths and deficiencies of the site from a security point of view? What is acceptable, and what has to be improved? Will the owner allow physical improvements to be made? How much will improvements cost, and are they affordable? Before signing a lease, negotiate in detail permission to make alterations to the building to increase its security. This should also be reflected in the lease contract.

9.2 Physical perimeter reinforcement

9.2.1 The outer perimeter

Several factors need to be taken into account when considering the outer perimeter of a site. If vegetation on the approach to the site or at the outer perimeter offers hiding places for robbers and assailants, have it trimmed or cut or replace it with thorn bushes. Consider whether rubbish and rubble are going to be more of a hindrance to an assailant, or will help a malicious person to monitor or gain access to the building, and whether it will be a hindrance to guards. If there is a risk of an explosive device being placed, all rubble and rubbish need to be removed.

Walling off the site increases protection. Walls should be at least 2.5 metres high, and may be topped with barbed wire or broken glass. Any nearby trees that could be used to help in scaling the wall need to be dealt with. High walls are of little use if gates are a weak point because they are easy to scale or are only secured with a padlock and chain, either of which can be broken open quickly. Ensure peepholes are fitted to check who is at the gate without having to open it. In some circumstances – for instance if an area is prone to mob violence or if armed robbery is a risk – it may be a good idea to have a second exit point. This too should be secure against incursion.

Improved lighting may reduce certain risks, but it may also make a site more prominent and draw attention to the fact that there is something inside worth protecting. Sensor lights that activate only when someone approaches may be a good compromise, though like any lighting they rely on a reliable electricity supply. Ideally, lights should only illuminate dark areas within the compound, rather than the facility itself or its occupants. In the absence of electricity, or if there are regular power cuts, consider using a generator, especially if this is anyway a common practice within the neighbourhood. A less expensive and more modest alternative is the strategic placement of hurricane lanterns, if there is a guard to monitor them. Solar energy lighting is becoming more common and affordable. Remember that security lighting is only really useful if there is somebody present to monitor the area.

Whether the agency logo is fixed to the outer perimeter depends on the circumstances, and whether doing so will reduce or increase risks. As a general rule, logos are appropriate where there is a high level of acceptance of the agency's work and presence. If a logo is displayed, add a translation of the agency's name and perhaps a short statement of its mission in the local language.

If a site is unoccupied for any period of time, a staff member should visit regularly to turn lights on and off and open and close the shutters, to give the impression that the site is in use.

Parking vehicles

Where vandalism, car theft, mob violence or bombing is a threat, vehicles must be parked in the compound at all times. Make sure that there is enough parking space when selecting the site. Vehicles should be locked when not in use, and operating procedures should be in place for vehicle key control, parking arrangements and emergency use. As a general rule parking and fuel arrangements should be conducive to easy departure from the compound, for instance ensuring that vehicles are fully fuelled at the end of each day, and parked in an arrangement that allows for quick loading and easy exit.

9.2.2 The inner perimeter

Walk around the building with the eye of an intruder and look for weak spots, particularly doors and windows. All entrance doors need to be strong, including the frames and hinges. Avoid or replace doors containing any glass, but do install an optical viewer (peephole) and a primary and auxiliary lock on outer doors. On the inside install a safety chain and a sliding dead-bolt or strong bar across the door. Heavy-duty padlocks on the inside, at the top and bottom of the door, add additional security, especially if the padlock rings are welded on. Don't place panic buttons or telephones close to the entrance door where an intruder could block access to them.

Windows can be protected with bars, grills or shutters, especially at ground level (provided they are easy to open from the inside in case of emergency). Check how easy it is to reach an upper floor window and respond accordingly. Thick thorn bushes under ground-floor windows can impede access. Make sure that bars or grills cannot be easily unscrewed or removed from the outside. Check whether it is possible to enter the house through garage doors, a cellar or a bathroom window. At night, routinely close curtains to make it difficult to observe who and how many are inside. When going out, leave a light on to give the impression that someone is in. Regularly check that all locks and bolts are in good working order and routinely lock everything as night falls or before going to bed. Limit the number of keys available and closely control who has access to them.

In case of fire, intrusion or rioting, an alternative exit from the house may be needed. The escape exit, including any bars or grills, must be easy to open from the inside. If bars are already fitted, they should be modified to allow exit from the inside. This may be done by hinging the bars on one side and using a padlock to secure them, and ensuring that occupants have quick access to the key to the padlock.

Burglar alarms and closed-circuit television (CCTV) cameras are uncommon in most aid contexts. Both typically depend on an electricity supply, although some burglar alarms work on batteries. A CCTV camera offers little deterrent if intruders do not know what it is and what it does, or if there is little chance that they will ever be apprehended. Very high-decibel devices can be a highly effective protection device. Remote operated and acting directionally, they create a sound that is unbearable (but does not damage the ear) and will effectively stop an intruder or even a rioting crowd from moving further into the premises. They have sabotage protection and run on batteries.

A note on basic fire safety is warranted here. Fit smoke and carbon monoxide alarms and provide fire extinguishers in the kitchen and on every floor. Electrical and oil fires require a CO_2 or powder-filled extinguisher; for other types of fire use a foam or water-filled extinguisher. Check the extinguishers and have them serviced at least once a year. Identify fire escape routes and ensure that, when locked from the inside, they can be opened instantly. In larger buildings organise fire drills regularly, especially if staff turnover is high. Make sure that gas room heaters are properly vented, and check whether they have thermal couplers (devices that prevent the gas supply from turning on without a pilot light or other source of ignition). Heaters without thermal couplers should not be left unattended, and should not be used at night.

9.2.3 The safe room

A safe room is a place where quick refuge can be found from intruders; it is not the same as a bomb shelter, and will not be bomb- or shell-proof. It should be easily and quickly accessible, and preferably located in the core of the building. Alternatively, an upper floor can be converted into a safe area by installing a grill on the staircase, which is locked at night. Safe rooms should have a reinforced door, a telephone or other means of communication (preferably un-interruptable), in order to call for help, and a list of key contact numbers, plus a torch or candles and matches. Consider storing a small quantity of water, food and sanitary items in the safe room as well. The purpose of a safe room is to protect people, not assets. Putting everything in the safe room is only likely to encourage robbers to make greater efforts to break in. Leave them something to steal, if not everything.

9.3 Site security management

Site security is everybody's responsibility. Everyone should remain attentive and report anything unusual or suspicious, as well as breaches in security procedures (doors or windows left open, keys left lying around). Try to cultivate good relations with your neighbours without being too intrusive. People are more likely to act on seeing something suspicious if a basic relationship has been established and they know at least a little about you.

9.3.1 Guards

Aid agencies commonly use guards and night-watchmen for their residences, warehouses and offices. Guards may either be hired directly, or contracted from a local provider. Too often, however, guards are ineffective because they are untrained, poorly instructed, poorly paid, poorly equipped and poorly managed. It is not uncommon to find a bed in the guardhouse of aid agency compounds, virtually guaranteeing that the guard will fall asleep on duty. During the day guards might be busy doing other things, and may be distracted. When hiring guards, provide clear terms of reference and make these part of the contract.

In recruiting and managing guards, consider the following:

- Select a physically fit person.
- Get reliable references, and if possible recruit staff from the immediate neighbourhood. This will ensure that they are familiar with the area and its regular occupants, and will increase their motivation to identify potential wrong-doers.
- The primary occupants of a building need to be able to communicate with the guard. Check the language abilities of potential recruits.
- Hire and deploy enough guards to challenge at least two intruders working together.
- As with all staff, ensure that the guards receive a full introduction to the agency.
- If the guard is to carry a weapon (lethal or otherwise), the circumstances under which it may be used must be governed by the contract signed with the individual or the guard provider, and must reflect the organisation's security policy. It is recommended that such policies be reviewed by the agency's legal adviser. Include contractual stipulations against the use of harmful substances (e.g. alcohol) while on duty, and against additional jobs that are likely to affect the guard's performance.
- Provide essential equipment, instruction and training: rain clothes, torches, a whistle or other alarm and a handheld radio or separate telephone in the guardhouse. Provide a logbook with instructions on keeping the log and on reporting, as well as a list of key contact numbers. Provide clear instructions and training on how to deal with visitors, and what to do if guards come across an intruder. Provide clear instructions about monitoring the surroundings, patrolling the compound and the rules regarding gates, doors, windows and keys.
- Guards should normally only have access to the outer, not the inner, perimeter, especially at residential premises. At the office compound they should have access to corridors, staircases and the roof, but not necessarily to the offices themselves.
- In areas where armed robbery is a high risk, consider deployment procedures, such as a routine inspection schedule alternated with rounds at less predictable times. Spread guards out, with at least one in a position

where he cannot be easily observed and overpowered, for example on a roof terrace.

- Being on guard for long periods can be boring, particularly if nothing is happening, and guards are likely to become less attentive and distracted. Try to keep them engaged: chat to them, show interest in them and ask them how they are and what they think about the situation in the neighbourhood.

Three other groups also play a direct and important role in site security: receptionists and telephone operators, relatives and household staff and office cleaners. Receptionists must monitor visitors and telephone calls and letters and parcels being delivered, and report anything and anybody that could be a security threat. Relatives of staff members must be aware of residential security, just like staff members themselves, and household staff, including gardeners, should not let unknown people in, give information to unknown callers, give details about the office layout or allow their keys to be duplicated. Anything unusual should be reported immediately.

Trained specifically for guarding purposes, dogs can be an excellent early warning help and often a deterrent. Remember that if the dog is potentially dangerous to people it does not know, some control measures will be necessary to protect legitimate visitors and staff.

9.3.2 Keys

Locks and keys are only useful when tightly managed. Keep a log of who has which keys. The number of keys, and access to them, must be tightly controlled. If in doubt, change the locks. Keys should be identified, generally in code. Spare keys should be locked away in a key box, with a glass front that can be broken in case of emergency. All personnel with keys, including household staff, should be clearly told that:

- Keys should be carried on the person and not left on desks, in cars or in unattended coats or bags.
- Keys should never be duplicated, except under specific instructions from the agency management.
- Any loss of keys has to be reported immediately.

On the other hand, being too strict may itself be hazardous, for instance if staff cannot escape from a burning building because they don't have the key to the emergency exit door, or cannot respond to an emergency call from a colleague because the car keys are locked away and the logistician lives on the other side of town.

Other technical access control measures include magnetic access cards, cipher locks (an electronic push-button access control system that permits entry only to those who know the code), magnetic readers, smart cards and biometric devices. Some of these systems can be expensive, and some will not work if the power supply fails or the mechanism malfunctions.

9.3.3 Managing access

Access control generally serves two functions: to establish the purpose and legitimacy of a visitor, and to ensure that visitors do not constitute a threat. How access is managed is delicate, and will affect how the agency is perceived. Generally speaking the majority of visitors will be welcome, though in some circumstances access may be very strictly controlled; visitors may be actively discouraged, or directed to a separate building away from the agency's main facility. In any case, it is helpful to have a designated visitor waiting space. This should be easily visible to security personnel and the receptionist. It should be connected to a toilet facility, but no uncontrolled access to the building should be possible for a visitor still waiting for clearance.

There are degrees of security control. For example, having visitors sign in and out is hardly a security measure in itself, as anyone can still get in. Stricter standard procedures include:

- All employees wear a visible photo ID when on the premises. These are collected upon termination of their contract or employment.
- All visitors show identification.
- All visitors are given ID or a pass, which is collected when they leave.
- No visitors are allowed in unless there is explicit authorisation from the person they want to see or who agrees to see them.
- No visitors are allowed in unless accompanied by a staff member.

Still stricter procedures include routine checks of visitors' bags and routine manual or electronic body searches (female guards and special training are needed here). Larger offices, typically in bigger cities, may control access by installing doors or turnstiles that operate with magnetic cards.

In high-risk environments, anyone unknown, unauthorised or unable to provide convincing identification should not be let in. The initial cursory check to establish whether a visitor could present a threat should therefore take place at the outer perimeter, before he or she is admitted into the compound. Only when a visitor does not seem to present a threat should they be let in. Establishing the exact purpose of the visit, contacting the host department and registration and issuing of a visitor's pass can then be done as a distinct second step within the premises, thereby minimising the number of people hanging around at the main entrance. If in doubt, guards should be instructed to contact a supervisor.

Access policy: questions to consider
- Are visitors' vehicles allowed into the compound? If they are, where should they park? For example, if there is a bomb threat make sure that there are no non-agency vehicles in the compound, and consider preventing visitors from parking around the compound. Guards may also be instructed to search vehicles, though this is a skilled job and they need to be trained to do it effectively.
- Should visitors who come with their own bodyguards be allowed to bring them in, and if so with or without their weapons? Are you liable in the case of an attempt on the life of the visitor whose bodyguards you did not allow in? Consider holding the meeting in an annex of the building or on a veranda, where bodyguards could be permitted.
- Think about service access, including maintenance, repair and utilities personnel and deliveries. Should service personnel be allowed into the premises in your absence? Can their arrival be planned and scheduled? What sort of ID should they provide? In the case of street vendors, tell guards and household staff that they should buy goods outside the gate.

9.3.4 Threatening phone calls and letters
Problematic phone calls can range from fairly innocent crank calls to sexual harassment and bomb threats. Staff receiving difficult calls should:

- insist that the caller identifies themselves and ascertain the purpose of the call;
- give as little information as possible about themselves and try to get as much as possible about the caller;
- give no information about their movements, when they will be in or out, and whether they are alone or not;
- request a number that they can call back on; and
- report all such calls to the security supervisor.

Sexual harassment calls can sometimes be stopped by having a male co-resident answer the phone. If the caller persists, change the telephone number. Female staff in particular should not put their home phone number on their business cards.

In the case of threatening calls, remain cool and polite. If the threat is vague and general try to elicit more detail about the motive, the precise target and whether the problem can be solved in another way. If the call is a bomb threat, the key question is when and where the bomb will explode. State the name of your organisation, followed by 'we have several premises – which one are you talking about?', and make the caller confirm the intended target. Ask the reason for the threat, and listen sympathetically. State that there are many people in and around the building who will be hurt if a bomb goes off. Try to write down exactly what is being said, or try to commit it to memory. Listen for any clues about the identity of the caller: male or female, tone of voice, agitated or calm, language and accent and specific background noises. Unless absolutely confident that the threat is not real, immediately evacuate the building.

If the office receives a threatening letter, it should be treated seriously and shared quickly with senior managers, the appropriate authorities and other organisations in the area. Any threat constitutes a security incident and should be reported.

9.3.5 Suspicious letters or parcels

While not a common threat to aid agencies, it is possible that a letter or parcel may be delivered that is deliberately contaminated with a poisonous chemical or biological substance (such as anthrax), or that contains explosives. Possible indicators are traces of powder on the envelope, a strange odour and, in the case of a bomb, a ticking sound or visible wires. The parcel may be unusually heavy for its size, the address may be misspelled or the mail may be addressed to someone who no longer works for the organisation. It may lack postage or may have excessive postage, indicating that it was not delivered for postage assessment at a post office.

Any such letters or parcels should be left where they are, the room vacated and security personnel alerted. Anyone who handled the object needs to be identified and must wash immediately with soap, especially their hands. The letter or parcel may have to be destroyed or opened by specially trained security personnel with proper equipment (contamination with a poisonous substance requires fully protective gloves as a minimum, and fully protective face masks as some substances enter the body through inhalation).

9.4 Areas under terrorist threat

Mitigating the threat of a terror attack is expensive and will generally require specialist advice and support. Some of the more common possible threats include staff in the building being fired upon from outside the perimeter; a suicide bombing at the entrance to the building; a car or truck bomb at the perimeter or rammed into the gate; armed attackers carrying explosives fighting their way into the building; and a visitor leaving a bomb package behind in the building. In dealing with such threats, the first question should always be: should we be here if the threat is so high?

The various elements listed here that help harden sites have important implications for site selection. It is unlikely that one building will meet all requirements, leaving certain vulnerabilities that will need to be addressed. In general, the building should have the following characteristics:

- It does not directly connect to space the agency cannot control, such as a public road. The building should be some distance from such spaces.
- The main entrances of the building are not in direct line of fire from a space that the agency cannot control.
- Offices are separated from warehouses and garages to which vehicles have access, and have their own security perimeter.
- There is an outer perimeter reducing the number of access points to the inner space and the site.
- Avoid underground garages. A car bomb under a building can do significant damage. If an underground garage is used, only staff (and in very exceptional circumstances visitors) should be allowed access; consider adding vehicle access barriers.
- Set up parking and drop-off spaces for visitors outside the external perimeter.

Speed limitation measures should be set up on access roads to all main entry points in the outer perimeter, to stop vehicles accelerating and ramming their way in. Specialised equipment can be installed, or alternatively use gravel- and stone-filled barrels or large concrete pots containing flowers or shrubs, chained together. If the outer perimeter is close to the building, erect additional stand-off measures such as concrete blocks or shrubs in a concrete block pot. The further from the building a blast occurs, the more its impact is lessened. A distance of 30m from the building is desirable, but will not often be feasible. If possible, separate staff and visitor entrances and staff parking from visitor parking. Staff vehicles still need to be carefully checked, in case a staff member's vehicle has been secretly loaded with explosives to be detonated by remote control, or a suicide bomber has requisitioned the car. Search vehicles and visitors authorised to enter the building at the outer perimeter.

Try to ensure an unobstructed space between the outer and inner perimeter of at least 10m. If vehicles or visitors have to move within that space, set up movement corridors. Any attempts to move outside these designated corridors should prompt an immediate response from security personnel. Within the building, separate spaces that are accessible to visitors from spaces that are restricted to staff. All visitors (and possibly also all staff) should be screened again on entry and any bags searched; the entrance point or lobby should be big enough to allow for this, and should not directly connect to other spaces in case a blast occurs in the lobby. Important assets such as the central computer system should be located deeper within the restricted area, and their location should not be identifiable by signs in the corridor.

If possible, create buffer rooms on the sides of the building to mitigate the effects of a bomb blast. Within rooms, people should not sit directly in line with windows. Good quality blast film will reduce the risk from flying glass, and objects outside the building that can turn into flying debris, such as rubbish bins, benches and flower pots, should be removed or solidly anchored in the ground. Refitting buildings to withstand blast waves would be costly and time-consuming, though consider reinforcing certain areas such as the entrance lobby, where a blast is more likely to occur.

9.5 Counter-surveillance

A serious attack or raid is likely to involve some forward planning. Counter-surveillance can identify a threat during the planning phase, before the attack takes place. [2] The planning phases of an attack will typically include:

- Initial target selection.
- Pre-attack surveillance.
- Planning the attack.
- Rehearsing the attack, perhaps including probes and drive-bys.

In its simplest terms, counter-surveillance involves watching to see if you are being watched. It can include:

- Identifying likely observation points, and pointing them out to staff.
- Instructing guards to patrol potential observation points.
- Instructing all staff to be on the alert for any behaviour that indicates active observation of the site or its traffic, such as the same vehicle passing by frequently or parked nearby for extended periods, and pedestrians loitering near the site.
- Building relationships with neighbours and local shop owners. Ask them if they have seen any suspicious behaviour or unfamiliar individuals near the site.

2 This section draws from 'Counter-surveillance and Surveillance Detection', presentation by John Schafer, Director of Security, InterAction, January 2010.

- Varying routines and routes taken to and from the office.

While counter-surveillance may have an unsavoury military ring to the humanitarian ear, it does not require heavy protective measures and materials or the use of force. Indeed, it may be a useful part of an acceptance strategy, requiring as it does daily interaction and communication with locals. Being of the community, observant of and familiar with your surroundings and co-inhabitants, you can potentially ward off threats – and your neighbours can help in this effort.

9.6 Distribution sites

A number of measures can increase security for aid agency staff and beneficiaries at distribution sites.

- Understand your beneficiaries. It is important to know how they view the distribution. Are they desperate for the items being distributed? Are there potential tensions between beneficiaries? Is political interference possible or likely? Are there elements that may have an interest in manipulating the distribution?
- Have a well-defined perimeter appropriate to the situation; in some instances fencing or walls may be necessary, in others barricades of some sort may be acceptable, with additional monitoring.
- The site should be in a place where ambient traffic (both vehicular and pedestrian) is not impeded. It should not invite unwanted bystanders.
- There should be one entry point and one exit point. Crowds at the entry point should be well managed so that the organisation can quickly separate legitimate beneficiaries from illegitimate ones – have a plan and staff on hand to deal with unruly individuals. Exit points should be managed with equal detail, ensuring that beneficiaries can leave the distribution site in an orderly and safe manner. Staff or the authorities should ensure that crowds (including family members that may come to help carry the load) do not gather and impede departure. It is very important to keep people moving. Agencies should be mindful of the potential protection issues for those leaving the distribution site, especially women and young children.
- Within the distribution site, the organisation should have a clear process that allows people to move on quickly – problems may occur when people are forced to wait in groups. Keep in mind how the distributed items will be bundled. Will the individuals receiving them be able to carry them in such a way that they are not made more vulnerable when they leave the distribution site? Think of ways to make distributed items less obvious as the beneficiary travels home.

Chapter 10
Crowds, mobs and looting

In tense and contested settings, crowds can turn menacing or violent. This can lead to looting of assets and aggression against staff. Common scenarios involve civil unrest, ethnic or communal violence, disorder around relief distributions and soldiers or armed fighters going on looting sprees. Such violence can erupt spontaneously, but it can also be planned and instigated.

10.1 Situational monitoring and analysis

Anticipating crowd and mob violence is not an exact science. However, the possibility needs to be considered as part of ongoing situational monitoring and analysis – at the general national level (with often a higher risk in cities), or at the local operational level (especially in camps of displaced people or in shanty towns). Growing tension and frustration can often be detected in advance. Local people, tuned into the local media and informal circuits of information, are often aware that something is brewing, although they are not necessarily better placed to predict exactly what will happen, when and where. It should be noted that tense situations can develop as a result of a particular event such as a distribution (e.g. a dispute about position in the queue, claims of fraud). Even in the absence of predictive factors, there should always be plans to defuse tensions (e.g. always having additional items to distribute, staff dedicated to watching and monitoring the mood of those in the queue).

Consider whether the agency is or might become a target, and where it is potentially exposed. What is the cause of the tension, and at whom is the resentment directed? Are foreigners or aid agencies the object? Can local authorities deflect resentment directed at them onto foreigners or aid agencies? Are local staff more at risk because of their ethnic or social identity? Has there been public unrest in the past? If so, where did it start, and how did it evolve? Is there a pattern that could repeat itself? Is the agency indirectly exposed, for example because offices or warehouses are close to an area where demonstrations take place, or located in a minority neighbourhood? Do staff have to travel through areas that could be flashpoints?

Tension that has been building for a long time can suddenly erupt into violence following a trigger event. Potential triggers can be identified, for example a decision by foreign powers to intervene militarily, a sudden economic crisis

---

Case example: WFP offices stormed

On 30 July 2006, an angry mob stormed WFP's building in Beirut, Lebanon. Demonstrations that morning against Israel and the United States had developed into protests targeting the UN. Feeling secure inside their office and perimeter gate, staff continued working, even as angry protesters began attempting to break into the building. Alarms sounded as the mob broke in, and security staff instructed workers to barricade themselves inside the WFP office. When the situation escalated further, security officers hurried staff down the back staircase to an underground parking garage, where they hid in locked vehicles. Eventually the situation was brought under control; although there were only a few minor injuries, two floors of offices were trashed. This incident shows how quickly a situation which might seem routine, in this case a street protest, can turn very threatening.

---

brought on by international trade conditions or a government decision to cut subsidies on essentials such as food or fuel, or to close a refugee camp before people are willing to go home. Others cannot be predicted but can be recognised as likely triggers, for example the arrest or assassination of a prominent figure.

10.2 Preventive action

The more misinformation that is spread about the agency, the greater the risk that collective frustration and anger will be directed against it. Expectations should be managed proactively. For example, discuss with people what they can realistically expect, and inform them immediately if there is a delay or a change of plan. Sitting together to listen to criticism and search for alternatives can help to prevent frustration from turning into anger. Don't just talk with a few representatives: try and make the information publicly known through a wide range of stakeholders, including local media.

Never encourage a crowd to gather unless you can meet their expectations. Organise in advance events (meetings, distributions) where crowds will gather. Work out procedures with local representatives. Try to avoid or minimise uncontrolled crowd movements, long queues and waiting times: multiply distribution points, schedule distributions throughout the day for different sections of the population, create waiting areas with shade and

---

Case example: a mob attack on aid agencies

In the latter half of 1995, an article appeared in the national press accusing the NGO Forum on Sri Lanka of supporting Tamil Tiger rebels in their war with the Sri Lankan government. The article appeared just days before the Forum's annual meeting, to be held in Sri Lanka, and alleged that the meeting was in fact a rally against the government and its war effort. The details of the meeting were broadcast by a local radio station. An angry mob of up to 3,000 people came to the venue and threatened the participants. The Forum moved to another venue, but again the details were broadcast over the local radio, and protesters once again disrupted the meeting. The hotel where some of the foreign participants were staying was also raided. The situation only eased after intervention by members of parliament and government ministers, and suspicion and hostility towards NGOs in Sri Lanka persisted for several weeks.

---

water and make those waiting sit down, provide precise information about the nature and quantity of hand-outs, designate crowd control staff who will turn back whoever does not belong there and further assist the crowd with information and movement procedures, physically channel people into a manageable queue or through small avenues and arrange for an exit route away from the entry points.

Pre-identification of beneficiaries is key to managing expectations. While many use lists, tension can rise when waiting in line if individuals are concerned about whether or not their name will be on the list. Coupons or tokens (with reasonable efforts to avoid fraudulent duplication) are a good way to reassure and calm those in line as they have a reasonable assurance that they will in fact receive their portion of whatever is being distributed. This worked well in the response to the earthquake in Haiti in 2010, for example.

10.3 Protection

Consider tactics such as cutting down on movements through risky areas, relocating sites away from risky areas, withdrawing staff considered to be at risk, limiting or reducing stocks in warehouses and temporarily moving valuables such as office equipment to the residences of local staff. Reduce visibility by removing agency logos and flags from buildings and cars, limiting the movements of international staff who stand out among local people and renting local cars or using taxis rather than conspicuous four-wheel-drive agency vehicles. Closely monitor any demonstrations.

The logistical movement of distribution items, especially food, needs to be carefully planned. Movements should be planned tactically to minimise visibility of cargo and timed to avoid passing through areas where beneficiaries in need may be tempted to loot (e.g. routes and time of day or night).

Inform the authorities of the situation, and consider asking for special protection. This can be a very effective strategy if the authorities are willing and able to control crowds. However, this may not always be the case: police from local stations may be part of the local community and unwilling to antagonise an angry local crowd. In addition, the government may be unwilling to intervene too quickly or too forcefully to control a crowd comprising possible supporters. On the other hand, the authorities may be willing to use excessive force to impose order, perhaps to the point of shooting into a crowd. When asking for armed protection from the authorities, make sure to discuss the rules of engagement, and indicate the agency's position with regard to the use of force.

10.3.1 Negotiating with crowds

It is very important to closely monitor crowd dynamics to identify indicators of problems well before they occur, for example in a distribution exercise. This may mean dedicating staff to this activity. Many unruly situations can start life as relatively small disturbances. Having agreed plans for stepping in early and purposefully to manage situations before they escalate is important.

When confronted with an angry crowd, try to defuse their anger. Key tactics include:

- Seek advice from local staff who can understand what is being shouted, and who may be able to identify who the demonstrators are and who appears to be controlling or driving them.
- Gain time: try to identify and negotiate with the group leader or spokesperson on the basis that talks should take place with a small number of their representatives. Have those representatives communicate the decision reached or information to share; people will be anxious and impatient to know the results if they know that a representative may be negotiating for them on their behalf; the message will also have more credibility. Consider that local programme staff may be perceived as biased if they have any ties to a particular element of the community.
- Hold these talks in the agency compound, but not in the heart of the

building. Consider the risk of going outside the compound to negotiate – be sure you won't be attacked.

- Listen attentively and respectfully; avoid making quick promises about the issue in contention. Signal that you are taking note of the grievances and are willing to pursue the discussion further, but not under threat or duress. In other words, try to negotiate an agreement for talks in a setting where the angry mob is not at the door.
- All employees should prepare for evacuation from the building. Consider whether to take essential items, such as laptops, satellite telephones, radio equipment and essential files. Lock the doors of all rooms that are vacated; exit the compound at a place where the crowd has not yet gathered and where staff are not visible to it. A well-chosen site should have a separate emergency exit which is not visible from the main entry and exit point. Staff should be familiar with alternative back routes in advance.
- If safe evacuation is not possible gather all staff in one place, where there is no easy access once all doors are locked.
- If local staffers believe that the crowds are being stirred up by trouble-makers who are not the normal community leaders, they may contact the latter and ask them to come to the scene of the confrontation to calm the crowd.
- Designate one person to contact other agencies that might be at similar risk.

Following an incident, make sure to:

- Maintain heightened security for some days until the situation has clearly calmed down and there is no perceived risk of individual retaliation.
- Consider the agency's public relations position and what messages, if any, the agency passes out.
- Keep your word: hold talks, even if police protection has now been increased. Communicate not just with the formal authorities but also with the wider environment of ordinary people; you will need to re-establish relationships and perhaps repair acceptance.

10.3.2 Surviving looting

Looting – of warehouses, convoys, offices and residences – is a frequent occurrence. As with surviving armed robbery, the key rule is don't resist, and try to prevent aggression against staff members by allowing the looters to take what they want. Don't show fear: signs of high vulnerability may give looters the confidence to turn on you (e.g. they may have only intended to take food but then decide to go for other assets). Remain calm, retain your dignity and try to defuse anger. In general, it is advisable to leave the place being looted in case the situation escalates. This may not always be possible, and it could be more dangerous outside. If this is the case, you will probably have to prepare for several hours, even days, of ongoing anarchy and widespread looting. Looters may come in waves, eventually stripping premises bare.

Anticipate that the risk may increase. Over time there will be fewer material possessions to satisfy looters. Try to keep a low profile and retain a means of communication. It may be possible to keep a hand-held radio, mobile phone or satellite phone, or negotiate for a telephone to be left (if the lines are not cut). Retain or re-establish contact with colleagues as soon as possible.

Chapter 11
Cash security

This chapter is only concerned with theft and armed robbery by persons external to the agency. Cash security is broader than this, however, and operational protocols should also include cash security in relation to events such as a fire or a natural disaster. Agencies should also be mindful of the need to protect staff from fraud and the temptation to misuse cash.

11.1 Reducing the use of cash

Of all forms of payment, cash is the most likely to be lost or stolen. Agencies can reduce their use of cash by using other formal financial mechanisms, such as payments by cheque or bank transfer, or via mobile phone banking, pre-paid cards, smart cards and credit cards. Where possible ask all staff to open a bank account, and consider meeting any costs involved. Bear in mind that company credit cards can be very vulnerable to fraud. Guidelines on using credit cards must be established, and credit card usage should be monitored regularly. Agencies with sizeable cashflows should inquire about taking out insurance specifically against loss or theft.

Informal credit and transaction mechanisms such as the *hawala* system offer another alternative to cash. Some of these networks only operate locally, while others have international connections. Local contacts should be able to advise. The *hawala* system has come under some pressure, especially post-9/11, regarding concerns that some transactions assist in the illegal transfer of funds to terrorist organisations, but it remains actively used in many developing countries.

11.2 Discretion

When dealing with cash, be discreet. The less people know, the less the risk. Communications over the telephone or radio should be in some form of code. If withdrawing money from a bank, arrange the transaction in advance and, again, be discreet. Paying suppliers is best done using one of the non-cash methods mentioned above, particularly for large sums. If staff regularly use the same hotel or supplier, consider setting up an account with them.

A common and sometimes unexpected problem is the actual bulk and volume of cash. In Somalia, for example, the monetisation of food aid in the early

1990s led to payments in Somali shillings that took up no less than 17 cubic metres of space. Even relatively modest amounts of international currency can translate into quite substantial bundles of local notes. Bear this in mind when withdrawing cash from a bank, and try to have money paid out in higher denomination notes.

11.3 Limiting exposure

There are several ways to reduce an organisation's exposure to loss or theft. Just-in-time payments to suppliers reduce the amount of time cash is held in the office. Another common practice is to set a ceiling on the amount of cash that can be withdrawn, transferred or kept in the agency safe, though bear in mind that reducing the size of individual transactions will probably increase the number of transactions that need to be made, raising transaction costs. If cash is at most risk when it is being physically moved, consider moving larger amounts less frequently, particularly if more secure ways of transporting cash are periodically available, such as helicopter flights or large convoys. Consider the various risks at different points in the transfer chain, from bank to agency safe to eventual recipient, and represent this chain in a flowchart. It may be possible to reduce the number of links in the chain, for instance by asking suppliers to come to the office to receive payment rather than taking cash out to them.

If burglary, hold-up and robbery are risk factors then it is advisable to spread the risk: do not keep all the money in one place, and have a certain amount to hand in an obvious place to mollify robbers and encourage them to leave you alone. Some money should be easily accessible on your person, in the car and at residences; the rest is better hidden. When travelling, secrete personal cash around your person, in a wallet, in a belt around your waist, in another pouch hanging around your neck, and perhaps in your shoes. If more than one person is travelling, spread the money between them. In periods of high tension, when withdrawal, relocation or evacuation might be necessary, distribute cash among departing staff, partly to spread the risk and partly to ensure that staff have some cash to hand in case they become separated. In countries where evacuation is a strong possibility, this should be prearranged and planned so that staff know what to expect. Check whether staff are prepared to carry large amounts of cash on them in situations of high tension.

11.3.1 Reducing predictability

Routine increases risk. Some of the more common predictable risk points include:

- The monthly payroll, for which cash is accumulated.
- Special payments to national staff just prior to evacuation.
- When international staff arrive at an airport and transfer to a hotel or the office in the city (professional robbers may monitor the arrival times of international flights, and may prey on vehicles on the main route into town).
- Trips by accountants or finance managers from the office to the bank and back, especially if they use the same route and travel at roughly the same time of day. Although the journey itself might not be problematic, being predictable with routes and times may increase the risk of robbery.
- Accountants or finance managers take another person with them to the bank, indicating that a larger than normal sum of money may be about to be withdrawn.

At times like these, take extra security precautions and try to reduce predictability. For instance:

- Use an unmarked rented or local staff vehicle or a back route to bring staff from the airport to the office or hotel.
- Change salary periods and payment times in order to reduce the predictability of the payroll, although this is unlikely to be popular with staff.
- Authorise additional staff members to go to the bank; change routes and travel times.

11.3.2 Reducing vulnerability

Ideally, anchor the safe to the floor so that it cannot be removed. Fit a lock that requires two keys to open, and give the keys to two separate people. Alternatively, use a key and combination lock. When thinking about safe security, consider whether armed robbers are likely to use violence against staff if the safe is not opened on demand. If one of the key-holders is about to go away or on leave, ensure that a proper cash count is done with the new key-holder, and signed off by both parties.

The most common method of transporting cash is by car. To reduce vulnerability at least two people, and preferably more than one car, should be involved, though again try to avoid predictability and consider varying the number of passengers and cars used. In extreme cases, an armed escort or an armoured vehicle might be used, though this is likely to attract unwanted attention. When withdrawing cash from an ATM, choose a machine in a busy street with a queue of others waiting to do the same, withdraw money during the day and ideally have a colleague with you to keep an eye on the surroundings.

11
Cash security

Remember that you can be observed taking out cash, and might be followed: don't enter quiet streets or more dubious areas after visiting an ATM.

11.4 Electronic money security

11.4.1 Online banking
Aid agencies increasingly use online banking for international money transfers, and in some countries this might also be a viable option for in-country financial operations. The normal rules of internet security apply (see Chapter 7): use an effective firewall and up-to-date security software, never download anything whose source you do not fully trust and delete temporary internet files. Never do online banking from a public computer, for instance in an internet café. Watch out for messages (known as 'phishing') that invite you to go to a website to check your account, or which ask you to confirm your password; such messages are designed to extract confidential information from you, and no bank would ever send them.

11.4.2 Identity theft
Identity theft and financial fraud, including credit card fraud, are large and growing industries. Some of the most common forms involve simple physical theft of cards; cheque fraud (printing fake cheques or stealing cheques); 'dumpster diving' (stealing financial documents from a trash can); account redirection (filling out a change-of-address form); and simply stealing a wallet or purse. In some cases, people have been detained, including in their homes,

---

Good practice in cash security

- Do everything possible to limit the use of cash.
- Do a risk assessment on the flow of cash around the organisation.
- At points of high risk, put in place actions and strategies to reduce that risk.
- Ensure reasonable credit limits and cash withdrawal limits.
- Check bank statements and investigate any unrecognised payments.
- Keep lists of phone numbers to call in case of loss or theft of credit cards.
- Keep PIN numbers safe (using a code in your address book is not safe).
- Block or cancel a credit card as soon as it is lost.
- When handing over a credit card to pay for a purchase, do not let it out of your sight.
- If you are forced by robbers to give up your PIN number for cash withdrawals, do so.

Mitigating the risks in cash programming

In Afghanistan and Somalia, agencies have successfully used local remittance companies to deliver money to people in remote and insecure areas. In Ethiopia, Save the Children takes out insurance coverage against the risk of loss in transporting cash to projects in areas where there are no banks. In Zambia, Oxfam sub-contracted delivery in remote rural areas to Standard Bank, which used security company vehicles to deliver the cash, accompanied by local policemen. Other security precautions include varying payment days and locations, minimising the number of people who know when cash is being withdrawn and transported and using different routes to reach distribution points.

while accomplices take their credit cards and PIN number to a nearby ATM. Where such a risk exists, agree a ceiling on cash withdrawals with your bank.

11.5 Cash programming

Cash programming is an option for agencies instead of providing in-kind assistance. Cash transfers are often seen as a more serious security risk than in-kind aid. Aid agencies implementing cash projects have developed a number of interesting and innovative ways to minimise potential security risks. Similar to internal organisational practices on the use of cash, the use of banks and other financial institutions potentially reduces the security risks associated with cash transfers to beneficiaries. That said, most cash projects in insecure environments have been relatively small-scale, and security risks may grow as programmes become larger.[1]

Cash
security

11

---

1 Paul Harvey, *Cash-based Responses in Emergencies*, HPG Report 24 (London: ODI, 2007).

Chapter 12
Sexual aggression

12.1 Definitions and scope

Rape and other forms of sexual assault and aggression must be addressed as a specific category of threat requiring distinct measures for prevention, mitigation, crisis management and after-care. Rape is understood here as sexual penetration (vaginal, anal or oral, with penis or object) without consent and against the will of the victim. Other types of sexual assault can include unwanted touching or forced removal of clothing. Rape and other sexual assault are usually carried out with the use or threat of violence.

Intimidation and sexual harassment have psychological effects that can turn into physical symptoms, sometimes long after the incident has occurred. The organisation should have a policy on sexual harassment, and should ensure that it is enforced among staff. This chapter, however, focuses specifically on direct assaults on the physical integrity of a person. While both males and females can be victims of sexual assault, it disproportionately affects women, so much of what follows is written from this perspective.

Sexual aggression is about power and humiliation, as well as sex. There are various motives for sexual aggression. Those common to the environments in which aid agencies often operate include:

- Certain categories of women (a particular ethnic group, a low caste or 'Western') are perceived as morally loose or not worthy of respect, and so can be sexually used.
- Rape and the domination of women enhance feelings of power in the rapist, which could extend to the social or ethnic group to which the rapist belongs.
- Gang rape may be used as a bonding ritual, to strengthen the cohesion and group identification of those participating in it.
- Rape may be a weapon of war, intended to destroy social bonds in the enemy society and weaken the resolve of men in the opposing group.
- Rape as a terror tactic can be politically motivated and designed to intimidate the agency or international interveners in general.

Hurting and demoralising the enemy by violating and degrading 'their' women is a common tactic of violence. Addressing rape may therefore become an

important part of civilian protection efforts. As noted in the Introduction, these protection challenges are outside the scope of this manual.

Sexual exploitation, such as the extortion of sexual favours for material and physical protection, often occurs when men control resources (e.g. food rations, access to a safe place or vital documents) or otherwise have power over women. Although there is no direct threat of violence, this remains a form of enforced consent. Women on the move – IDPs, returnees, those in refugee camps, economic migrants – may be particularly vulnerable, especially if their social or legal position is weak.

12.2 Risk reduction

12.2.1 Awareness and general risk appreciation

Risk reduction starts with the organisational and individual acknowledgement that sexual aggression constitutes a real threat. This is currently not the case: sexual assault and rape of aid workers are still highly sensitive subjects and often receive too little attention in security guidelines. Including clear guidelines on sexual aggression in the agency's security protocols can help to encourage increased attention, discussion and action on what is an uncomfortable subject for many staff members, including security coordinators.

It is important to recognise that males and females of all ages can be at risk. It is also important to recognise that working in violent environments can increase the risk of particularly traumatic forms of sexual assault and rape. During a period of captivity, for example, there may be a greater risk of gang rape or of repeated rape. Women – more often local women than foreigners – may be abducted and forced into sexual slavery or forced 'marriage' with a fighter.

12.2.2 Risk mapping and risk patterns

Acts of sexual aggression can occur in any society at any time. However, aid agencies should have a good idea of the countries where this form of violence constitutes a higher risk for aid workers than others: the DRC and Afghanistan as compared with Sri Lanka, for example. The lack of risk analysis and poor incident reporting mean that impressionistic assessments are often more common than informed ones. General contributing factors heighten risk, even without focused inquiry: the presence of many young men with access to arms; war or conflict in which rape has often been used as a weapon; areas in which a government has little or no control; a conservative society which restricts contact between unmarried men and women; or settings where it is common practice to extort sexual favours. It may be that there is systemic under-reporting of rape as part of this extortion.

Focused risk analysis will identify places, times, situations and categories of people at higher risk. Areas of higher risk may include districts in which militia operate; the area surrounding a refugee camp or the periphery of a camp; certain neighbourhoods in a town or city; prisons (men and women detained in police stations or in prison are often victims of rape); certain types of hotels; and border crossings and checkpoints. There may be certain times when risk is heightened: after dark; during festivals and celebrations; during aid distributions; when women go to collect water or firewood or go to the toilet; when armed groups are fleeing in defeat; or when troops enter a town they have just captured. Certain categories of people may be at higher risk: national staff of a particular ethnic group; local female (or young male) staff who have been relocated and are living in an environment where they have few or no social ties; Western women; widows or female heads of household; or teenage girls (because they are thought less likely to have HIV).

Certain groups or individuals may be more likely to commit sexual assault and rape than others, e.g. paramilitaries or police reputed to breach international standards of law; undisciplined government soldiers; rebel groups and violent youth movements; demobilised and unemployed soldiers; and armed robbers whose primary intent is to steal but who will often rape if they find a woman in the residence.

12.2.3 Sources of information

Owing to the sensitive nature of the subject, it is not always easy to obtain reliable information or accurate statistics on incidents of sexual aggression. Possible sources include local female staff, local women's groups, human rights organisations and human rights lawyers, women's groups in refugee camps, expatriates with good contacts in the community, such as religious workers or long-term aid workers, and security focal points at embassies. It may not always be advisable to ask straightforward questions; instead, approach the topic discreetly and be sensitive to cultural and social norms. One approach would be to ask local authorities and local health centres for statistics: their reactions might provide an indication of the sensitivity surrounding the subject. This could also lead to a discussion about legal requirements and local responses to sexual violence, and provide additional local legal and medical resources.

12.2.4 Reducing vulnerability

Individual measures

General recommendations about personal competence with regard to security (see Chapter 6 on 'People in security management') are also relevant here. Staff should dress and behave inconspicuously, and strive not to attract attention.

12 Sexual aggression

However, it is also important to display clear determination, familiarity with the environment and self-confidence. The aim is to give the impression to anyone watching that you cannot be easily surprised or overwhelmed.

Personal appearance is a sensitive issue as it is regarded as within the private realm. At the same time a woman's dress, hairstyle and behaviour can be misinterpreted by others as overtly sexual, or used as an excuse for aggression. This can happen in any society, though it may be especially common in communities opposed to Western-style dress, which can be seen as more casual. Both male and female staff members should adopt a culturally sensitive approach to their appearance, and err on the side of modesty. In many social and cultural contexts this will facilitate the social acceptability of male and female staff, which in general contributes to acceptance for their role and their work.

In social situations, the excessive consumption of alcohol renders those indulging in it particularly vulnerable to a range of threats, including sexual aggression. Sexual assaults have also been committed after drugging the victim's drink. Basic guidelines are: don't accept drinks from strangers (or even acquaintances that you do not yet fully trust), be acutely aware of your surroundings in drinking venues and never leave your drink unattended.

Organisational measures

Look carefully at hotels used by staff, and insist on a room that offers maximum protection from intruders. In some cases the risk assessment may indicate that female staff should be lodged with colleagues. Normal residence security and site selection guidelines should be observed (see Chapter 9 on 'Site security'). In particularly risky environments, female staff should be seen with male colleagues from the community or local partner agency staff often enough to provide the impression that they are not alone or isolated. Gender identifications (Miss, Mrs., Ms., or a recognisably female first name) should not be displayed outside the residence or listed in the telephone directory. Consider employing a male housekeeper to answer the door during the day. If using an answering machine, a male voice should record the outgoing message.

Possible incremental policy measures could include:

- Female staff considered at risk (international or national) should be accompanied from home to work in an agency vehicle. Where a female staff member lives alone or stays in a hotel, the driver should be instructed to take her to the door of the residence and even to check the house or flat to make sure that intruders are not waiting inside.

- In situations of high risk, female staff should travel either in groups or accompanied by a female or (if this is culturally acceptable) male staff member – during both work and off-hours. They should be briefed on appropriate security procedures and not pose a risk themselves to the persons they are accompanying.
- In a hostile environment, female staff members should not be left on their own in any way, even for short periods of time.

Differential security procedures

In certain circumstances security procedures may be different for men and women. For example, it could be a policy that no female staff should stay overnight in a project area even if male staff do. Such measures tend to be contested as discriminatory. Their intent, however, is to reduce an identified risk, not to discriminate. One perspective would hold that individuals, when fully informed of the risk, should be able to make their own decisions. The counter to that is that the repercussions of an incident go beyond the individual and would affect the operations of the agency as a whole, which justifies the agency taking the final decision. Examples of such decisions may include female staff being relocated away from high-risk neighbourhoods or camp areas, or the withdrawal or evacuation of female staff at times of higher risk. Such policies should be supported by an up-to-date risk assessment for the locality in question, and can be selectively applied depending on that assessment. For example, measures might be adopted for national female staff only, for younger women or for women of a particular ethnic group.

12.3 Surviving sexual assault

The available guidelines on surviving a sexual assault are primarily based on Western psychological models. These are centred on the individual and concentrate on talk therapy, whereby the survivor is helped to put the incident and their emotions and reactions into perspective. People with different cultural backgrounds may deal differently with the experience of sexual violence. For example, it may affect not only their psychological wellbeing but also their social future, including marriage. They may seek to forget or repress the experience as opposed to reframing it, or seek out traditional healing practices. In offering support, agencies need to be open and sensitive to other means of recovery.

12.3.1 Experiencing sexual assault

The key message to staff should be: protect and preserve your life. Beyond that, however, there is no general rule on how to behave when faced with the imminent threat of sexual assault and rape. The most common reactions are:

Sexual aggression

12

Active resistance
- screaming, blowing the car horn, shouting for help;
- running away; and
- fighting back.

Passive resistance
- talking to the assailant to try to make him change his mind (knowing a few sentences in the local language would help greatly in this regard).

What happens and what the staff member does will depend on the circumstances, e.g. if there is a gradual build-up of the threat; how many assailants there are; if they are armed; where the attack happens (a public or private area); how far away help is; and an individual's mental preparedness. (It is also important to remember that the assailant may be someone who is known to the victim.) Survival should be the priority, followed by minimising the physical and psychological harm done during the sexual assault or rape. This may mean submitting, and not resisting physically.

Possible psychological responses
As in other acute situations it is likely that psychological defence mechanisms will be active. These include:

- Dissociation: it is as if the victim is watching a film and experiences it as an observer.
- Denial: 'this is not happening to me'.
- Suppression: 'it will be over in a few minutes; this isn't the end of the world'.
- Rationalisation: 'what a cheap way of satisfying your need to feel power. You can't really hurt me'.

While these are healthy responses during an attack they should not mislead the victim into believing that she has not been deeply hurt.

Possible physical responses
There can also be physiological or psychosomatic responses during or immediately after a rape, such as vomiting, diarrhoea, hyperventilating, choking or having difficulty swallowing one's saliva, losing consciousness and disorientation. These are normal reactions to the psychological and physical experience of sexual assault. Physiological and psychosomatic responses will be affected by the scale of the attack, the location, the type of assailant and the length of the attack. In some cases victims may be overwhelmed to the point of psychological trauma. Staff members involved in providing immediate support should be aware of the possible implications.

Sexual assaults are commonly under-reported, due to feelings of shame and fear of the reactions of family, friends and colleagues. Other staff members may want to abet the silence out of sensitivity to the victim's feelings or their own discomfort with the subject. These are understandable reactions, but failure to report a sexual assault may deprive the survivor of the medical assistance and psychological support necessary for recovery. It will also deprive others of critical security information, and could result in further similar assaults.

12.3.2 Witnessing a sexual assault

Attention also needs to be paid to people – it is often men – who may be forced by the assailants to witness the rape taking place, or who might be prevented from stopping the rape of a co-worker, mother, wife or daughter in another room or in their vicinity. This risk is real, and awareness and preparedness are needed. Being unable to prevent a rape is in itself a deeply shocking experience. The witness will have to deal with his or her own emotions afterwards, and will require support.

As with victims, the key message to witnesses must be protect and preserve life. Staff should be advised:

- To make efforts not to be separated from the female staffer under threat of rape, to reason with assailants if something else can be offered to forestall the intended aggression, and to insist that they cannot leave the woman on her own.
- If resistance becomes life-threatening, desist. No one is helped if witnesses are badly injured or killed; if violence is used first against male colleagues or relatives there is a greater chance that it will subsequently be used against the woman, either during or after the rape. Colleagues in such situations should be advised to avoid provoking assailants into unnecessary violence, but rather focus on preparing themselves mentally to help and support the rape victim when the attack is over. Concentrating on how best to support the rape survivor immediately after the attack can be a strong coping mechanism during the ordeal.

12.4 Crisis management

From a management point of view sexual assault and rape should be treated as a medical emergency and as a serious security threat. There are four major areas that need careful management following sexual assault and rape: medical care, psychological support, legal action and confidentiality issues. All of these need to be initiated immediately and simultaneously; this is easier if a crisis management team is already in place prior to an incident.

Sexual aggression 12

12.4.1 Medical care

A victim may have suffered injury as a result of violence by the assailant, and is at further risk from involuntary pregnancy and infectious disease. Victims should be given immediate access to medical care to treat acute injuries. In addition, the following steps can be taken, with the agreement of the victim.

Post-coital contraception

Post-coital contraception (also known as emergency contraception or the morning-after pill) can be administered within 72 hours of intercourse. The decision to take it rests with the person concerned, but should not await the results of a pregnancy test, as tests are generally not reliable within this short timespan.

Prophylactic treatment of HIV and other sexually transmitted diseases

Medication can prevent chlamydia, gonorrhea and trichomonas. If it is not known whether the assailant is HIV-positive assume he was, and care needs to be taken during the medical treatment of the survivor. The risk of contracting HIV increases if penetration was violent and caused tissue damage. No preventive medication which is 100% effective exists. Some agencies offer medication that consists of a combination of AZT/3TC, to be started within 72 hours and continued for four weeks. The medication can cause side-effects such as stomach aches, nausea, headaches and liver inflammation, and must only be taken under medical supervision. Medical tests for sexually transmitted diseases and HIV have to be repeated intermittently for up to a year after the incident.

Post-exposure prophylaxis (PEP) is an emergency medical response that can be used to protect individuals exposed to HIV. PEP consists of medication, laboratory tests and counselling. Ideally PEP should be initiated within 2–24 hours (and no later than 48–72 hours) of possible exposure to HIV, and must continue for approximately four weeks. Although PEP has not been conclusively proven to prevent the transmission of HIV infection, research studies suggest that, if medication is initiated quickly after possible exposure, it may be beneficial. The efficacy of PEP is probably higher if treatment is started within the first few hours of exposure and is probably progressively reduced if started later. After 48–72 hours, the benefits are probably minimal or non-existent, and the risk of intolerance and side-effects associated with antiretroviral treatments will outweigh any potential preventive benefit.

Some UN agencies and NGOs keep PEP starter kits in offices for the benefit of staff and associated personnel. Each PEP kit contains the medication required for the first five days of PEP, a pregnancy test kit and emergency oral contraception, guidelines for the attending physician and the patient and a consent form.

Hepatitis B infection

If the rape victim is not immune due to prior Hepatitis B infection, and has not received a complete Hepatitis B vaccine series, then vaccination should be offered. This is effective when started within 14 days of exposure. Additional protection can be gained from Hepatitis B immunoglobuline.

12.4.2 Psychological support

The key objectives for those providing immediate help are to create a sense of safety, empathy and positive support. It will also be important to provide support to the rest of the team. The principal person providing the support should be someone with maturity and sensitivity, whom the victim trusts. This is not necessarily their manager.

Restoring a sense of safety

It will be important to find a place where the victim can rest and recover with a sense of total safety and security. This will be influenced by physical location, which must feel secure, and by those surrounding the victim. An expatriate can be relocated in-country or to a neighbouring country. The person affected is best placed to indicate where she feels safest and most secure, so should be consulted and encouraged to be part of the decision-making process. Ask her whom she feels most comfortable with and trusts. This person should be in the vicinity and should maintain close contact.

Positive support

Immediate emotional responses following rape can vary: one survivor may cry copiously and suffer from feelings of acute anxiety; another might be very calm and apparently composed, and keen to carry on as normal as if nothing had happened. Whatever the reaction:

- Empathise with the survivor and help her to identify and recognise her own emotions. Don't impose on her.
- Avoid saying or doing anything that could imply blame or criticism of the victim. There is no question about who is to blame: the rapist. While the survivor may have made herself more vulnerable by her actions, she did not ask to be attacked and did not consent to what happened.
- Allow the survivor to be in control as much as possible. Experiencing sexual assault and rape is disempowering, both in a physical and a psychological sense. Always ask, consult and seek consent, rather than making decisions on the victim's behalf.

Key messages for the survivors of sexual aggression:

- The attack was not about sex but about power.
- You are not to blame, the assailant is to blame.
- You are not alone. There are people who support and care for you.
- You can survive this and recover from it. It will take time and needs attention, but this is not the end of your life or happiness.
- Others who have gone through the same experience will work with you through this when you are ready to speak with them.

Support for the rest of the team

Those who were present and unable to prevent the aggression will also need support. If what has happened is known to a larger segment of the team the agency will have to attend to the sense of shock, disorientation, depression, anger and confusion that this may cause in the wider group. Other members of the team may have been victims of rape in the past. Depending on their own healing process they may or may not be well placed to provide support for the new survivor. If the incident reawakens their own trauma they will then require support themselves.

Helping the helpers

Supporting rape victims is stressful and demanding. Those doing so should also monitor their own emotions, which may become turbulent. They should find someone they can share their feelings with confidentially, and who has the maturity to talk the helper through a constructive evaluation of their emotions.

Dealing with the family

The responsibility for dealing with the victim's family will lie with headquarters unless the victim's partner and possibly her children are also in the country of operations, as would certainly be the case for national staff. Seek the advice and consent of the victim about this. She must be allowed to decide who should know what when. In the case of a repatriation, however, a reason will have to be given to the family, and close consultation with the victim is required for this. If the press takes up the incident a more proactive approach towards the family will be required, with the organisation probably designating a contact person to liaise regularly and closely with the family, as in the case of a kidnapping (see Chapter 14).

12.4.3 Legal pursuit and confidentiality issues

Reporting the incident to the police

The question of whether or not to inform the police is also sensitive. Ask the agency's legal adviser in advance what the procedures and time limits are with regard to making a declaration to the police. Obtaining official documentation might seem bureaucratic, insensitive and less of a priority, yet it may turn out to be important at a later stage, for example if the victim decides to press charges and initiate prosecution, to access legal abortion services or to obtain HIV treatment at an affordable price.

Forensic evidence admissible in court

If legal proceedings are desired, prosecution would be in the country where the assault occurred. Prosecution in court requires medical evidence; to be acceptable, such evidence needs to be collected and handled under certain prescribed conditions. Seek out a reliable and experienced lawyer in advance (the embassy may help find one). Find out from the lawyer:

- who has the legal authority to collect forensic evidence in the case of rape;
- what forensic evidence is admissible in the prosecution of a rape; and
- what procedures of collection, examination and storage must be followed to ensure that the evidence will be admissible.

If a recognised medical professional is required consider identifying one (preferably a woman) before any incident occurs.

This whole process is a delicate matter and requires sensitive handling. Two key principles are:

- Forensic evidence should not be collected without first informing the victim fully of why this is being done and what, in practice, it consists of. It should only be done with the victim's written consent.
- Collecting evidence does not commit the victim to future legal action, but preserves the possibility of such action should she wish to pursue it at a later date.

Typical items of evidence include the victim's clothes (unlaundered), pubic hair, evidence of genital or other injury and semen. Three common problems in collecting this evidence are:

- The victim wants to wash and change her clothes as soon as possible, and she may want to dispose of everything that reminds her of her ordeal. This does not destroy all evidence, but it will make it more difficult to collect.
- Collecting certain physical evidence will require a medically trained person and appropriate equipment.
- The evidence has to be sealed, handled and stored in a correct and appropriate manner, for example in paper not plastic bags, sealed and

Sexual aggression

12

Case example: a second traumatic experience

It is not uncommon for the victim to suffer a second trauma as a result of insensitive treatment by the police. In one case a female expatriate aid worker was sexually assaulted during aid work overseas. No one in the (well-established) organisation knew what to do immediately after the incident – not her female field manager or the human resource team at headquarters. The next day she was sent, alone, to her embassy to report the incident. The embassy sent her to the local police accompanied by the embassy security officer, a national. Once at the police station, four armed policemen interrogated her, asking detailed questions about the incident. When she hesitated in her answers, they accused her of lying. During the interrogation other policemen kept coming in for a look, as they were curious. The police undertaking the interrogation insisted that she show them her injuries before she was allowed to leave the station. They then insisted on her taking them to the place where the incident took place, for a re-enactment which they claimed was essential to the investigation. No real investigation ever took place. The assailant was never caught and the survivor learned later that it is very rare for anyone in that country to be tried or convicted of sexual assault. Her experience at the police station was effectively a second assault and resulted in a second trauma.

A well-informed and trusted individual should always accompany the victim to the police station, to ensure that the survivor is not intimidated or further victimised at any stage, that interviews are conducted in a language that the victim understands, and that the appropriate documentation and assistance are provided. The protector should be prepared to intervene when the victim's rights and dignity are not respected. It is important that the protector takes on the role as an organisational representative, and is not perceived as acting in their individual capacity.

marked; some needs to be refrigerated. There should be a minimum of transfers and as few people as possible should handle the evidence, and a log should be kept of who handled it and when (the chain of custody of specimens must be preserved). Time limits on collection may be imposed, after which evidence is inadmissible in court.

Prosecution

The decision to prosecute should be made by the victim, and the victim should be in a position to make an informed choice. To assist in this decision the manager has to inquire about the practical details of an arrest and court proceedings. Will the victim have to identify a suspect before he can be charged? How does this happen in practice? Can a suspect be released on bail? Does the victim have to testify in court, possibly in front of the assailant? Can the prosecution proceed if the victim does not reside permanently in the country, or will it involve her having to return several times? What are the penalties if the assailant is convicted? Given the facts of the case, what are the chances of conviction? What is the country's record with regard to international human rights standards and prosecution of sexual assault? Are the courts predisposed to dismiss sexual assault or rape cases? A sexual assault survivor should have the help of someone competent and objective enough to review all of this information and sort through it with her.

Managers also need to consider the possible security implications for the survivor and for other staff members if a prosecution takes place – and if it does not take place. Bringing and pressing charges may expose the survivor, her relatives and those supporting and accompanying her to further threats and aggression.

Medical confidentiality

To the extent that rape constitutes a medical emergency, the survivor must enjoy medical confidentiality. This is often guaranteed by law (e.g. by the Privacy Act in the US). The purpose of confidentiality is to make it possible for the person seeking medical help to discuss their medical and psychological concerns and problems openly and fully. Feelings of shame, guilt and humiliation, and the fear of being judged by others, will all dictate that the survivor will want to keep her experience as private as possible. This is a legitimate concern.

Even if it is known that someone in the agency has been sexually assaulted, the survivor will not want the details to be widely broadcast and discussed. It is the responsibility of the whole team, the manager and the organisation to protect the individual identity of the victim and the confidentiality of the details of the ordeal. The manager must take immediate action:

- Ensure that other staff members do not mention the incident. It is advisable to give them a standard response if questions are asked (e.g. 'I cannot answer this question, please contact the resident representative').
- Establish a direct line of communication with a designated focal point at headquarters. Communications between the field and headquarters should be managed and controlled and should not involve a series of intermediaries or a large number of alternates. The situation should not be discussed where such discussion can be overheard.

- Take proactive action towards the press if it looks like the incident will get press coverage, impressing on editors and journalists to use at most only the initials of the victim, and not her full name.

It is advisable to agree upon a code name, a code word or a case number to refer to the victim, in place of their name.

Alerting others

As with any security incident, it is important that rape and other sexual assaults, including attempted assaults and threats or intimidation, are reported not only within the organisation but to other relevant field organisations (withholding the name of the victim for purposes of confidentiality). This will enable other organisations to assess the risk and adjust their security plans accordingly.

While confidentiality can be protected in various ways, it is extremely important that the incident is reported and shared with other organisations operating in the area. It must be understood and explained to the rape victim that failing to make any mention of the incident could prevent others from taking precautions, and thus could be a contributory factor in other rapes in the future. The strategy therefore should be one in which the confidentiality of the victim is protected, while the alert is sounded to prevent others from suffering the same ordeal.

Case example: the obligation to sound the alert

A number of organisations have field offices in a city which, while outside the war zone, is subject to tensions between the local population and the authorities, who are seen as an occupying force. After nearly 20 years of war, many male civilians have been brutalised and are armed. One night, three armed robbers break into an agency residence. While there they rape an expatriate woman while her colleague is held at gunpoint. The woman is repatriated, but in order to protect her privacy the agency decides not to mention the incident. Three weeks later armed robbers break into another residence. This agency subsequently reports that an expatriate woman was threatened with rape, but that one of the robbers had stopped his fellow assailants from going through with the attack. The staff are shaken and the agency decides to withdraw them from the city. Only now does the earlier rape become more widely known among agencies operating in the city, and steps are taken to reduce the vulnerability of staff.

It will also be important to write a full report which can be handed over to an incoming manager. The new manager may have to follow up any legal proceedings, and will have to deal with any longer-term emotional effects on remaining staff. It may also be advisable to inform the embassy, even if embassy assistance is not being sought (in which case it will not be necessary to disclose the identity of the victim).

12.5 Preparation and training

12.5.1 At organisational level
- An aid organisation that deploys staff in an environment where rape is a known risk must be able to mobilise expert and effective support to field managers dealing with rape victims. If this expertise cannot be developed or retained in-house, it must be readily accessible from external sources.
- As a matter of policy, all expatriate staff members (not just women) should be informed about the risk of rape, as well as other assessed risks, prior to signing the contract, rather than merely prior to deployment.
- Good organisational practice should include clear policy statements about what support a rape victim can expect from the organisation, and how the organisation intends to reconcile the need for confidentiality with the need to alert others to the threat.
- There should be detailed guidelines for field managers and, whether male or female, they should be prepared to deal with a rape situation through training and simulation.
- There should be clear guidelines on how the organisation will protect and support national staff in the specific context.
- Managers should consider possible differences in leave entitlements or rest and recuperation breaks for women operating in areas at high risk of sexual aggression.

12.5.2 At field level
- Guidelines for responding to rape and sexual assault must be clear, documented and readily available to all staff members. Guidelines could include policy or practice on repatriation, relocation (temporary or permanent), available HQ and local legal support and compassionate leave.
- Managers are advised to discuss with staff the threat of rape, and the basic guidelines for proper conduct as suggested in this chapter. At field level, if rape is no longer ignored or discussion of it is no longer seen as taboo, and if staff are sensitised to the risk and the requirements for proper support, it will become much easier to employ measures to handle a situation should it arise. There should be active sensitisation of male staff members, including those responsible for security, to the risks and

stress experienced by female staff members operating in high-risk areas.

- It will be important to discuss with staff from other cultural backgrounds what protocols and support they find most appropriate. Local female staff may be less able to control outcomes and therefore more reticent about reporting sexual violence within the agency, and may be very concerned about confidentiality.
- The senior management team should discuss who should handle the various aspects of immediate crisis management.
- In a high-risk area couples should be advised to discuss between themselves their understanding of sexual aggression and their mutual expectations in case of an incident.
- As a rule, detailed knowledge should be sought about local legal requirements and police and judicial practices and specialist medical support. This knowledge will then be available if an incident occurs.
- If post-coital contraception and other specialised medication are not readily available from medical institutions in the operational area, ensure that these are at hand in the office and can be dispensed under medical supervision, or that the victim can be transported immediately to somewhere where they are available.

12.5.3 At individual level

Individual aid workers, but especially women, need to examine their own preparedness. Women usually have a heightened awareness of the risk of sexual aggression wherever they are, but it is important to note that, in conflict-ridden environments, there may be a higher risk of gang rape, aggravated assault (i.e. being threatened by weapons) and HIV infection as a result of rape.

- It is important to recognise your own emotional strengths and limitations. Can you cope with the risk? Would you be able to survive emotionally and recover from the experience?
- Decide whether you are genuinely prepared to accept a posting that may present a heightened risk of sexual assault.
- Will you be prepared to observe security measures intended to control the risk, even if they feel like an infringement of your personal liberty or of equal rights?
- Consider how you would deal with your partner, your family and your children if you are raped. Could you discuss the risk and the potential aftermath of an incident with your partner, and find clarity about what you can expect from each other, so that this does not become an additional worry and anxiety?
- Knowing some sentences in the local language may be critical in changing the intent of a potential assailant. Get some language training and discuss with colleagues what you should say or do if threatened.

Chapter 13
Detention, arrest and abduction

This and the following chapter address detention, arrest and abduction and kidnapping and hostage situations. These terms are often used in different ways. All have in common the characteristic that people are deprived of their freedom of movement and could experience anything from polite pressure to a life threat, but the nature and motivation of the captors will differ in each type of scenario. As such, crisis management response strategies will not necessarily be the same.

The effective management of all these incidents demands an advanced state of readiness and a high degree of expertise and experience, either in-house or on call. This includes appropriate training as a prerequisite for all staff engaging in operations in kidnapping- or abduction-prone locations. An organisation should also have a fully elaborated incident management plan (see Chapter 5 on 'Incident reporting and critical incident management'), which establishes the roles and responsibilities of the organisation (HQ and in the field) and staff in such circumstances. In all of these scenarios organisations could also consider seeking assistance from third parties, for example the UN, international governments and the Red Cross.

13.1 Terminology

In legal terms, 'detention' has a specific meaning, but here we simply refer to staff members being kept under the control of an individual or a group and prevented from leaving. While there is no serious or immediate threat to life, there is also no clear precondition for release. Being detained can be a common part of aid work. Agency staff can be detained by a group of villagers, a local authority or a group of soldiers or militia. Triggers for detention may include local discontent with the project or programme of the agency or another agency (people often do not differentiate between agencies), resentment that others are receiving project aid or frustration that the authorities are not engaging with the particular group, or are not doing so in a satisfactory manner.

'Arrest' is used to describe detention by government authorities (normally the police, but also the army) or the presumptive authorities. What distinguishes it from the more general type of detention mentioned above is the involvement of official authorities. This means that, in principle, the law can be invoked. The

situation can be more difficult and dangerous when the government authorities arrest someone extra-legally (i.e. without a proper arrest warrant), or where the arrested person 'disappears'. The authorities may then deny that the arrest took place, and may refuse to reveal the whereabouts of the arrestee.

'Abduction' refers to the forcible capture and removal of a person in an illegal way, but which does not lead to any ransom demand. There can be various motives for abduction: for forced labour, conscription, sex, or political reasons.

13.2 Risk reduction

Be aware of which areas and groups benefit from aid and which do not, and therefore might feel discriminated against, and make sure that as many people as possible in the area of operations understand the agency and the role it is playing. The way in which programmes are executed and the interactional skills of programme staff are important here, as is awareness of local laws and regulations. Transparency, good communications, integrity, even-handedness and respectful attitudes help as well.

Preventing an arrest that follows legal procedure is obviously not normally possible. An arrest that does not follow proper legal procedure can be challenged, but may not be preventable. Where there is concern about possible 'disappearance' after arrest, the agency should immediately mobilise for a very active engagement that signals that the situation is being closely monitored.

National staff may be detained, arrested or abducted for political reasons extraneous to the work of the aid agency, and aid agencies may be wary of being seen to meddle in local politics. This should not, however, be an excuse for failing to assume full responsibility for any staff member in this situation, and making every effort to ensure their safe return.

13.3 Incident response and crisis management

When staff members go missing, the first challenge for a field manager is to find out the exact nature of the situation. This might take hours to become clear, or it may take several weeks. Basic information needs to be established and communicated in an incident report. Key elements include:

- A statement of the problem (someone is missing, arrested or detained).
- The victim (name, nationality, age, gender, position in the office, affiliation, known condition (medical, etc.), family, clan, tribe).
- What happened (what is known, what is speculation, what is not known).

- Where it occurred, as precisely as possible.
- When it occurred, as precisely as possible.
- Who did it (known, suspected, speculation, unknown).
- Why it occurred (motive stated, speculation).
- Whether witnesses have been identified.
- Whether anyone else was involved or injured in the incident.
- Who has been notified/who knows outside the organisation/who you propose to notify outside the organisation, including whether the police, security forces or authorities are aware or have or will be informed; whether the press or any third parties are aware of the incident; what the rest of the team know; whether next of kin have been notified.
- What actions are under way or proposed.
- Monitoring of the local and national press and media to gauge impact, if any.

13.3.1 Detention

In the case of detention the key issue for those detained should be to observe the guidelines for surviving as a hostage (see Chapter 14). As and when appropriate, the detainee might be able to seek unconditional release (see below). For the organisation, calling upon national authorities or adopting a heavy-handed approach can be counter-productive, and can increase rather than decrease antagonism towards the agency. Generally, the purpose of the detention is to force the agency or another entity to pay attention to and engage in serious conversation with those doing the detaining. Responding to this expectation and engaging in serious dialogue is usually enough to end the incident, though bear in mind that in some circumstances what begins as a detention can escalate into a much more serious and prolonged incident.

When negotiating their release, detainees should:

- Remember that the objective of the negotiation should be securing permission to return safely and quickly to base.
- Emphasise their humanitarian work and the neutral, impartial and independent nature of their organisation and its activities.
- Remain conciliatory; avoid becoming antagonistic.
- Listen to their captors and try to find out what is motivating them and what they want or hope for.
- Do not make promises in order to obtain a quick release, and always be clear that they are not in a position to make final decisions or firm commitments.
- Request permission to contact their agency or embassy.

13.3.2 Arrest

If a staff member is arrested and their whereabouts are unknown, the first priority is to establish where they are and under whose authority. Be assertive and visit all relevant local authorities, inform the embassy (in the case of an international staff member) and be very persistent and insistent in seeking information. Remember that a staff member may be arrested for legitimate reasons and may have to account for their actions. Either way, engage a good local lawyer, who knows the local languages and the local system, has experience with this type of situation and perhaps has useful connections.

When it is clear who has arrested the staff member and where they are, seek to ensure that their rights are protected. Insist on their right to be visited and to medical and legal assistance, and request improvements in the conditions in which they are being kept, if these are not acceptable. Protest if these requests are not met. People are often arrested without formal charges being brought, in which case insist that a charge is articulated within a specified period of time. The charge may relate to the individual (for example they are accused of being involved in a crime) or the organisation (for example an accusation of spying under cover of humanitarian work). In any scenario the main priority is to work towards the safe and speedy release of the staff member. In most circumstances, only once a staff member is freed from wrongful charges should efforts be made to clear the name of the individual or the organisation.

In the case of an arrest liaise with, and manage, the staff member's family (see Chapter 14). Tell them the steps being taken, maintain a direct regular line of communication, remain aware of what steps the family intends or has taken, and warn them if what they plan to do looks like it may be counter-productive.

13.3.3 Abduction

An abduction can be an extremely challenging situation. The whereabouts of the abductee may be unknown, and it may be impossible to contact their captors. The targeted agency may seek to generate high-level publicity about the incident, but as with any media engagement this may be counter-productive if it unnecessarily raises the profile of the abductee and heightens their value. Alternatively this may be a good approach if it signals to the authorities that there is widespread awareness of the fate of the person concerned and that their continued abduction would seriously damage the image of the authorities and their capacity to establish or maintain the rule of law. Human rights and other advocacy organisations are generally better at creating this type of publicity than humanitarian agencies, and it may be possible to cooperate with them. In other cases there may be little that can be done beyond circulating information and pictures of the abductee, and trying to find someone who can eventually provide a lead or a contact.

Chapter 14
Kidnapping and hostage situations

14.1 Definitions

Kidnapping refers to forced capture and detention with the explicit purpose of obtaining something in return for the captive's release. The objective and hence the motive for kidnapping vary: often it is money, though kidnappers may also demand political concessions. In other cases, what may ostensibly be a political cause may in fact be little more than an extortion racket.

The terms 'hostage-taking' and 'kidnapping' are sometimes used interchangeably, but here hostage-taking is used to describe a situation of siege. In essence, the perpetrators and their hostages have been located and surrounded by security forces and the captors threaten to kill hostages unless they are given a means of escape. A kidnapping can turn into a hostage or siege situation when the security forces trace the whereabouts of the kidnappers and surround their location.

Globally, kidnapping has become increasingly common in recent years, including in the aid world. High-risk countries include Yemen, Iraq, Somalia, Darfur (Sudan), Afghanistan and Pakistan. Kidnapping can be hard to prevent, at least against a well-organised and determined group of perpetrators, and can be a very effective way of raising funds or increasing political visibility. It is therefore a very serious threat.

14.2 Risk reduction

A number of measures can help reduce the risk, including programme risk assessment, specialised training and orientation for staff and well-designed standard operating procedures (SOPs). Agencies may also declare certain areas temporarily off-limits.

14.2.1 Preparation, coordination and cultural awareness
Preparation includes the establishment of an incident management plan (see Chapter 5) and related specialised training for field and headquarters staff. Constantly reinforce the importance of staff adhering to security procedures. Coordination includes establishing links locally and internationally to ensure expertise for effective incident management support as and when required. Cultural awareness is critical, as the behaviour of staff is never so closely scrutinised as when they are abducted, taken hostage or kidnapped. This

should apply equally to national and international staff, as national staff are often recruited elsewhere in the country and may be just as unfamiliar with the operational area as their international counterparts, and to staff visiting a country only for a limited period of time, as well as those living and working there on a more long-term basis. Cultural awareness includes all the aspects you may include in an acceptance strategy, such as understanding the kind of behaviour that is considered appropriate or inappropriate in a particular social or cultural environment, as well as gender dimensions and a respect for cultural and religious norms.

14.2.2 Reducing exposure
Avoid routines

Avoid predictability when moving between residences and offices, as well as in off-hours activities, such as taking children to school and going shopping. Vary travel times and take different routes. This is easier said than done – and very difficult to maintain over an extended period of time.

Reduce visibility

Expatriate aid workers have been kidnapped on their way to and from airports. Reducing visibility might mean staff travelling in a taxi rather than an easily identifiable agency vehicle (ensure it is a bone fide taxi). If there is a suspicion that radio communications may be overheard, expatriate staff should not identify themselves when travelling. For example, only local staff might be allowed to talk over the radio (in their own language), as they would when travelling without an expatriate colleague. Information about movement plans, routes and travel times should be encoded (see Chapter 8 on 'Travel and movement security').

In-country vetting of personnel

The easiest way for kidnappers to obtain information about a potential target is to place a contact within the agency. In-country vetting can help defend against this, but it is not easy and is often overlooked, and expediency may preclude it (for instance the agency's driver is sick, so he calls his brother to fill in for him).

Remove potential vulnerabilities

A more drastic measure is to withdraw those staff members considered at risk. As the kidnap risk in Chechnya grew from the late 1990s, agencies relocated first to Nazran in Ingushetia, and then to Vladikavkaz in North Ossetia. Following a spate of bomb attacks and kidnaps in Iraq in 2003 and 2004, most international staff relocated outside the country. The same has happened in the Somali regions. Note that national staff can be at similar or

greater risk than internationals; indeed, the long-term trend shows nationals at growing risk relative to internationals.[1]

Site protection

Site protection and strict rules governing the identification of strangers and limits on access (including access control measures and procedures – see Chapter 9 on 'Site security') complicate the situation for potential kidnappers. While kidnapping is still a risk in residences, hotels and guest houses, most incidents take place when the target is on the move, typically in a car.

Heightened awareness and counter-surveillance

In simple terms this means 'watch to see if someone is watching you'. A successful kidnapping normally needs planning, and the perpetrators will be watching the residence, office and movements of their identified target for some time before making their move. They may try to find out more about the residence by presenting themselves as servicemen, or checking the locks of doors and windows while staff are away. They may follow a target in a car to establish routines and identify the ideal point at which to strike. Be observant and watch for anything unusual. Doing this effectively requires constant attention and knowledge about the local environment, including who belongs in the locality and who does not. See Chapter 9 for further discussion on counter-surveillance methods.

Seek local support and protection

In environments where a host is responsible for the wellbeing of his guest and will mobilise his men to protect his guest as if they were one of his own, it might be a good idea to obtain local (traditional) protection. Likewise, asking respected elders to join a site visit may offer a form of protection. Some agencies have a policy that expatriate staff are always accompanied by a local person when they travel; consider too co-residing with local staff. However, in contexts where in the past this tactic has been successful, including Yemen, Somalia and Afghanistan, it no longer guarantees protection as the control of the traditional authorities and the social norms they uphold has eroded with the influx of criminal elements and foreign fighters. Only good knowledge of the context will determine whether this tactic will reduce the risk.

Armed protection

Another option is to have armed protection at the residence, in the office and on the move, including during leisure time (see Chapter 3 for detailed discussion on armed protection). This could mean armed guards around sites or close

1 A. Stoddard, A. Harmer and V. DiDomenico, *Providing Aid in Insecure Environments: 2009 Update*, HPG Policy Brief 34 (London: ODI, 2009).

protection (bodyguards). There are however examples of incidents in which a target was captured, even when under armed protection. Armed guards may be surprised, outnumbered and outgunned, and may surrender or be killed.

A public policy of 'no ransom' or other substantial concessions

In their policy documents and public communications, governments and aid agencies often state that under no circumstances will they pay ransoms or make substantial concessions to resolve a kidnap incident. Publicly, of course, it could not be otherwise: openly stating that ransoms will be paid would be tantamount to declaring open season on your agency and its staff. In reality, however, some money is in many cases paid, by families, private companies, governments and aid agencies. Do not overestimate the deterrent effect of a public policy of non-payment: mitigation measures, training and preparation are still required.

Kidnap and ransom (K&R) insurance has become more widespread in recent years. The costs range significantly and primarily depend on the size of the organisation, locations of field staff and whether the insurance covers national as well as international staff. Depending on the policy, some insurance plans allow for 10% of the annual premium to be deducted for preparation and training. They can also support evacuation costs, communication costs, medical costs, trauma counselling and other contingencies outside the scope of the agency, as well as access to a case manager to handle negotiations.

14.3 Surviving a kidnapping or hostage situation

In general terms there are four main phases to a kidnapping:

1. The moment of capture.
2. The period in which the kidnapped person is held and negotiations take place.
3. The release of the victim (or confirmation of their killing).
4. The aftermath.

Being kidnapped is a huge psychological and sometimes also physical ordeal. A kidnap may last anywhere from a day or two to as long as months and sometimes years. The most dangerous moments are the immediate period after the victim is taken, during a siege situation and during release. At these times kidnappers will feel threatened and tense, and will therefore be more prone to violence. Stay calm and avoid adding to the kidnappers' tension. Other extremely difficult moments include speaking to relatives or colleagues, perhaps to show that the victim is still alive, or being forced to

make a scripted statement on video, for release to the media. Learning that others taken at the same time have been either released or killed can also be extremely difficult. Victims may also be submitted to psychological torture, such as false promises of imminent release or fake executions.

Prepare yourself mentally as best you can. Remind yourself that the vast majority of kidnap victims are ultimately released, and that the human body and mind have considerable powers of adaptation and resilience, allowing victims even of long-term hostage situations to endure the ordeal physically and psychologically, and to recover from it once it is over.

14.3.1 The moment of kidnap

People may be shot and injured or killed during a kidnapping: a driver, household staff, a residential guard, a bodyguard. Expect to be threatened with weapons, possibly blindfolded and perhaps beaten, and in some circumstances even tortured or raped. This is to break down physical and mental resistance and signal the dire consequences of any attempt to escape or otherwise trick the captors. In addition victims may be drugged. These tactics are all designed to keep victims quiet. Do not resist; indeed, staying quiet will help you regain composure, pick up information about where you are and who your captors are, and adjust to the shocking change in your situation. In the initial hours and days, victims are likely to be moved several times as the kidnappers seek to cover their tracks. Be calm and cooperative, speak only when spoken to, listen carefully and attentively and avoid sudden moves. Do not behave aggressively or try to be a hero: accept the situation. Your actions can and will affect your safety and wellbeing.

14.3.2 While being held

Be prepared to be held for a long period of time, and possibly by more than one group. Victims may be sold on by their kidnappers, perhaps to another criminal gang or to a political group seeking to use the kidnapping to obtain political concessions. Where and in what conditions victims are held can vary widely. They may be kept in the same place or moved several times; they may be held alone or with other captives. In some situations captives have walked with their captors for weeks through the bush or mountains. Some are held in reasonable conditions, while others are kept chained to a bed or a radiator. If in a group, try not to be separated. Being confined with someone else, probably in difficult circumstances and perhaps for a prolonged period, creates its own pressures, but by and large the ability to share experiences with at least one other person will be a source of support. If you are kept together as a larger group, identify a spokesperson to liaise with the captors, selected on the basis of ability rather than formal rank.

Case example: surviving a kidnapping in Pakistan

In late 2008, a doctor working as a national staff member of an organisation with an operation in the North-West Frontier Province of Pakistan was kidnapped by a group of armed assailants in an unidentified white Toyota station wagon. He was moved to multiple locations over the course of the kidnapping. Throughout his ordeal he was polite and followed the instructions of his abductors. He asked them what day of the week it was and what time of day, and prayed when they did, helping to establish their trust and respect. He tried to maintain good spirits and a positive attitude. One day the doctor was informed that his family had been contacted and that agreement on his release had been reached. Although the kidnappers had demanded a substantial ransom the doctor's family refused. Instead, all the doctors in the area went on strike and declared that local hospitals and clinics would remain closed until such time as the victim was released.

Remind yourself that securing release is not your problem but your organisation's. Remain confident that your organisation (as well as your government and your host nation) is doing everything possible on your behalf, and providing support to your friends and relatives – even if you don't hear anything or your captors tell you otherwise. Anticipate periods of isolation and other methods of intimidation and prepare for a long wait. Do not believe everything you are told.

Try to build a relationship of respect whilst keeping your dignity: do not beg or plead, be cooperative and obey demands without being servile or aggressive; do not discuss politics or religion, keep to mutual subjects such as family and children and encourage your abductors to view you as a person. Avoid exchanging clothes with your abductors, as this may hinder your identification in a rescue attempt or clothes can be misused if they are branded. Be aware of body language and non-verbal communication styles; do not threaten to testify against abductors; if they are concealing their identity, do not indicate that you recognise them; eat and drink even if you have no appetite or it is unpalatable; maintain a routine of rest and activity; try to exercise every day and keep track of time; maintain personal hygiene and maintain your values, and ask for medication if needed. Keep a low profile and avoid appearing to study your abductors. Never get directly involved in the negotiations for your release. This will only complicate matters. If asked to speak on the radio, telephone or on video say only what you are asked or allowed to say and refuse to negotiate, even if pushed forward by your captors.

14.3.3 While being released

Victims may be driven (possibly blindfolded) to an unknown location and put out of the car, or they may be picked up by a third party charged with taking them to the authorities. It is less likely that there will be a form of direct exchange, as this is a high-risk situation for both sides. In a rescue operation, the location may be assaulted by the security forces, or it may be surrounded and a siege situation may ensue. These are very dangerous times:

- As noted, try to avoid changing clothes with your captors: rescuers may mistake you for them.
- In the event of a rescue attempt, drop to the ground, seek cover and cover your head with your hands.
- Be ready to shout out your name. You will not be immediately recognised by your rescuers, and you may be roughly handled until you are identified as the kidnap victim and not one of the perpetrators.

14.3.4 After being freed

Once released, your focus will probably be on your loved ones, and you will probably want quiet time to recover. In the immediate aftermath of an incident, however, there is likely to be a great deal of press attention, and the authorities will also want to speak to you to get information about the captors and the circumstances of the kidnapping. You will not immediately get all the quietness and privacy you may want. Being kidnapped is a huge psychological ordeal: expect to feel its impact for months and perhaps even years to come, but feel confident that, with the right help, you can recover and get on with your life.

14.4 Critical incident management

Generally speaking, kidnap situations cannot be dealt with only at field level, but must involve the agency's headquarters and regional offices. A kidnapping is a very complex and challenging situation, and inevitably requires the involvement of a wide range of people and organisations, including law enforcement, government agencies, the media and insurance companies. Critical incident management capabilities will be required, including training, planning, preparedness exercises and the proper allocation of resources.

14.4.1 The immediate response

The first thing to do is establish the facts and prepare a critical incident report. The basic elements are covered in Chapter 5. Next, secure the rest of the agency's staff, perhaps confining them to their residences or moving them to a different, more secure location. Consider whether the risk is such that programmes should be suspended. Alert other organisations that a kidnap has taken place, so that they can take precautionary measures to protect their own staff.

14.4.2 Critical incident management teams

The next step is to mobilise or constitute the critical incident management team (CIMT). Decide too how the agency will communicate with key stakeholders, including the victim's family, other agency staff, the host and home government and the media. A senior manager will also inform the organisation's Board, and where applicable contact the insurance company and donors.

Several incident management teams may be required, one at field level and one at headquarters, and perhaps a third at the country head office. Key team members should have been identified in advance, and resources allocated and procedures established. Team members should have received training, ideally including a simulation. The CIMT at headquarters normally has overriding authority – i.e. the field team does not take decisions without its approval.

The core of the headquarters team should remain small. The team needs to include one or more senior managers, one or two security staff with relevant experience (previous experience with kidnap and hostage situations, or sound knowledge of the environment where the incident occurred). Other candidates include legal advisors, human resources personnel and media managers. A specialist in kidnapping and hostage situations may join the team from outside the organisation, either from the host or home government or from the insurance company, or contracted from a private security company. The organisation's director may or may not be on the team, depending on the other demands on his or her time. Each critical incident management team should keep a detailed log in which all events are precisely documented and recorded: what happened and what was said, at what date and time, who was involved, what was discussed and what was decided on the basis of which arguments, and who was given responsibility for what. The confidentiality of this information must be respected.

Incident management of a kidnapping is initially at least a full-time job. Staff involved need to be released from their other duties and shielded from unnecessary intrusions so that they can concentrate on the task at hand. They will need their own working space and facilities, including a temporary crisis room, and should monitor the situation on a daily basis, and decide on and review policy towards captors, relatives, the authorities, the press and the other agencies involved. Team members will need regular rest and relaxation, and support during and after the crisis. If the crisis continues over an extended period, members of the CIMT may have to be replaced. At the outset

of the crisis prepare for a smooth changeover: make sure that a handover file is kept updated with reports and analysis, and plan the handover so that team members overlap.

Critical incident management becomes extremely challenging when people of different nationalities and from different agencies have been kidnapped together, or are being held by the same captors. Different home governments and families will be involved, and the agencies affected will need to adopt a collaborative approach. Individual agency approaches clearly risk undermining each other or giving captors room to play one agency off against the other. Ideally, the different stakeholders should constitute joint critical incident management teams at field and HQ level. While each relevant agency will want to be involved, team members must be chosen for their skill and competence in managing incidents, rather than as representatives of their respective agencies. Outside experts not affiliated with any agency could be brought in, to help the team maintain its objectivity and focus.

14.4.3 Managing relations with the victim's family

This section focuses on the families of international staff. It can also apply to national staff, though there is additional specific guidance on this at the end of the section.

Immediate contact

As with any other serious incident, the victim's family must be informed immediately. It is vital that they hear about the kidnapping from the organisation first, and not through the press or a third party. Every effort should be made to arrange a personal visit to close family members, though this may not always be possible. If the initial conversation has to be by phone, arrange a face-to-face encounter as quickly as possible thereafter, and consider inviting relatives to headquarters to see at first-hand how the incident is being handled.

In the first contacts with the family, try to find out about the kidnapped person, including their general personality, mental state prior to the kidnapping, physical condition and any special needs. Clarify the organisation's commitment to the victim, including continuing to pay their salary, and indicate what costs the organisation is prepared to bear on the family's behalf, such as periodic trips to headquarters or travel to the country where the incident took place. Inform them too about any psychological support the organisation is able to offer them and their loved one upon their release. Stress counselling may be required, and advance coordination with other organisations can bolster in-house resources in this regard.

Develop a clear approach towards the family

The family has a right to know what is happening. It will be vital to develop and maintain a relationship of trust. If the family has no trust in the organisation it may act on its own initiative. Even if the situation ends well, the family may still turn against the organisation with a public or legal complaint about alleged mismanagement. That said, try to avoid saying too much about the organisation's critical incident management and negotiation strategy lest a relative lets this slip and it reaches the captors or the media. Be aware that the home government and the media will also make contact with the family, or vice-versa. For the family's sake it would be ideal if there was a joint or at least a coherent approach between the agency and the home government.

Family liaison

A relatively senior agency staff member with good interpersonal skills should be designated as the focal point for the family. Some agencies have a family liaison post on staff expressly for circumstances such as these. One function of this post is to act as the designated contact person for the family. The same individual should play this role throughout the incident. This is a demanding responsibility, and will require support from the organisation.

It is important to schedule a time slot for briefing families, and as far as possible try to ensure that the agency calls them, rather than the other way around. In long-running cases, clearly explain to the family that daily calls in the first days of the incident will gradually become less frequent when there is nothing special to report. It is also useful to encourage the family to appoint a focal point themselves, who can act as a point of contact for the organisation and as a spokesperson for the family. As the incident develops, it is likely that the family's mood will fluctuate, and they may come to voice doubts about the agency, the authorities or the strategy being pursued. This is normal, but should nonetheless be monitored.

Expect initiatives from the family

Relatives and close friends of the victim may be tempted to take action themselves, particularly if the incident is dragging on: they may go to the press, visit the country where the kidnap took place or try to establish their own line of negotiation. The family will also be more prepared than the agency to pay any ransom, and may start selling assets to collect the money. Families have their own right of initiative, but advise them about the possible consequences of their actions and the risks to any negotiations by other parties.

The families of national staff

In the case of national staff, families may prefer to deal with the case themselves. Indeed, they may be better placed due to their knowledge of the local culture and society and their own networks of contacts, particularly if the kidnapping is motivated by social or political rivalries between local social groups or clans. In the case of a criminally or politically motivated kidnap, however, the family may be no better equipped than the agency.

When nationals are kidnapped for financial gain, their families will often pay a ransom, though they may ask the organisation for support such as compensation. In such circumstances it is important to advise families that payment does not guarantee release, and may encourage further demands. Remind the family too that the release of the victim is one of the most critical and risky stages of any kidnapping. Families should be aware of the position of the employing organisation, and the support it can provide. However, the final decision on whether to involve the organisation rests with the family. Coordination of activities with the family can be difficult, as abductors will often only want to deal with a family member. It will also inevitably be more stressful as the family members themselves can also feel under direct threat. Another factor to consider is that K&R insurance often does not cover national staff, or has limitations and restrictions in its coverage.

14.4.4 Critical incident management and the authorities

'Authorities' here refers to the host government and, in the case of an international staff member, the home government. In practice, a range of different government departments and institutions may become involved.

In situations of detention an agency may try to solve the situation by itself. When it comes to kidnapping, however, it is generally advisable to inform the authorities at once as they will, in all likelihood, get to know at some point and will be unhappy that they were not informed. Even if a kidnapping occurs in an area of the country not under the control of the government, it should still be informed. Provide the facts about the kidnapping as well as any details about the victim.

Headquarters and field staff will need to decide upon a policy towards the host and home governments. The national authorities will have access to information and intelligence, networks and services (e.g. phone-tapping and GSM networks) that are not available to foreigners or individual nationals, and therefore may be in the best position to secure a release. At the same time, their decisions may be guided by considerations other than simply the wellbeing of the victim. They may wish to be seen as assuming their responsibilities for law and order, or as tough on terrorism. They may be primarily concerned with deterring other would-be kidnappers, or using the incident to justify strong-arm tactics against known opponents. They may also be mistrustful of the capacity of an aid agency to handle the kidnapping properly, or may want to prevent it from entering into dialogue with kidnappers whom they may regard as terrorists or rebels (in some countries it is illegal to make contact with kidnappers). If the authorities are keen to bring the incident to a rapid conclusion they may be predisposed to use force instead of, or in conjunction with, any negotiations, presenting potential risks to the victim's safety.

Agree and confirm with the authorities:

- The overall strategy to be pursued.
- That the safety and wellbeing of the kidnap victim should be the primary concern.
- That the authorities will refrain from a rescue attempt by force without the consent of the family and the agency.
- Confidentiality vis-à-vis the media, unless a different strategy is agreed.
- Agency involvement in the incident management team set up by the authorities. If that is not acceptable, then try to ensure the involvement of an embassy official or at least an agreed framework of contact between the national authorities and the aid agency.
- A joint approach to the family.
- Agreement on the choice of an interlocutor (see below).

The same issues need to be discussed and ideally agreed with the home government. Obtain advice from the embassy and enlist embassy support in dealing with the national authorities. The primary concerns of the home government tend to be the safe return of the captive and bringing the captors to justice. Depending on the wider political context, however, and the relationship between the home and host government, other – not necessarily stated – considerations may also come into play. Collaboration will also be required between headquarters and the home government regarding the victim's family. In some contexts the home government may establish direct contact with the family, and may not involve the agency in this process.

It is possible that the national authorities or the home government simply tell the agency that they are taking the lead in managing the kidnap situation. Ideally, a member of the agency's staff will be accepted as part of the government's crisis management team. Failing that, seek as a minimum the guarantees outlined above, and try to ensure regular briefings and prior

consultation with the agency ahead of key decisions. Clarify for the family who has responsibility for managing the situation.

14.4.5 Outside experts

Experts in kidnap management may present themselves spontaneously, be proposed by the host or home government or sought out by the agency itself. They may also be available through the insurance provider. Such experts can play a useful role by offering an objective perspective based on wider experience, anticipating scenarios and ensuring greater preparedness, articulating options and their respective advantages and risks and by confirming that what has been done has been done well, and that ups and downs are normal. Expert support is useful if the expert acts as advisor and coach, including offering advice to the media team, legal and psychological support to the CIMT and regional or local expertise. The expert may however become a problem if they pursue someone else's agenda. A government-provided expert, especially a government official, will follow official government policy, which might not be entirely in line with the organisation's approach. No external adviser should enter into direct negotiations with the captors.

14.4.6 Managing the press

Designate a media liaison at headquarters and field level. If the kidnapping involves an international staff member, the international media and home country media are likely to pick it up. How long they will sustain the story will depend on what other newsworthy events take place, and the political importance of the incident. Since the story is going to come out anyway, be proactive and try to influence the message. All messages should be kept concise. A key message should be that the agency holds the kidnappers responsible for the safety and wellbeing of their captives. The national media (radio, TV, newspapers, the internet in local languages) may put a different slant on the story. Always consult the local media liaison on media statements.

One way of dealing with media inquiries and public interest is to post weekly updates on the organisation's website. This will help to reduce the number of phone calls, and to ensure that the messages coming out of the organisation are coherent. Always assume that the kidnappers monitor the news and may hear what you are reported to have said in the home country. It is not advisable to try to communicate, let alone negotiate, with the captors through the public media. Media messages get distorted and undermine 'genuine' messages as well as the negotiation process. Engage with editors and journalists so that they work with the organisation rather than against it. The family may insist on making a public appeal through the press: manage that request constructively.

Whether media publicity helps or hinders the management of a kidnap situation depends on the circumstances. Publicity may help if the kidnappers are concerned about their reputation. This is unlikely to be the case for criminal gangs, or for terrorist groups that use kidnapping precisely to generate publicity, in which case it is the captors who bring in the press. This is highly dangerous; it turns the situation into an international spectacle, with the killing of the captive as a possible 'dramatic climax'. Countering this entails persuading the press not to go along with it. As noted above, the family and friends of a captive may launch a publicity campaign to exert pressure on the home and host governments. The target audience here are not the kidnappers but the authorities that are formally responsible for security, and messages are designed to ensure that they continue their efforts to resolve the situation. There may be indications that captives are allowed to read newspapers, listen to the radio, watch television or browse the internet. If so consider using the press to send a supportive message. There is evidence that hearing themselves mentioned in the news can boost captives' morale.

14.4.7 Attending to other staff

Internal communication with other agency staff is important, and needs to be proactive and well-managed. Anticipate questions and maintain staff morale and confidence in the agency, while at the same time trying to keep non-core staff at arm's-length from the crisis management effort. Communication should involve:

- Weekly information sessions for all at HQ, given by the head of the crisis team.
- A weekly information sheet drafted by the head of internal communications, accessible to all at HQ and field level (i.e. in multiple languages if necessary), posted on the intranet or through another communications medium.
- Provide staff with opportunities to feel engaged and to show their support for the victim, for instance by signing messages of support. Former captives seem to be very appreciative of these efforts.

14.4.8 Informing other agencies

Kidnap situations are highly sensitive and need to be handled discreetly. As with sexual assault and rape, however, the need for discretion has to be balanced with the agency's responsibility for the security of all aid workers, including those of other agencies. This is not generally understood. Discussions may arise between different agencies about risk-control strategies and aspects of the management of the situation, especially the role of the authorities and the issue of a ransom. It is difficult to be prescriptive here, but guiding principles could include:

- What one agency does has implications for the security of others in the same area. There is therefore a collective responsibility for security.
- An agency whose staff member has been kidnapped is responsible for choosing the approach it wants to take. However, it may be sensible to listen to advice from others with experience in the area, especially with regard to the possible security implications of particular strategies.
- In principle no ransom should ever be paid, as this increases the general risk of repeated or copycat incidents targeting the same agency or others in the region. The reality is that in many cases some ransom is paid, though agencies deny this. While this reluctance is understandable, it is still the case that paying a ransom dramatically changes the overall situation, and it may be advisable to inform others in strictest confidence that a ransom is being paid. At the very least, if a staff member of another agency is subsequently kidnapped that agency should be informed if a ransom was paid to resolve an earlier incident.

14.5 Communicating and negotiating with the captors

14.5.1 Communicating with the captors

A critical element in the negotiations will be what the demands are – and who in practice can or must meet them. We have already indicated that kidnappers' objectives and demands can change, and a detention can turn into a kidnapping. There are also many examples where the original political demands in the end withered away, leaving only a demand for money. But the reverse can also be true: a criminal gang may 'sell on' a captive to a politically motivated group if no ransom is forthcoming. If the kidnappers ask for political concessions from the host or home government, this will be beyond the agency's control.

As soon as a kidnapping is suspected or reported, a logbook should be started at field level and at HQ to record the time and means of any communication with the kidnappers, the names of those involved and the contents of the communications. This is as a complement to the critical incident management logbook. The authorities may advise recording communications, as the choice of a particular word, the tone of voice used and any background noises may all provide useful clues to the identity and location of the kidnappers. This can be done on most telecommunications equipment, including mobile phones. In many instances all parties, including the captors, will expect conversations to be recorded.

14.5.2 Negotiating with the captors

The CIMT at headquarters should retain control over any negotiations, at least as regards the broader strategic and policy issues involved (whether direct contact is allowed, for instance, and standard procedures). This can also serve to create a time lag to allow for internal and external consultation and analysis before responding. Key principles for communicating with kidnappers include:

- Examine the motivations of the kidnappers, and consider whether they follow the same pattern over time. How do the captors appear – do they seem aggressive and threatening, rational and factual or highly emotional? What tone of voice and style of speech would be most effective in defusing the situation and establishing rapport?
- Examine the profile of the captors and how they have operated in the past.
- Ask for proof of identity and possession to be sure that the victim has not been killed or passed on to another set of captors. A tape or video recording is not absolute proof that the victim is still alive. From the family or a close friend obtain an intimate detail that the captors cannot possibly know (e.g. the name of a close friend at school or something that happened during a memorable family holiday). As the situation continues, check regularly to remain sure that the captive is still alive. The best proof is to directly hear the kidnapped person speak. If no proof of identity and life is provided do not pursue negotiations.
- Agree a code word with the captors that identifies them, to ensure that you are speaking with the genuine kidnappers and not impostors.
- Always refer to the captives by name. Encourage good treatment: indicate any special needs they may have, for example spectacles or special medical treatment. Signal their human concerns (for family or children), and whether a way can be found to arrange an exchange of messages.
- Emphasise that you have no decision-making authority and need to consult with others, whom you might not be able to reach immediately. This provides time to think and gives the agency some room for manoeuvre. Do not give any indication that a third party (the authorities or a security expert, for instance) is advising you. In some circumstances the kidnappers may demand to speak with the decision-maker rather than the messenger. Be prepared for this, and agree on an approach beforehand.
- Restate the no-ransom policy to show that the organisation remains consistent and that the passage of time is not weakening its resolve.
- Agree communications times. Try to get agreement about the next contact; ask how you can contact the captors, for example through a third party or a message in a specific newspaper. Prepare contingencies for communications problems, including loss of cell coverage or network disruption.
- Sustain the communication: do not on your own initiative break off contact unless you are certain that your interlocutor is not the real captor or that the captives are no longer alive. Make it clear to the captors that you want them to communicate with you.

- Do not agree to go to a specified place for an encounter. If there is very strong pressure to do so, insist on detailed guarantees for your own safety. You may be kidnapped as well.

14.5.3 Communicating with the victim

At some point the interlocutor may talk directly to the kidnapped staff member. Here it is very important to be clear on what kind of information and messages should be passed on. Do not provide the victim with any information that the kidnappers should not know, but reassure them that everything possible is being done to secure their release. One of the main concerns of kidnap victims is how their family is coping back home. Try to alleviate this fear as far as possible.

14.5.4 The interlocutor

Interlocutors act as a link between the decision-makers (the incident management group) and the captors; they are not decision-makers themselves. As kidnappings can last for a long time, more than one interlocutor may be required. The interlocutor's task is simply to convey messages. In order to fulfil this task, however, they will need to be well prepared through, for example, simulation exercises, as inevitably there will be unexpected demands and pressures from the captors.

The interlocutor should be a local from the country, who is fluent in the local language and understands the culture and the character of the people. He or she needs to be reliable, intelligent, balanced, even-tempered, able to work under extreme pressure, available 24 hours a day, seven days a week, and willing to act under instructions from the CIMT. Interlocutors are not privy to the discussions of the CIMT, which considers scenarios and hypotheses and formulates responses. If the captors insist on speaking to a particular individual who is not the designated interlocutor, ensure that the preferred interlocutor discreetly listens in to the conversation.

Using a local intermediary

An intermediary can also come forward from within the community, or one can be sought out by the agency, proposed or approached by the authorities or even put forward by the captors. It is not uncommon for locally respected and influential people to involve themselves in kidnap resolution. Elders have played an influential role in Somalia and Afghanistan, for example, as have local businessmen in the Caucasus.

In a situation of high acceptance, and where the community retains a measure of influence over the captors, a trustworthy local may be able to secure the release of the captives. It should be made clear, however, that they cannot make commitments on the agency's behalf without its prior consent. In the face of well-organised criminals who are more autonomous from the community, traditional leaders may be ineffective. The question of trust is crucial. On whose behalf is the intermediary acting? Are they on your side, or do they have connections with the captors? Who controls the negotiations? There will also be a question of payment. Consider reimbursing some operating expenses, in line with local rates. This may cover travel, accommodation and food and communications. Such payment may not be appropriate if the agency is dealing with a person who, in local terms, is known to be relatively wealthy already.

Official negotiators

The authorities may put forward an official negotiator. The negotiator's first step will probably be to establish a climate for dialogue. Initially, the focus will probably be on minor issues on which agreement can be reached. This will establish firm ground on which to base discussion of more difficult issues. If the negotiator is fielded by the authorities there is always a risk that other considerations will come into play other than a concern for the safety and release of the captives. Alternatively, a prestigious non-governmental entity may propose an envoy to try to mediate the release of the captives.

14.5.5 Obtaining release by force

It is not uncommon for the security forces to try to trace captives and attempt either to rescue them, or to create a siege situation and try to force the captors to surrender. This is a high-risk strategy as the captives may be killed by their captors when they find themselves trapped. Alternatively, one or more captives may be injured or killed in the confusion and crossfire that often accompany a forced release. Siege situations or attempts at forced liberation should not be attempted without the agreement of the family and of the agency. However, the approach should not be totally rejected: if the captors start maiming or killing captives to step up the pressure, or if there is a risk that the captives may die through weakness or exhaustion after a prolonged captivity, a rescue attempt by force may be the option of last resort.

There are a number of reasons why siege situations can go wrong. From the agency's point of view, two elements are particularly important:

- Do those carrying out the siege have a clear overall command? If they do not, uncoordinated actions could imperil the lives of the hostages.
- Do troops have a clear description of the hostages in order to be able to differentiate them from the captors, and have they been given clear

instructions only to fire on those firing at them? Remember, captives may be wearing the same kind of clothes as their captors.

14.6 Managing the aftermath of a kidnapping

14.6.1 Managing the return of a kidnap victim

The return of kidnapped staff also needs to be properly organised and managed. Several competing demands will have to be taken into account:

- The emotional needs of the captive, and their family and friends.
- Communications between the captive and their family and friends.
- The need for rest and a medical check-up, as well as possible medical care.
- The wish of the authorities (host and home governments) to debrief those released.
- The desire of the press to get hold of the story.
- Relocation of the victim out of the country, for extended rest and recuperation.
- The need to inform other agencies that the situation has been resolved.

Be aware that if multiple staff from differing agencies were involved in the kidnapping then the situation might not be resolved for all stakeholders. If this is the case extreme care needs to be taken with public statements until the crisis is resolved for all parties.

CIMTs, at both field and HQ level, therefore need to be prepared to:

- Attend to the needs of the victim, including making arrangements for them to speak to their loved ones and for their physical reunion.

Case example: controlling rumour

During the final phase of negotiations with the kidnappers of an aid worker in Somalia, controlling rumours became a real challenge. While the situation was still tense another aid agency unexpectedly announced that the captives had been released and had left on a plane the previous day. This rumour circulated immediately within the aid community and was taken up by the local press. It took the agency involved in the kidnapping two frantic hours to find out where the announcement had come from, and to issue a correction.

- Provide accurate information to other agencies; if deemed necessary, ask them to refrain from public comment, and indicate when further information will be provided.
- Manage the press; organise a press conference with the victim and/ or their family, and retain control over press contacts (e.g. how long interviews last, and how many questions will be allowed).
- Arrange for the authorities to meet and interview the victim.

Ideally, the kidnap victim will be received by someone they know, perhaps a close colleague. A female colleague would be best when the victim is also female. Allow victims to regain control of their situation as quickly as possible. Bring them into decision-making directly affecting them, but do so progressively and in accordance with medical advice. In addition, the organisation will need to arrange:

- A flight home 48–72 hours after release (assuming the kidnapped staff member was not a local). The staff member should be accompanied.
- A private welcome at the airport (in the VIP lounge), with no press.
- A debriefing at HQ.
- A press conference at HQ (one hour maximum).
- Time off, with full insurance coverage and no loss of income.

A kidnapping or hostage situation is a traumatic experience. Survivors will need long-term help and access to professional support; so may their loved ones, who have also lived through a very anxious experience. Choose professional counsellors with care: the wrong type of counselling can itself become a stressful and disorienting experience.

14.6.2 After-action reviews and accountability

Once a kidnap incident is resolved, the agency involved is likely to want to conduct an after-action review, to see what lessons can be learned. If things went badly – if the captive was injured or killed, for example – the victim's family may question how the agency handled the crisis, and may take legal action against it. In this case the records the agency kept as the incident unfolded will be an important source of evidence. If things go wrong in a kidnap incident managed by the authorities, the agency may insist upon an inquiry into how the operation was conducted and whether what went wrong could have been avoided. If hostages are killed, their families may also call for an inquiry.

Specific preparations need to be made in case of a negative outcome. Mortal remains must be dealt with, as well as an autopsy, conducted either in the country concerned or elsewhere, particularly for expatriate staff and if objectivity is a concern. It will be important for the organisation to know how the deceased died, and who killed them.

14.7 Preparation and training

14.7.1 At organisational level

- Identify the members of a CIMT and their alternates.
- Train them, including using simulations of kidnap scenarios, and involve operations, IT, personnel, finance, press and legal department staff as well as senior managers.
- Discuss with your government what help can be expected if a staff member is kidnapped.
- Identify qualified external experts for crisis management and post-crisis support to potential victims and their families.
- Keep a record of all international staff, the contact details of close relatives and any special medical conditions.
- Be clear who is responsible for what in case of an abduction, arrest or kidnapping under agreements with other agencies governing the secondment of staff.
- Spell out the responsibilities and obligations the agency assumes with regard to staff who have been abducted, kidnapped or arrested, and their relatives.
- Have a clear policy that staff should not be deployed in high-risk areas without being fully informed of the risk in advance, and without their explicit consent.
- Constantly monitor high-risk zones for possible kidnapping threats.

14.7.2 At field-office level

- Establish and maintain contact with the embassy and other diplomatic actors, such as the UN.
- In a high-risk environment, know who to contact in the host government in the event of a kidnapping.
- Find out the command structure of the national security forces in the agency's area of operation.
- Identify and get acquainted with a reliable and competent local criminal lawyer.
- Be clear about the legal procedures governing arrest in the country.
- Understand the government's policy on contacts with kidnappers, if it has one.
- Constitute a CIMT, prepare and regularly update the plan and provide specialist training.
- Keep a full record of staff details, including ID and family contact details and medical information.

14.7.3 At individual level

- Prior to deployment make sure your domestic affairs are in order. Ideally the following should be readily accessible: birth certificate; marriage/divorce certificate; insurance policies; medical and dental records; naturalisation papers; adoption/guardianship records; military record; power of attorney; key financial papers; and contact details of doctors, lawyers and other key professionals.
- Be aware of the risks and how to control them.
- Be alert, all the time.
- Familiarise yourself with the physical environment; carry a map if possible.
- Carry with you a list of key telephone numbers and radio frequencies; memorise the most important ones in case you lose the list.
- Carry family pictures, including children.
- If on medication, carry a small supply; carry a spare set of contact lenses or spectacles. Carry a note on any special medical requirements, in local languages as well.
- Wear good walking boots.
- Hide a small amount of money on your person.

Basic check list

These key points could be followed or adapted by field staff in the first few critical hours of an incident, when time is precious and everyone is under pressure.

The field CIMT's terms of reference are:

- Management of the crisis at the local level.
- Contacts with intermediaries.
- Contacts with the abductors.
- Liaison with the authorities, especially the police.
- Contacts with embassies.
- Provision of information to the UN and NGOs.
- Providing support for the family, if present, and moral and material support for the hostage, if possible.
- Contacts with the local media.
- Referring other contacts to the CIMT at headquarters.
- Information and assessment of risks for the CIMT at headquarters.

Basic check list (continued)

Immediate action following an abduction:

- Set up the CIMT.
- Confirm that the abduction has taken place.
- Inform headquarters.
- Inform family members present on the spot.
- Inform local staff.
- Inform/brief the authorities.
- Organise 24-hour telecom cover.
- Review security measures.
- Start logbook.
- If possible, fit a recorder to the telephone or radio.

Initial contact with the abductors

- Record the conversation.
- Adopt a cooperative attitude.
- Ask to speak to the abductees.
- Insist on proof that they are alive.
- Explain the limited responsibilities of the interlocutor.
- Set a deadline for a reply.
- Establish a procedure for return calls (telephone number, code word).

Initial contact with the local authorities

- Discuss with headquarters the line to be taken.
- Get in touch with a contact, who should already be known.
- Inform the authorities of the facts.
- Insist that the security of the hostages is the top priority.
- Obtain a guarantee of confidentiality, especially with regard to the media.
- Establish a contact procedure.

Proof that the victim is alive

The following may serve the purpose:

- A photograph of the victim holding a recent edition of a newspaper.
- A recorded or handwritten message.
- Correct answers to questions that only the abducted person could know.

Basic check list (continued)

Proof that victims are alive is important:

- To make sure that they have not been killed.
- To make sure that you are dealing with a genuine intermediary and not a hoaxer.
- To contribute to the hostage's wellbeing.
- To give the hostage moral support.
- To establish a link, however tenuous, with the hostage.

Chapter 15
Combat-related threats and remnants of war

This chapter considers combat-related threats, including bombing, missiles and shelling, crossfire and sniper fire, landmines, improvised explosive devices and unexploded ordnance (UXOs) and white phosphorus. It also includes an important discussion of the dangers of 'remnants of war'.[1]

15.1 Core questions

Key issues to consider in active combat areas include whether the agency should be there at all (the threshold of acceptable risk), and whether the benefits of staying (i.e. the programme impact) outweigh the risks. Is the risk of shelling and bombing, crossfire and sniper fire still within the agency's threshold of acceptable risk? Are there significant assistance and protection needs that warrant the agency's presence? Are the conditions such that you can still effectively programme, or are you staying out of solidarity alone? How many staff have to remain to fulfil this function? Medical personnel in particular tend to stay or even move in closer to help the casualties of conflict. Again, the same key questions should be considered.

Core advice for staff when coming under fire includes:

- Don't be macho or try to be a hero.
- Don't stand around trying to find out where the firing is coming from, who is firing or what sort of weapon is being fired.
- Your immediate survival decision is whether to stay or to leave, followed by the logical steps resulting from that decision.
- Use the best natural defences you have: your own fear and common sense.
- Seek cover, get out of sight, get out of the line of fire.

15.2 Shelling and bombing

15.2.1 Types and tactics
Shelling and rockets may come from howitzers and heavy artillery, from tanks and rocket launchers, or from smaller portable mortars. The most common

---

1 A particularly useful publication dealing with these and related issues is *Landmine and Explosive Remnants of War Safety Handbook* (2005), published by the UN Mine Action Service and CARE, and available in English and French. In addition to the Handbook there is a training module and powerpoint suite, a training video and a CD-ROM in various languages. See also ICRC's *Staying Alive: Safety and Security Guidelines for Humanitarian Volunteers in Conflict Areas* (2006).

mortars have a range of about 6km, whereas other types of artillery can have a range of up to 50km. Being behind a hill is no protection as shells can be lobbed over the top. Missiles can cover much greater distances than artillery. Home-made rockets and some military-issue weapons, for instance the *Scud* missile, are very inaccurate. Others are satellite- or laser-guided, and are in principle at least reasonably precise. Fighter planes can drop bombs, shoot rockets or pepper the ground with machinegun fire. Helicopters can fire rockets or use machine guns. Drones or unmanned and remote-controlled aerial vehicles are often used for reconnaissance, but can also launch missiles. They have been used in Iraq, Afghanistan, Pakistan and Somalia, as well as in the Israeli–Palestinian conflict. Since planes and drones can launch their weapons from a distance they may be out of earshot; the explosion may well be the first you know of a missile attack.

In terms of tactics, basic distinctions can be made between random or saturation fire, predicted fire and observed fire. Technological developments are increasing the ability to carry out precision strikes. Random or saturation fire is highly inaccurate. It can be a result of the type of weapon used, such as multiple rocket launchers which saturate an area with shells (used by the Russians against the Chechen capital Grozny), or cluster bombs which scatter hundreds of smaller bomblets (used by NATO over Kosovo and by Israel at the end of its 2006 war with Hezbollah in Lebanon). It can also be a deliberate tactic, such as an artillery barrage or so-called carpet-bombing.

Predicted fire means that the artillery crew is aiming on the basis of calculations from a map, with no capacity to adjust to a specific target, or that pilots are shooting rockets or dropping bombs at a target in a single overflight. The behaviour of pilots and therefore the accuracy of fire from a plane or helicopter depend very much on whether the enemy can detect them early by radar, and whether they expect to be attacked by anti-aircraft fire or by enemy fighter planes. Radar installations, enemy airfields and anti-aircraft installations are primary targets. While the enemy may not have the technical means just described, it may still dispose of shoulder-fired surface-to-air missiles. Planes and helicopter gunships then tend to reduce their vulnerability by dropping bombs from high altitude, standing off the target or coming in low in an attempt to surprise. This does not help the accuracy of fire.

Observed artillery fire or air attack means that there are one or more observers who watch where shells, rockets or bombs are landing, and relay directions for more accurate targeting to the firing crew. There are two commonly used techniques to adjust artillery fire on to the target: 'walking' towards it, and 'bracketing'. In both cases the observer first directs the artillery crew to a firing line – an imaginary line between the observer and the target – and then closes in on the target. Walking towards the target means that the shells get successively closer. In bracketing, the shells are fired alternately before and beyond the target, with the 'bracket' getting smaller and smaller.

Laser and satellite technology have enabled wholly new types of bombs and missiles that in principle can strike a designated target with great precision, even in built-up areas.

15.2.2 Risk reduction
The first step is to think carefully about your location:

- Do not locate offices and warehouses close to obvious or likely military targets, such as airfields, barracks, fuel depots, official buildings or strategic points such as crossroads, railheads, power stations and radio and TV buildings. Avoid hotels near potential targets.
- If the agency is working in a town of strategic military value that is likely to come under fire, move as far to the outskirts as operational requirements permit, or to nearby countryside.
- In hilly or mountainous areas avoid stopping on high ground where you will be very exposed. Find relative safety from shelling and bombing at the foot of a steep hill or mountain.
- Identify the agency: paint the logo in bright colours on roofs and on the walls of the agency compound. Remember that the agency flag will not be visible from a distance or on a windless day. Long-distance artillery fire and missiles or laser-guided bombs do not rely on visual identification but on pre-programmed coordinates of the target. If you are in contact with the combatants, consider providing them with the GPS coordinates of your premises, and advance information about the routes and timings of vehicle movements.

Bear in mind that, if the area comes under fire, civilians are likely to seek shelter in the agency compound, in the belief that it is better protected and may not be targeted. Consider whether the compound has the capacity to accommodate large numbers of extra people. Will access be denied, and who is responsible for enforcing that decision? If access is granted, should people be allowed into the more protected spaces, or should they be left out in the compound?

Physical protection
Physical steps to reduce the potential impact of a strike may not help much against a direct hit, but they can reduce the damage from near-misses and the effects of blast and shrapnel. For shelters and bunkers, the best place

is underground, often a cellar. Second best is a reinforced room on the ground floor. Concrete and steel beams provide the most solid structure, but the ceiling can also be reinforced with logs or tree trunks. The larger the shelter, the weaker the construction is likely to be. It would be better to have two smaller shelters, though obviously they need to be large enough to accommodate everyone on the staff, along with vital equipment, a toilet and possibly food and water. Ideally they should have two exits, in case one is blocked by rubble. Shovels and pick-axes may be needed if the occupants have to dig themselves out. No shelter, not even a concrete bunker, will protect against very heavy bombs.

A shelter will not be very helpful if staff have to run 800 metres to get to it. Set a time-limit for reaching the bunker, say one or two minutes. Staff who cannot reach a bunker in that time from their usual place of work need their own shelter nearer at hand. If the authorities have identified or constructed public shelters, make sure that staff know where they are.

Refuge trenches and foxholes can provide cover against mortar shells and strafing by low-flying planes or helicopters. Make them deep (2 metres), narrow and large enough for up to four people. A good construction is an L-shaped small trench, with two entry and exit points. The top can be protected with logs and two layers of sandbags. Remember that these too need maintenance: rain can cause the entrances to crumble and flood the trench. Watch out for snakes, which may make nests in trenches or foxholes.

Despite their name, blast walls are designed to stop shrapnel and bullets, not necessarily the blast wave of a bomb. Use sandbags (alternate between 'stretchers' and 'headers' and build solid corners to strengthen the construction), oil drums or boxes filled with earth or rubble or strips of grass pods reinforced by vertical timber stakes. Build blast walls higher than a standing person, except perhaps for the wall protecting the route to the shelter, behind which people can run crouching. Blast walls should not block passages, in particular passages to the shelter. Areas to protect with blast walls include the guardhouse, a building's doors and windows, the radio room and fuel depot and the entrance route to a shelter. You may also want to create a blast wall 'bay' in the house, ideally on the ground floor and in an inner room, i.e. with at least two walls between the shell and you. Building a good blast wall requires some expertise. Poorly built walls can collapse, and therefore can themselves become a danger.

The primary threat in the explosion of large Improvised Explosive Devices (IEDs – as opposed to exploding mortar or artillery shells) is the blast wave itself, not fragmentation and shrapnel. Unlike shrapnel, a blast wave will roll over and around obstacles largely unhindered. To mitigate the effects the blast wall will have to be at least twice as high and wide as the structure that it is intended to protect, and would need to be placed right next to it, or right next to the explosion itself.

The vast majority of injuries in a blast event are caused by fragments of window glass, which are propelled into occupied areas by the force of the explosion. This can be mitigated by the application of Fragmentation Retention Film (FRF), also known as Shatter Resistant Film (SRF), to the inside of the windowpane. Note that FRF applied to a window with double glazing is largely ineffective, as is FRF applied to the outside of a window. FRF will also not stop shrapnel or bullets. If FRF is not available, or is too expensive, several layers of regular adhesive film (or the film used to cover books), applied in a criss-cross fashion on both sides of the window, can be used. While FRF is designed to keep the glass together, it is not meant to keep it in its frame. In a large explosion the entire window pane will be propelled into the room, and could cause serious injury or even kill someone. Short of having no windows at all the simplest way to mitigate this risk is to arrange desks such that nobody is sitting in the direct path of a window should one be blown into the room. Alternatively, consider installing blast curtains or catcher cables or bars. Windows can also be kept open. Consider leaving outside or exposed rooms unoccupied, i.e. by using them as storage areas instead of office space. In areas with a high risk of indirect fire, the top floor of a building may also be used in a similar way.

Finally, ensure that the physical environments of offices and compounds do not provide sources of secondary fragmentation, such as gravel.

What to do under fire (shelling, missiles and bombing)

What you do when under fire will depend partly on where you are when the shelling or bombing starts, where the missiles land, where fire is directed (if at all), and where the nearest effective cover is. In general:

- Seek immediate cover in the nearest shelter or emergency trench.
- If you cannot reach a bomb shelter seek other, solid cover. A tree, a wooden fence or a car won't do. Something much more solid is needed, for example walls, concrete, rock or a deep hole, such as a ditch on the side of the road. If you are exposed, lie down flat. Exposure to blast can damage eardrums: remember to cover your ears with your hands and keep your mouth slightly open.
- If driving, decide whether to accelerate out of the firing zone, or abandon the vehicle and seek cover. If the shelling is close by or you are stuck in a convoy

you should get out and seek cover away from the vehicle. (Inside the vehicle you are at risk of flying glass, shrapnel piercing the car or the fuel tank exploding if the car is hit by a shell.) If the artillery fire is not too close and you can drive away, try to reach a safer location that offers proper cover.
- Under air attack always assume that your vehicle will be targeted. Get out and seek cover.
- If you have to drive around in a danger zone keep the radio volume low and the window slightly open, and stay alert.

15.3 Crossfire and sniper fire

Crossfire refers to any small-arms fire, either exchanged between combatants or used indiscriminately. This includes machine guns, grenades and rocket-propelled grenades (RPGs). Sniper fire is targeted. Snipers are very good shots, and can pick out an individual target from long range. They may be active while no general combat is ongoing, and may use special rifles with telescopic and night sights. Snipers are deployed to harass the enemy force and disrupt its movement, or to terrorise a larger enemy population. They do this by taking up advanced positions or by infiltrating enemy territory, for example to target officers or delay a convoy by killing the driver of the lead truck, or simply to cause terror by suddenly and unexpectedly killing a civilian. They operate by stealth and surprise. If their position is distant and not threatened they may maintain it for a long period. In other circumstances, they may fire and then shift position to strike from somewhere else.

15.3.1 Risk reduction
The best defence against crossfire and snipers is to stay away from areas where small-arms fire is being exchanged or where snipers are operating. In contemporary warfare, however, this may not be easy: you may get caught in sudden crossfire, and it is only possible to avoid snipers if they are static or are only covering an identified area, and if you know where they are and how far their rifles can reach. Although small-arms fire is usually effective only up to 100m, rifle bullets may travel more than 3km and heavy machine gun bullets over 6km.

Physical protection
Remember that protective gear is not a solution in itself. Overall security planning should never be marginalised by the provision of protective equipment.

When well-made and sufficiently thick, blast walls offer protection from small-arms fire (though not from a direct hit by an RPG, and possibly not from sustained heavy machine gun fire). Snipers can use armour-piercing bullets which pierce normal blast walls. The best option in these circumstances is to keep out of sight: stay away from windows and doorways, and try to get at least two walls between you and the bullets. This will also increase protection from ricocheting bullets.

Flakjackets are designed to protect parts of the body from blast, flying glass and shrapnel. They will not stop a bullet. Ballistic or bullet-proof jackets give more protection. Basic jackets should be worn with ballistic plates and a helmet. They are heavy (up to 12kg) and expensive.

Armoured vehicles can offer some protection from rifle fire and from the blast effects of shells and smaller mines. They will not provide adequate protection from a direct hit by artillery, a bomb or an RPG, or from specialist sniper fire, which may use armour-piercing bullets. Unless specifically designed as a mine-proof vehicle (with a V-shaped under-body), they will also not provide adequate protection from the blast and shrapnel of an anti-tank mine or a well-made roadside bomb. Armoured vehicles are significantly heavier than normal vehicles and very expensive. Generally, the heavier the vehicle the more protection it offers. Given the additional weight and the resulting longer braking distance, special driver training is recommended. When travelling in an armoured vehicle a helmet and flakjacket or ballistic jacket should be worn. Like other vehicles, armoured vehicles should move around in pairs.

Evasive action: reducing exposure

If you or your staff come under sudden close fire, how you respond will depend on where you are, how far it is to cover, how close the firing is and whether you are being targeted.

If under close frontal fire while driving, you will probably need to stop the vehicle, jump out and seek cover; stopping and reversing or turning and exposing the flank of the vehicle will take too long and will present an easy target. When taking evasive action from small-arms fire, go for speed. Avoid swerving or zigzagging; it does not make you harder to hit.

When seeking cover remember that solid cover is what is needed. Crouching behind an ordinary car may keep you out of sight but will not protect you from bullets. As with rockets and bombs, solid cover means rocks, holes, a crest of soil, concrete or several layers of bricks. Bushes, trees, wooden fences and ordinary cars are not solid cover. If you have reasonable cover, take time to consider your position and options. Is it general small-arms fire? Where is it coming from, and is it targeted at you? If it is aimed at you, is it meant as a warning shot to make you retreat, or is it intended to hit you? Is it general small-arms fire, or precise sniper fire? Soldiers say that if you don't know whether or not you are being targeted, then you're not. In other words, you will know when you are. Experience will teach you the different sounds made by a very close bullet and bullets some distance away (the former makes a whiplike cracking sound, the latter a hissing or whining sound). Remember, a firefight is in many ways like a boxing match, with frequent lulls while the parties reposition themselves or gauge the other side's response. Stay under cover until you are certain that it is safe to emerge.

15.4 Mines, booby traps and unexploded ordnance

15.4.1 Mines

Mines generally come in two categories: anti-tank mines and anti-personnel mines. Anti-tank mines are larger and have greater explosive power. They typically require a heavier weight or movement to activate, but this may not be the case if they are old and unstable. They will break a tank track and damage part of its suspension, but will cause almost total destruction to a non-armoured vehicle. Anti-personnel mines are smaller. Some are designed to cause injury by blowing off a hand or foot. Others can do much more serious, even lethal, damage.

Anti-personnel mines injure or kill through blast or fragmentation. Fragmentation mines are mines whose casing breaks into small fragments or which contain fragments that are dispersed upon explosion. Most anti-personnel mines are buried in the ground. Some have a first explosive charge underneath which, when activated, makes the mine jump about a metre above the ground, where it then explodes. Some mines are detonated by trip wires, which are generally hard to see and are very dangerous. Others have fusing systems that are pull-activated, detonating when pressure is put on the trip wire, or are triggered by pressure release, and detonate when the trip wire is cut. If you come across a trip wire, never try to cut it, do not approach it and do not touch it. Leave the area in the direction you came from, checking systematically for trip wires along your extraction route. Note that trip wires are not put only at ankle height, but can be higher, for example at chest level. Some anti-personnel mine systems are interconnected and have sensors. If someone approaches one mine will explode. The others will explode when a second person approaches – for example, a rescue team – to help the victim of the first mine.

Directional mines are positioned above ground and attached to trees or fixed objects. They are normally remote-activated but can also be linked to trip wires or booby traps. Some anti-personnel mines can kill up to a range of

35–50 metres, and cause severe injury up to 100 metres. If you find yourself in a minefield or think that you might be in one, careful extraction is the only option (see below, Section 15.4.3). Simply walking in single file does not significantly reduce the risk.

Anti-tank mines do not normally explode when a person walks on them as they need heavier pressure to activate. Sometimes an anti-personnel mine is put on top of an anti-tank mine, the smaller explosion causing the detonation of the larger mine. Some anti-personnel and anti-tank mines have protective mechanisms to prevent them from being recovered or disarmed (they explode if tampered with).

Many mines have a metallic content, which is why metal detectors are used. In some situations, notably with some mine types that have no or minimal metal content or in metal-saturated ground, metal detectors will be of limited use. Some mines have a magnetic-influenced, anti-handling device – i.e. the magnetic field of the metal detector will trigger detonation. Fortunately these are rare.

Where mines might be
Mines are generally laid for three purposes:

- As part of a battle strategy. Armed groups lay mines to defend their military positions, to disrupt enemy movements, to deny the enemy access to a certain route or to channel the enemy onto a certain route. Minefields can therefore be expected around bunkers and trenches, static tank positions and on or alongside bridges and roads. Where towns and cities are besieged both sides may be laying mines: the defenders to disrupt an attack, the attackers to prevent the defenders from getting supplies and from breaking out. Mines are often laid in non-systematic ways: they can be scattered into enemy territory from planes and helicopters, or delivered by artillery. In guerrilla or insurgency warfare, many groups plant mines indiscriminately without ever keeping or passing on records. It is not surprising therefore that forces of the same group wander into minefields laid by their colleagues. Knowledge of where major sieges and battles have taken place and where major defensive positions were, as well as day-to-day terrain awareness, will make you more alert to obvious risk areas.
- Around socioeconomic targets. Targets such as power pylons, water and electricity plants and railroad junctions can also be surrounded by mines to protect them from sabotage and attack.
- To cause general terror and dislocation. Mines are also used in more generalised warfare to target civilians and their assets: grazing and agricultural land, irrigation canals, wells, forest areas where firewood is

Case study: 'anticipatory' mining

In 1995 an NGO vehicle hit an anti-tank mine on a road in Central Africa. The force of the explosion hurled the vehicle 12 metres and turned it round completely. Two passengers were killed and three injured. During the night anti-personnel mines were planted around the wreckage. The next day a local woman who had come to look stepped on one and lost her leg.

collected, temples and even village paths can all be mined. The purpose is to dislocate a local population which may be providing support to the enemy, and to create discontent.

People planting mines will anticipate the reactions of an enemy force, or of civilians. Hence a bridge over a shallow river may be mined, but so too will the slopes next to it, to target people who avoid the bridge and cross through the water instead. A major access road may be mined – with alternative access roads possibly mined as well. In an ongoing conflict, even a low-intensity one, cleared areas may be re-mined. Mines also 'migrate', moved by rain, flooding, mudslides or tidal action on a beach. Eight years after the war in Mozambique, heavy flooding in early 2000 swept mines potentially anywhere and destroyed the existing markings of identified mined areas. Finally, local people may also plant or replant mines to protect their assets. Ask about this, and only move around with local people on their own terrain.

Finding and sharing information

However attentive, you cannot know about every mined area unless someone knowledgeable tells you where they are. People are unlikely to come to you and volunteer information or ask what your movement plans are in order to give you warning. You must inquire yourself, collate information from various sources, and hand this on to new staff with similar responsibilities. Prior to departure, obtain general information about the mines in a country, for example from the annual reports published by the International Campaign to Ban Landmines. Specialist humanitarian de-mining agencies, such as the HALO Trust, the Mines Advisory Group, Handicap International and Norwegian People's Aid, may be able to provide useful information.

In the country itself, the main sources of general and locality-specific information will be:

- The national mine action agency or the local authorities and security forces.
- De-mining organisations, and a central UN mine action centre, if there is one.
- UN military observers or peacekeepers.
- Hospitals and health posts where mine casualties may be seen.
- The agency's own staff.
- Local people.

Local knowledge is especially important: when venturing into a new area where there is active fighting or there has been in the past, stop regularly and ask local people about mines in the vicinity. While this takes time, it may save lives. Build this extra time into the journey plan. The more precise the questions, the more precise the answers are likely to be. Inquire about:

- How long the respondent has been in the area.
- The local history of fighting.
- The local history of accidents: have vehicles, people or animals been hit by mines, and if so when and where?
- Where do local people go, and what areas do they avoid?
- Has the respondent used the road, and if so when and how far along it have they gone?
- How do people use the road? If they only walk or use bicycles, anti-tank mines may not have been detonated and will remain a danger. Be careful about definitions: in Mozambique, for example, people classify a bicycle as a vehicle.

Important though it is, do not overestimate the reliability of local knowledge. For example, if people were refugees and have only recently returned they will not know where mined areas are. Even if they have been in the area for a long time they may not know every location.

Marked minefields

Those laying mines are obviously not going to mark them. Local people often create their own warning signs, but these are hard for outsiders to identify and can be ambiguous or unclear. Signs may be nothing more than a small heap of pebbles or two crossed branches lying at the start of a path. Ask local people what signs they use, and whether they have a common system (if everybody does it their own way, there is no common signal). De-mining operations mark identified fields in different ways in different countries, but usually the signs are clear enough. The colour red is normally used in markings. Note, however, that signs could have fallen down or become less visible, or may be obscured.

15.4.2 Booby traps and unexploded ordnance

The purpose of booby traps can be to prevent the removal of other explosives. More commonly they are planted by a retreating force to complicate reoccupation of an area – usually a built-up area – and render it more costly. Many booby traps are improvised, but are planted and disguised with great – and cruel – creativity: a door or window of a house can be booby trapped, as can a well, an abandoned rifle or a dead body. A booby trap can be attached to an innocent-looking household item, even a toy. The guidance is straightforward: don't go wandering about in abandoned areas, and don't pick anything up. If involved in the removal of dead bodies, check them carefully before moving them.

Unexploded ordnance (UXO) refers to material that was intended to explode on impact but failed to do so. This includes bullets, rockets, missiles, bombs, grenades, cluster munitions and shells. UXO may pose a much greater threat than landmines, because the dispersion may be more random and unpredictable, and because the munitions themselves are likely to be unstable. A particular risk are cluster munitions delivered by artillery shells or from a plane. In mid-air the containers break up and then distribute a multitude of bomblets that can saturate a whole area. Cluster munitions were used by the Soviets in Afghanistan, by NATO in Kosovo and by the Israeli air force over southern Lebanon.

15.4.3 Risk reduction

When driving, try to use tarmac roads only, and avoid driving into potholes as these may be mined. If the tarmac suddenly ends and becomes a dirt track, it may be wiser to turn back if you don't know what lies ahead. Watch for obvious signs of mines: a crater from an explosion, a torn shoe, the carcass of an animal, a wrecked vehicle, a road that appears not to be used, a field that is overgrown and not cultivated in an otherwise populated area or a building with the roof, shutters and doors intact while other buildings have had these looted or removed. Stay on the beaten track. Never walk off a road or path and look out for marked areas. If being driven, instruct the driver to:

- Keep to well-travelled routes and not to go cross-country.
- Drive in existing tracks and not drive over obstacles on the road (a big branch or some debris that may conceal a mine) or drive around them without first checking whether the road surface has been disturbed.

- Not to drive on to the sides of the road to avoid an obstacle, to turn round, to overtake another vehicle or to give way to an oncoming vehicle: the sides of the road may be mined.

Above all: if in doubt, turn back.

A non-armoured vehicle cannot be protected from an anti-tank mine. However, the risk of serious injury may be reduced by putting sandbags about 10cm thick on the cabin floor under each passenger, as well as a layer or two of sandbags in the back of a truck. Unfortunately this will also increase the weight of the vehicle, and may be enough to make an anti-tank mine explode. You also risk being blinded by sandblast if you run over a mine. A marginally better trick might be to fill the wheels with water, although this works best with larger truck wheels because of the volume needed to make a difference.

Mines are seldom planted alone. The basic assumption must be: where there is one mine, there are more. If a mine explodes or you suspect that you are in a mined area, never act impulsively:

- Do not jump out of your vehicle if it has detonated a smaller mine but is not on fire.
- Do not drive impulsively up to another vehicle that has hit a mine.
- Control yourself and your colleagues and act carefully and cautiously to avoid more casualties.

Evacuating a vehicle

If your vehicle hits a mine but is not on fire or at risk of further explosion, leave it in a controlled manner. Do not step on the ground around it except in the tracks where you have driven, behind the vehicle. Climb out through the rear door, or from the back by first getting on the roof, and step in your own tracks. When you are on solid tarmac or the vehicle tracks are sufficiently visible, you can walk back – in single file and spaced out – to the last known safe point, or to a point where you think there is no more risk of mines. When the tracks are not clearly visible you must prepare yourselves for an extraction process with prodding that will probably take several hours. If night falls you must prepare for a probably uncomfortable night until dawn allows you to get back to work.

Extraction

The basic principle of extraction is to retrace your steps or return along the tracks that you followed to get to where you became stuck. This is easier in theory than in practice.

Prodding

Prodding means searching cautiously every inch of ground before you step on to it. You should first ascertain that there are no trip wires before you start prodding. Mines can be triggered by trip wires. Trip wires look like fishing lines or thick spider threads; they are barely visible and can be covered by leaves and branches. A trip wire feeler – a thin branch which will bend when touching a trip wire – helps you identify them. Place it horizontally in front of you, holding it between thumb and forefinger, then gently raise it, keeping it horizontal. As soon as you encounter any resistance immediately release the pressure and check whether it is a trip wire. Try and find another path avoiding the trip wire. Never touch or try to cut a trip wire: some will cause a mine to detonate when pressure is put on them, but some work through tension release. If you cut a tight trip wire the mine will explode.

If there are no trip wires, the next thing to do is delineate a space shoulder-length wide and systematically prod it. The best way is to lie prone (first clear an area before you stretch out), otherwise do this kneeling or crouching. Prodding means sticking the prodder carefully into the soil at an angle of 30 degrees, gently feeling for any hard object. If you come upon a hard object – and in stony ground there may be hundreds – very carefully clear the side of it until you can see what it is. If it is a mine never touch it or try to remove it, but mark it and move your prodding path around it.

Rescue

Few situations are as difficult to confront as someone stepping on a mine in your vicinity. Staff should be instructed:

- Never rush in to assist, even if the victim is screaming for help and risks bleeding to death. Always remember that where there is one mine there are likely to be others, and increasing the number of victims helps no one.
- Only attempt a planned and controlled rescue operation when the victim is still alive, when no specialist teams can be called to the site within a reasonable time and when there is a reasonable chance that they themselves will not become further victims.

In essence, a rescue operation consists of:

- Talking to the victim and getting the message across that they should not move as there may be more mines in the vicinity.
- From the closest safe spot checking an access area of about 1.5 metres wide by prodding.

- Clearing an area around the victim to allow first aid to be administered.
- Checking carefully under the limbs and body of the victim for other mines.
- Administering first aid.
- Extracting the victim along a cleared path.

Reporting

Any indication that there may be mines, booby traps or other explosive ordnance in an area, and of course any actual incidents, must be reported to the relevant authorities (including a mine action centre) and at interagency forums. Make a sketch map of the approximate location and consider putting up a marker, but leave the actual investigation of the area to the professionals. Aid agencies involved in curative medical work should report any mine-related cases they treat.

Essential guidance: Don't touch, don't approach, mark if possible, report

- UXOs: Generally visible, although they can be partly or even wholly buried. Presume that they are unstable and can explode if touched. Never touch them. Mark their position and inform the authorities. In certain countries there is an active scrap metal/recycling industry and UXOs are touched and handled. Even when handled several times, they may still contain explosive and can detonate at any time.
- Booby traps: The object that is booby-trapped is generally visible, but not the explosive linked to it. Presume that virtually anything in an uncleared and not yet reinhabited, or only recently and partially reinhabited, area, can be booby trapped. Don't touch anything, don't pick anything up, do not open shutters or doors. Don't enter empty buildings or ruins, even for a call of nature.
- Mines: Generally not visible. Never touch them; don't try to remove them; don't try to make them explode by throwing rocks at them. If you know that mines have been used in a conflict, and you are not absolutely certain that a road is clear, don't venture onto it. If you see a mine, mark the location very clearly and inform the authorities.
- Local people may become over-confident and act foolishly. Do not trust untrained people to handle mines and UXOs. You may be invited by villagers to take a look at their cupboard full of such curiosities or recycled pieces, or visit a work party digging up mines. Items may be unstable and may explode, even if they have been handled before. Stay away or leave immediately.

15.5 White phosphorus

The stated use of white phosporus in a combat zone is to provide a smoke-screen. It is one of the most effective smoke-screen producers because it clouds very quickly and because it not only obstructs visual contact but also scrambles infrared radiation, thereby interfering with infrared optics and weapon-tracking systems, such as those used by guided weapons like anti-tank missiles. It can be delivered by small smoke grenades, tank cannons and mortars or other artillery. Upon explosion, burning particles spray outward, followed closely by streamers of white smoke, which then coalesce into a very white cloud. Recent uses of white phosphorus include the Israel–Hezbollah war of 2006, Iraq and during the war in Gaza in 2008–2009.

The problem with white phosphorus concerns its use in populated areas and its effects on people. The burning particles stick to skin and can produce serious burns. Particles continue burning until completely consumed or until they are deprived of oxygen. In addition, phosphorus can be absorbed into the body through the burned areas and cause liver, kidney and heart damage or even organ failure. The second potentially fatal contact is through oral ingestion of the phosphorus particles. Inhalation of the smoke is hazardous and will irritate the eyes, nose and respiratory tract, but does not pose the same lethal threat as burns and ingestion.

15.6 Remnants of war: a reminder

15.6.1 Explosive remnants of war

You are not safe just because the war is over: landmines and cluster munitions will remain dangerous for years and even decades to come. Artillery and mortar shells, and even bullets, may seem like nice souvenirs, but can remain explosive and are likely to become increasingly unstable over time. Other bombs and shells may have buried themselves deep in the ground, presenting a continuing danger to farmers and builders. Destroyed or abandoned military or militarised vehicles and buildings used by armed groups may contain unexploded ordnance, as well as volatile fuels, chemical residues (including depleted uranium, a material used for armour-piercing munitions) and booby traps. The general advice is to stay away from them.

15.6.2 Preparation and training

Preparing for operations in a potentially mined area demands good knowledge and an emphasis on personal movement and behavioural discipline.

Core knowledge about mines, UXO and booby traps includes where one might expect them and therefore how to avoid them; locally used warning signs; misconceptions about mines; mine clearance and local knowledge, and what to do if it is uncertain whether or not an area is mined; the do's and don'ts when one is confronted with mines; how to get out of a minefield; and reporting on identified or suspected mined areas. Above all, mine training should emphasise behavioural discipline. Aid agency staff will generally not heed advice to turn back when in doubt, unless that message has been instilled in them through simulation exercises and reinforced in daily operations by programme managers. In high-risk areas, the drill should include making inquiries of local people, discipline while moving and then extraction from a vehicle and then from an area by feeling for trip wires and prodding. If the agency is operating in an area where specialist rescue is more or less everywhere at hand, as in Kosovo in late 1999/early 2000, staff may not need training in first aid. That will, however, be the exception. Staff operating in areas away from specialist support will need basic medical training. This is staff- and time-intensive, and likely to be costly.

New staff arriving in an operational area where there are known to be minefields and mine risks should be briefed in detail. Familiarise them with the vicinity and point out known mine areas and the signs that help to identify them. Real-life exposure and visual memory will stick more thoroughly than verbal or written information. A proper briefing should also instil the necessity of marking any suspect areas that the staff member comes across, and reporting in detail on this. Staff should be reminded regularly of the importance of remaining alert to the dangers of mines.

Essential equipment includes:

- A radio in the car.
- If possible hand-held radios for use away from the car.
- A good first aid kit.
- Prodding and feeling equipment (a prodder can be a long screwdriver or a strong knife with a blade 12–15cm long. For a trip wire feeler, use a light, flexible rod 100–130cm long, a thin piece of strong wire or a flexible stalk or branch).

Section 6
Annexes

Annex 1
Global trends in aid worker security

When the first edition of this Good Practice Review was published in 2000, the majority of aid agencies were only just beginning to take serious notice of the realities and challenges of operational insecurity. Spurred into action by high-profile attacks, such as the 1996 assassination of six ICRC workers in Chechnya, international aid organisations had started collaborative learning initiatives aimed at enhancing operational security, resulting in the earliest interagency security training as well as the first edition of this GPR. At that time most international organisations still had no designated security responsibilities or security coordinator positions, no risk assessment tools or good practice guidelines and limited if any organisational policies or protocols on how to manage the risks of deliberate violence against staff and operations.

The ten years that have passed since the first edition have seen a good deal of development in humanitarian security management, as well as changes in the global security environment. These changes have had serious implications for international humanitarian assistance. The beginning of the decade brought the attacks of 11 September 2001 and the subsequent wars in Afghanistan and Iraq, prompting large humanitarian relief interventions in areas of active confict. These largely Western-based humanitarian operations suffered a continuous and rising number of attacks partly because they were perceived by some as instruments of a Western political agenda. Subsequent years saw devastating bomb attacks against the UN and ICRC in Baghdad, a rise in kidnappings and lethal armed attacks affecting aid workers and another major bombing of UN aid offices in the Algerian capital Algiers.

This annex provides a short examination of the trends in the international security environment for aid workers since the time of the first publication, and the developing culture of security management within the humanitarian community.

By the numbers: the revelations – and limitations – of global statistics

It wasn't until 2005 that a global retrospective mapping of major attacks against aid workers worldwide was compiled, in the form of the Aid

Worker Security Database (AWSD). Since then the database has been kept current and made freely available online at www.aidworkersecurity.org. Other statistical research projects on the topic include Insecurity Insight (www.insecurityinsight.org).

Such global statistics, it should be noted, usually have little direct operational relevance to staff in the field. Their main function is to raise awareness within and among organisations, governments and the wider public, to increase understanding of the scope and depth of the operational challenges facing aid work and to provide information on big-picture trends and issues within the international humanitarian and political spheres. They provide an essential base of evidence for a discussion that had previously been driven by anecdote and speculation.

The AWSD's findings over the past decade point to the following broad trends:[1]

- An increasing rate of major attacks against aid workers, but with most attacks concentrated in a small number of highly violent conflict settings, notably Afghanistan (and more recently Pakistan), Iraq, Somalia and Darfur.
- In some of the most violent settings, the increasing use of more sophisticated, organised and lethal tactics, the evident targeting of internationals and more politically oriented motivations among perpetrators.
- An overall slight decline in aid worker casualties in other aid settings around the world, despite growing numbers of field staff, indicating better security management within the sector.
- A long-term trend of increasing attack rates for national staff relative to their international counterparts.

These trends reflect the changing geostrategic and security environment and the policy and operational responses of international aid agencies. They can be summarised in three main issue areas.

Strengthening security management: expansions in organisational policy, training, interagency collaboration and overall duty of care

First, the good news: aid agencies have come a very long way over the past ten years in terms of creating and strengthening security management within their organisations. General awareness and professionalism in attitudes towards security have greatly increased across the sector, reflected in the development

---

1 Findings have been published in the *Providing Aid in Insecure Environments* reports of 2006 and 2009, available at http://www.odi.org.uk/programmes/humanitarian-policy-group.

Aid Worker Security Database: summary statistics as of October 2010

Incidents of major violence against aid workers	1997	1998	1999	2000	2001	2002	2003	2004	2005	2006	2007	2008	2009*
Total incidents	35	27	32	42	29	46	63	63	75	106	119	161	139
Total aid worker victims	73	69	65	91	90	85	143	125	172	239	208	274	278
Total killed	39	36	30	57	27	38	87	56	54	86	78	127	102
Total wounded	6	15	15	23	20	23	49	46	95	87	84	87	84
Total kidnapped	28	18	20	11	43	24	7	23	23	66	46	60	92
Total national staff victims	40	52	40	70	62	68	116	101	157	213	173	227	205
Total international staff victims	33	17	25	21	28	17	27	24	15	26	35	47	73

* Provisional figures

of policies, protocols and practical tools for use in the field. From a small minority of agencies in 2000, virtually every major humanitarian organisation now has formalised security responsibilities in organisational policy, although these vary in their quality and implementation.

Many more field staff are undergoing training in security matters, and resources for such training have proliferated in the field. One of the major training providers is RedR (www.redr.org.uk), which runs training sessions in home countries and in field settings around the world. Training, information and education in operational security are offered by a growing number of other organisations, such as Security Management Initiative, based in Geneva (www.securitymanagementinitiative.org).

Security-themed international consortia of humanitarian agencies include the London-based European Interagency Security Forum (EISF) and the Security Advisory Group of the US NGO consortium InterAction. These groups provide platforms for information-sharing and policy development, and are also increasingly seen in field settings. The reporting, tracking and sharing of security incident information is not yet what it should be, and in certain areas agencies are still reluctant to engage in frank and open discussions (such as on the issue of the use of armed protection in humanitarian operations). Overall, however, progress has been unmistakable. It is not unreasonable to conclude that the strengthening of security management capacity in the humanitarian community is at least partially responsible for the flattening out of the rate of major incidents around the world, when controlling for the most violent contexts.

The increasing politicisation of aid worker violence in settings of 'globalised' threat

Now the bad news: unfortunately these improvements in operational security management have been dwarfed by the rising level of threat in the highest-risk aid settings. The combination of rising numbers of attacks on aid workers in a small number of places, the increased targeting of internationals there and the increased use of 'terror tactics', such as suicide bombings, coordinated armed attacks and IEDs, all suggest that aid workers have become political targets. This is borne out by the available data pertaining to the attackers' allegiances and objectives (when it is possible to determine them). In these highly violent settings, international aid operations face an unprecedented level of threat and are finding it increasingly difficult to access populations in need. In these places the humanitarian footprint is shrinking, as aid workers lose secure access and programmes are scaled back or halted altogether.

Continued weaknesses: shifting the burden of risk to national staff, and the need for more active acceptance approaches

Aid agencies seeking to continue humanitarian operations in violent environments commonly respond to serious threats by relocating or restricting the movement of certain categories of staff, while shifting more responsibility to local staff or local partner organisations. Relief operations continue, often at a lower or simplified level, while being managed from a distance. This practice, known as remote management and covered in Chapter 4, can keep aid flowing to meet vital needs, but it can also place an unacceptable burden of risk on national or local personnel, who often have the least access to training, equipment and other resources for security. The statistical evidence of a long-term increase in attack rates for nationals underscores the seriousness of this issue, and the ethical implications it holds for aid agencies. The GPR has highlighted this issue in the foregoing pages, emphasising the need to properly assess risks for national and local staff members, to mitigate them accordingly and to provide equitable levels of security input for both international and national staff.

This review has also highlighted the need for a more analytical and proactive acceptance approach by humanitarian agencies in contested areas (see Chapter 3). This may prove unfeasible in settings where the aid community at large is already viewed as a tool of Western political and cultural domination. Nonetheless, aid practitioners are again looking to acceptance to secure consent and enhance security. By doing so, they are seeking solutions in the security approach most grounded in humanitarianism's core values and principles, rather than short-term solutions such as extreme protective and deterrent measures. Current practitioner and academic research, such as an initiative spearheaded by Save the Children US into how to measure acceptance and actively apply acceptance strategies, is an important step in this direction.

Annex 2
The United Nations security management system[1]

The primary responsibility for the security and protection of personnel employed by United Nations system organisations[2] rests with the Host Government. In the case of international organisations and their officials, the government is considered to have a special responsibility under the Charter of the United Nations or the government's agreements (called Host Country Agreements) with the individual organisations.

Headquarters architecture of the security management system

The United Nations security management system was restructured after the 2003 Baghdad bombing. This established an Under Secretary General-level headed Department called the United Nations Department of Safety and Security (UNDSS). The Under Secretary General (USG) for Safety and Security is responsible for the executive direction and control of the United Nations security management system (UNSMS) and the overall safety and security of United Nations civilian personnel and their dependants at both headquarters locations and in the field, as well as United Nations premises and assets at field and headquarters locations. He/she is directly accountable to the Secretary General on all security-related matters, and is responsible for developing security policies, practices and procedures for United Nations system personnel worldwide. Executive Heads of the United Nations funds and programmes are responsible and accountable to the Secretary-General for ensuring that the goals of the UNSMS are met within their respective organisations.

The Inter-Agency Security Management Network (IASMN) brings together UNDSS, relevant departments of the Secretariat and the UN agencies regarding security policy and guidelines within the UN. It meets in full forum twice a year to discuss and endorse recommendations that go to the High Level Committee on Management (HLCM) and in turn the Chief Executives Board for Coordination (CEB), however special committees and coordination mechanisms function throughout the year. While the USG for Safety and Security has overall responsibility for the security management system, the IASMN supports the HLCM in its review of policies and resource-related

---

1 This annex was drafted in collaboration with the UN Department of Safety and Security (UNDSS).
2 This includes the spouses of UN personnel and other recognised dependants and property and the organisations' property.

issues for the entire UN security management system. The IAMSN monitors the implementation of UN security management policies, practices and procedures by all actors of the UN system, including the related programme budget. It reports and makes recommendations to the HLCM.

Financing of the UN security management system

UNDSS receives a portion of its biennial budget from the UN Regular Budget. The other portion (45% of total expenditure) comes from agency cost-sharing contributions that are calculated on a per capita staffing basis at both the global level and for field-level operations. Originally it had been hoped that UNDSS would be fully funded from the Regular Budget, but Member States through the General Assembly opposed this on grounds that cost-sharing would increase a sense of 'ownership' and encourage participation in decision-making.

The security management system at the country level

In each country or designated area where the United Nations is present, the most senior official is normally appointed as the Designated Official (DO) for Security. The Designated Official is accountable to the Secretary General, through the USG for Safety and Security, and is responsible for the security of personnel employed by the organisations of the United Nations system and their recognised dependants throughout the country or designated area.

Representatives of organisations (the 'country representative', 'agency head' or 'head of mission') of the United Nations system participating in the United Nations security management system are accountable to the Secretary General through their respective executive heads, under the overall guidance of the USG for Safety and Security, for all matters related to the security of their personnel at the duty station. Each agency head will also be represented at the field level in the Security Management Team (SMT), which is chaired by the Designated Official, and includes the Security Advisor (see below). The SMT advises the Designated Official on all security-related matters. In peacekeeping missions, where the Head of Mission serves as the Designated Official, the Security Management Team may also include Heads of Offices or Sections of the mission.

The Chief Security Adviser or Security Adviser is a security professional appointed by the USG for Safety and Security to advise the Designated Official and the SMT in their security functions. The Security Adviser reports to the Designated Official and maintains a technical line of communication to the Department of Safety and Security. In the absence of a Security Adviser, the Designated Official, in consultation with the Department of Safety and

Security, should appoint a Country Security Focal Point for the SMT. The Country Security Focal Point could be someone employed by another UN organisation who primarily has other responsibilities.

Area Security Coordinators are staff members appointed by the Designated Official, in consultation with the SMT, in areas of larger countries that are separated from the capital in terms of both distance and exposure, in order to coordinate and control security arrangements applicable to all personnel employed by organisations of the United Nations system and their recognised dependants in their area of responsibility. Area Security Coordinators are accountable to the Designated Official for their security-related responsibilities. The Area Security Advisor may benefit from the services and advice of an FSCO, or Field Security Coordination Officer, a security professional deployed by UNDSS.

Wardens are appointed by the Designated Official, in consultation with the Security Management Team, to ensure proper implementation of the security plan in a predetermined zone of a large city. Wardens are accountable to the Designated Official/Area Security Coordinator for their security-related functions, irrespective of their employing organisation.

Staff member responsibilities

All individuals employed by the organisations of the United Nations system are responsible for their own safety and security, irrespective of their location of assignment, and must comply with all security policies and procedures. Personnel employed by UN system organisations must:

- Familiarise themselves with information provided to them regarding the UN security management system at their location.
- Receive a security clearance prior to travelling to a country in which a security phase has been declared, and inform the Designated Official in the country of destination when travelling to a country where a phase is not in effect.
- Attend security briefings and certify their participation.
- Know who their warden and/or agency security focal point is and how to contact them.
- Be appropriately equipped for service at the duty station (e.g. ensure all required vaccinations have been received, appropriate transportation arrangements for travel within the duty station have been made).
- Apply and comply with all security regulations and procedures at the duty station, whether on or off duty.

- Behave in a manner which will not endanger their own safety and security or that of others.
- Complete all required security training.

UN Security Phases and the new UN Security Level System

The current UN Security Phase system was created in 1980 in response to emergency and crisis situations that threatened the security of UN personnel. As a primary security management tool for preparedness at duty stations the Security Phase system was associated with appropriate security measures, depending on the level of classification of the duty station (from 1 to 5), which were articulated in the security plan.

During 2010, the UN was set to introduce a new Security Level System (SLS), which contains six levels, to replace the Security Phase system. It was to be officially implemented UN-wide on 1 January 2011. The SLS sits within the Security Risk Assessment of the UN Security Risk Management model, allowing a more objective assessment of the security environment in which the UN operates. It provides a structured threat assessment which describes the general security environment in a geographical area or location, and gives staff and managers an overall impression of how the security environment in one area or location compares with another. The SLS is intended to be more objective, fact-based, logical and systematic, and removes the automatic security measures and human resources entitlements found in the Security Phase system.

Minimum Operating Security Standards (MOSS)

MOSS is the primary mechanism for managing and mitigating security risks to personnel, property and assets of the organisations of the UN. MOSS encompasses a range of measures designed to reduce the level of risk. A single MOSS system applies throughout the UN.

Security training

The United Nations system has initiated mandatory security training for UN staff members. Completion of this training by non-UN personnel is strongly encouraged. The course, entitled 'Basic Security in the Field: Staff Safety, Health and Welfare', is available on CD ROM in the six official languages of the UN, and is recommended for all personnel, regardless of whether they travel outside the duty station. The course 'Advanced Security in the Field' is strongly recommended for personnel who travel to locations in Phase One or higher. A certificate is generated after a test is successfully completed, and is valid for three years. See Annex 7 for information on how to access this training.

Annex 3
Saving Lives Together: a framework for security collaboration

In 2001, the Inter-Agency Standing Committee (IASC), in close collaboration with the UN Security Coordinator (UNSECOORD, the forerunner of the UN Department of Safety and Security (UNDSS)) established a 'Menu of Options' for security collaboration between the UN, NGOs and inter-governmental organisations. The Menu of Options was a list of potential risk-mitigating strategies to improve the collective security of the humanitarian community. The Menu was not a great success for a variety of reasons, including resource constraints, diverse approaches to security and a lack of trust and understanding among the participants, and it was little known in the field.

In 2006, the Menu was revised and renamed *Saving Lives Together (SLT): A Framework for Improving Security Arrangements among IGOs, NGOs and the UN in the Field*. The SLT established ten non-binding recommendations on how the UN, other inter-governmental organisations such as the International Organisation for Migration (IOM) and NGOs could collaborate on behalf of their common security. The SLT framework seeks to encourage this collaboration without compromising the neutrality or independence of humanitarian efforts or imposing on institutional mandates. The underlying premise is that, through joint efforts, the humanitarian community can minimise risks in insecure environments.

Despite being revised and relaunched, uptake of the SLT framework has been slow at the field level, where knowledge of the existence and purpose of the framework remains limited. This has partly been a resourcing and staffing problem. While the SLT has support from UN member states, it remains informal and non-binding, and as such any additional resources required to implement its recommendations must come from extra-budgetary sources. In addition, in some field contexts it has proved difficult to recruit and deploy UNDSS staff, even when financing is available.

Saving Lives Together: A Framework for Improving Security Arrangements among IGOs, NGOs and the UN in the Field

1. Collaboration in the UN Security Management Team, with the participation of NGOs and IGOs

a) IGOs and NGOs may participate in relevant meetings of the UN Security Management Team (SMT) on an ex-officio, representative basis.[1]

b) UN/NGO/IGO security collaboration is to be taken as a regular agenda item at UN Security Management Team meetings. As permitted within the framework of the UN Security Management System, consideration should be given to inviting Senior Managers of the NGO and IGO Communities to attend relevant portions of Security Management Team meetings.

c) That Protocols for sharing and dissemination of information discussed in Security Management Team meetings shall be agreed to in advance by all parties in attendance.

d) That where appropriate, the DO[2] should coordinate security decisions with non-UN humanitarian actors.

e) That IGO/NGO partners to UN organisations in specific humanitarian operations select among themselves one or a limited number of field security focal points.

2. Convening broad-based forums for field security collaboration and information sharing

a) That fora for practical security collaboration among all humanitarian actors at area, country and sub-office level be convened, at regular intervals, in order to address practical security issues of common concern.

b) That the fora may include the following regular participants: DO/FSO[3]/ Area Security Coordinator or other DO Designee; Members of the SMT as appropriate; NGO field security focal point(s); Representatives of IGOs. The chairperson may be chosen on a rotating basis.

c) That the fora may include topics of discussion, such as:
The exchange of security-related information; incident reports; security and trend analysis; joint operational planning, as appropriate; protocols for the sharing and further dissemination of information and documents presented or discussed.

---

1 Ex officio refers to the fact that representatives of non-UN organisations are not bound by and do not participate formally in SMT decisions on UN security policy.
2 Designated Official, the senior UN official with overall responsibility for the security and protection of personnel of the UN system.
3 Field Security Officer, the UN official responsible for security at his or her duty station.

Saving Lives Together (continued)

3. Including staff security concerns in the Consolidated Appeals

That structured efforts to include well conceived and developed UN/NGO/IGO security projects within Consolidated Appeals Processes (CAPs) to cover the additional resources potentially required for enhanced collaboration on staff security by UN Agencies and NGOs/IGOs, such as telecommunications and security training.

4. Meeting common security-related needs and sharing resources

That whilst recognising that individual NGOs' financial resources are often more modest than those of the UN or IGOs, their contributions are nonetheless needed and that consideration should be given to what resources could be made available to help address common security-related needs.

That UN organisations and their IGO/NGO partners, committed to security collaboration in each specific humanitarian operation, participate, to the extent feasible and based on the extent of their involvement, in meeting the uncovered, security-related needs of the humanitarian community.

5. Sharing resources

That UN organisations and their IGO/NGO partners cooperating in humanitarian field operations develop a local inventory for the sharing of their specialised, security-related human and material resources.

6. Facilitating inter-agency security and emergency telecommunications

That telecommunication among UN organisations and their IGO/NGO partners at field level be facilitated by:

a) The DO advocating with the relevant authorities for the use of telecommunication equipment within the framework of existing international agreements.

b) The relevant UN body negotiating with the authorities a common, inter-agency frequency to facilitate greater interoperability for security collaboration for UN organisations and IGOs/NGOs operating in the same area without denying the need for agencies to have their own internal and integral communications infrastructure.

c) Humanitarian actors committing to security collaboration using standard communication procedures and, to the extent possible, providing staff with compatible communication systems.

Saving Lives Together (continued)

7. Collaborating and consulting in security training

That all UN organisations and their IGO/NGO partners at HQ and at field level:
a) Carry out joint security training in collaboration and/or consultation with other agencies to the extent possible.
b) When feasible, pool necessary resources to conduct field security training.
c) Seek to increase their capacity for security training at all levels.
d) Give consideration to the development of training packages that focus specifically on improving security collaboration.

8. Sharing information

That security-related information be shared among UN organisations and their IGO/NGO partners while respecting the humanitarian character of the participants as well as the confidentiality required when dealing with sensitive information.

9. Identifying minimum security standards

That UN organisations and their IGO/NGO partners jointly identify and agree on how to apply minimum security standards, principles, and/or guidelines adapted to local circumstances. In so doing, humanitarian actors will take into consideration already existing standards, principles, and/or guidelines for example the UN MOSS (Minimum Operational Security Standards) that are binding for the members of the UN system and InterAction's Security Planning Guidelines.

10. Seeking adherence to common humanitarian ground-rules

That the security collaboration of the UN organisations and their IGO/NGO partners in specific field operations, to the extent possible, rest on respect for common, locally developed ground-rules for humanitarian action.

Annex 4
Private security providers

Private commercial security is a growing industry, with numbers of internationally operating companies spiking in the early years of the Afghanistan and Iraq operations. Projections suggest that the private military and security industry worldwide is expected to reach $202bn in 2010.[1] The term 'private security provider' is used rather than private security or military companies to include hired militia that are not necessarily incorporated and registered, but provide similar services. The range of services PSPs provide is broad: static protection (typically of offices and residences), mobile protection (escorts), personal protection (bodyguards), risk assessments and threat analysis, security audits, training, consultancy (i.e. advice on security protocols), critical incident management, logistics and the provision of equipment. A sub-category of PSPs, commonly referred to as Private Military Companies (PMCs), can also offer services to governments and militaries, such as security sector reform, military advisors, military training, command and control of military operations, major logistical support, the administration of prisons and interrogation.

A 2008 study of the role of PSPs in humanitarian action showed that the main services they provided consisted of unarmed protection, training and consultancy.[2] Although the provision of armed protection remains exceptional, all major humanitarian actors have used PSPs for this purpose in at least one context. As unarmed guarding is the most frequently contracted security service, most PSPs hired by humanitarian agencies are local, not international, companies. The study also found that decisions to contract a PSP are often taken at the field level, with little or no policy or practical guidance from the agency's headquarters.

Considerations in hiring private security providers

A number of assumptions influence the decision to hire a PSP: it provides know-how that does not exist in-house; it may save time; and it is more cost-effective. These assumptions should be carefully examined.

Outsourcing to the private sector is often assumed to be a cheaper option, reducing training, insurance and administration costs, and freeing up staff

---

1 D. Avant, 'Privatizing Military Training', *Foreign Policy in Focus*, vol. 7, issue 3, May 2002.
2 A. Stoddard, A. Harmer and V. DiDomenico, *The Use of Private Security Providers and Services in Humanitarian Operations*, HPG Report 27 (London: ODI, 2008).

to concentrate on core tasks. This type of reasoning may hold in the narrow accounting terms of most international (and probably also many national) humanitarian agencies. Over the long term, however, hidden costs may include the failure to invest in incorporating skills and expertise within the organisation (because security competence remains with the contractor); the possible damage to an agency's reputation; and potential legal fees and even compensatory payouts if something goes wrong. Another consideration is the possible longer-term cost implications for the agency if it is following a predominantly protection and deterrence security approach. There is a risk that this approach will perpetuate itself partly because it will become increasingly difficult to return to an acceptance approach, which can be less expensive. Finally, where a PSP has a virtual monopoly prices are likely to be high and could evolve into an extortion racket.

Another crucial question is the perceived association of these entities (and by extension humanitarian agencies) with military and political actors. Private security providers can have links with state security, police or military services or actors with a past record of illegal, criminal or abusive behaviour, including human rights violations. It can be extremely difficult to assess the wider practices of some PSPs, because companies tend not to publicise activities whose legality may be questioned, and information about other clients is generally regarded as confidential. PSPs may also be subsidiaries of larger holding companies, making it difficult to ascertain ownership.

Another concern regarding private security services is the generally detrimental impact they can have on public security:

- The presence of many private security providers is an indirect sign that the authorities are not able to provide public security.
- Better remuneration in the private sector may lead members of the public security sector to quit and take up opportunities with private companies.
- If private security personnel cannot be easily distinguished from public security forces, any misconduct will create more generalised distrust.
- Where government officials (civil or security forces, active or retired) have business interests in private security services, the incentive to strengthen the public sector will not be high and there may be conflicts of interest.
- Post-conflict states may not have a regulatory framework for private security providers; even where such regulation is in place it may not be effectively applied or enforced.

Exploratory research in Angola and Afghanistan indicates that local people generally distrust PSPs, and regard them as increasing, rather than reducing, insecurity.[3]

In sum, hiring a PSP is not just about the short-term reduction of risk for staff and assets or lower costs. It can have profound implications not only for the agency's own security strategy in the longer term, but also for other aid agencies and for the wider goal of restoring an effective and accountable state.

The following is an outline of steps that aid agency personnel can take to improve their decision-making on the use of PSPs, and their management of their relations with these providers.

Strategic implications
- How does this option fit with your security strategy? Could using a PSP undermine your strategy or require a different approach?
- Will it reduce direct physical risk in the long term, as well as the short?
- How are PSPs perceived by the local public? What are the reputational risks, locally and internationally?
- Do you have a policy on the use of PSPs – both armed and unarmed?
- Do you have the competence to manage a PSP? How are you going to develop in-house competencies if you outsource your security (especially the management of your security)?
- Are you creating a precedent that may affect other aid agencies?
- Are you contributing to market inflation (higher prices) or a lowering of standards? Could collective bargaining by humanitarian actors be an option?
- Are there ways to use PSPs that also strengthen public security services or that deliver more public benefits (e.g. static guards that help secure a whole neighbourhood rather than just individual houses)?
- Are there government policies or regulations regarding PSPs that you are required to follow?
- What is the direct financial cost compared to your overall operating budget in-country? How will you determine the cost-effectiveness of the investment?

Questions to consider during the background check and hiring of a PSP
- Do you have guidelines for conducting due diligence in the background checks and quality control of PSPs? Do you have templates of contracts for the purchase of PSP services? Do you have a record-keeping system covering the PSPs you hire?

---

3 Ulrike Joras and Adrian Schuster (eds), *Private Security Companies and Local Populations: An Exploratory Study of Afghanistan and Angola*, Swisspeace Working Paper 1, 2008.

- What services does the PSP provide?
- If the PSP offers armed protection, do you know how they should handle, maintain and use their weapons? Do they have rules of engagement?
- Are they registered, and where? International companies can be registered in different countries: one question will be where their headquarters is registered, another whether they are registered in the country where you operate. National entities may or may not be registered, possibly under different legal provisions.
- Who are their other clients?
- Who owns the company (or commands the personnel for a group that is not incorporated)?
- What can you find out about their past record and reputation? Are they perceived as close to special interests, such as a prominent individual, elite group or local faction? Has the company been involved in any notable incidents or has it been accused of misconduct?
- Is the PSP fully compliant with national laws and regulations?

Reliability and professionalism

- Does the PSP have a statement of ethics or corporate social responsibility, including a commitment to abide by national laws, international human rights laws and any other applicable international legal frameworks?
- Does it perform detailed background checks and keep up-to-date records on its personnel?
- Does it require personnel to be clearly identifiable as belonging to the entity?
- Does it have licences for arms or dual-use equipment, and does it use any weaponry prohibited by international law?
- Is there an up-to-date register for all weapons and ammunition?
- Does the PSP provide comprehensive training for its personnel covering the use of equipment, including clear rules on the use of weapons and interaction with the general public?
- Does it provide adequate salaries and benefits for its personnel?
- Does it provide its personnel with a contract in a language they can understand?
- Does it regularly monitor the conduct of the personnel it provides?
- Are effective measures in place against bribery and corruption?
- Are there complaints mechanisms, investigative capacities and disciplinary procedures for the conduct of personnel?
- Does the PSP sub-contract to others, and if so does it have effective procedures to screen and hold accountable its sub-contractors?
- Does it have the financial capacity to absorb any liabilities?
- Is it adequately insured?

You can ask a potential provider about these issues during preliminary discussions. These discussions will provide a basis for drawing up a contract, which can include many of the above details. The contract should also specify conditions that allow you as client to revoke the contract, and which clauses may involve penalties for the contractor.

Monitoring, complaints investigation and reporting

Clients of PSPs have a responsibility to oversee the conduct and performance of their security providers, not only as regards their own interests but also those of third parties, including the population at large. When hiring a PSP, consider establishing a monitoring and complaints mechanism that is accessible and safe for the public at large.

Clients of PSPs also have an ethical obligation to contribute to the strengthening of a national and international regime to regulate and oversee private security providers. Negative experiences with PSPs need to be reported and communicated, as appropriate, to the relevant authorities in the country of operation and/or the PSP's headquarters. International mechanisms are another means to ensure that PSPs are guided by global standards of good conduct. These include the Global Code of Conduct for Private Security Companies and Private Military Companies, due to be launched in 2010.[4] Another mechanism, the Montreux Document (September 2008), reminds states of their obligations towards private military and security companies (both those they have contracted and those that are incorporated in their territory) and lists a set of good practices. The document is also seen as a valuable reference for aid agencies. It includes a reminder that senior managers of a private military and security company can be held liable for the conduct of their personnel, as can a government official who has entered into a relationship with the company.[5]

---

4 See http://www.dcaf.ch/privatisation-security/_index.cfm.
5 Letter dated 2 October 2008 from the Permanent Representative of Switzerland to the United Nations addressed to the Secretary-General. New York, UN A/63/467-S/2008/636 (http://www.icrc.org/web/eng/siteeng0.nsf/htmlall/montreux-document-170908/$FILE/Montreux-Document-eng.pdf).

Annex 5
Insurance

This annex highlights some of the key issues that individual aid workers, security managers and agency headquarters need to consider. It is not meant to be a specialised examination of accident and war-risk or malicious acts insurance policies.

For employers, insuring staff against safety and security incidents is an important part of due diligence in safety and security. Aid workers should be fully briefed on the details of the insurance coverage the agency provides. As an individual aid worker, you have personal responsibility to inquire into the insurance coverage being provided to you. In addition to obtaining details from your organisation, it is also advisable to contact insurance companies and professional bodies to find out yourself about what is available.

It is important for all to remember that insurance cover provides compensation, not protection.

The costs of not having insurance

Safety and security accidents and incidents can have major financial consequences for the aid workers concerned, for their families and for the agency. There are immediate costs, such as medical evacuation and emergency treatment, which can quickly run into very large sums of money. There are also potential long-term costs, such as those resulting from permanent disability (for example following the loss of limbs) and long-term care needs.

In the past, many aid agencies did not have adequate insurance cover for war risk and malicious acts, either because they were unaware that their standard policies did not cover such incidents, or because of the high costs involved. Predictably, this led to cases where insurance companies refused to pay out and injured aid workers, or the families of deceased aid workers, sued the agency for compensation. Such direct compensation claims can leave small agencies facing bankruptcy.

What do you need?

Different agencies will have different insurance needs. Insurance should be considered a component of a mitigation strategy, and like everything else requires a full appreciation of risks, derived from a comprehensive assessment. After learning some costly lessons about the dangers of being under-insured, agencies today are clearer about the extent of coverage it is prudent to have. Most large international aid agencies with staff deployed to difficult environments, such as conflict or high-crime contexts, have insurance policies with the following types of coverage:

- Standard health insurance.
- Standard accident insurance, including accidental death or dismemberment.
- Disability insurance: partial or total, long-term or short-term.
- Medical emergency insurance, including coverage for medical evacuation and emergency care in situ and in transit.
- War risk insurance. This is often a separate policy, or a supplement at an additional cost. It covers injuries or deaths caused by acts of war or terrorism. This can be in the form of a personal accident policy covering malicious acts or terror tactics that pays out a lump sum, for example five times the annual salary.
- Kidnap and ransom (K&R) insurance covering technical expertise for crisis management and contingencies to facilitate safe release.
- Legal liability insurance. This is generally intended for senior staff and executives, should they be sued as individuals by staff members or others seeking damages.

What you need to know

Overall, as insurance coverage for aid workers has increased, so it has become more complex. It is more important than ever to read the fine print and inquire explicitly about what is and isn't covered.

Exclusion clauses

Insurance policies may not apply under certain conditions, and the details and interpretation of these exclusion clauses can be vitally important. Examples include:

- Coverage applies only during work assignments (e.g. in Somalia, but not during a period of rest and relaxation in Nairobi).
- Coverage applies only during working hours (e.g. up to 18.00, but not afterwards or during weekends).
- Coverage excludes certain types of war risk or malicious acts, particularly 'acts of terror', for instance a bombing in a public place.
- Coverage excludes specific war zones (you will need to ensure that how such zones are defined is clearly specified).

- Coverage applies only if the agency has written security guidelines which are demonstrably enforced (here the security manager may be held accountable) and followed, and/or provides security training to staff.
- Coverage excludes staff on short-term contracts or staff older than a certain age (often 59 years).
- Political exclusions: for US-based organisations, countries that are under sanctions by the Office of Foreign Assets Control (OFAC) are usually not covered by insurance policies, unless a special waiver is obtained from the US government.

Invalidation of other insurance policies

Check not only the extent of accident and insurance coverage while working in risk areas, but also the potential impact of taking out more than one insurance policy. Sometimes life assurance policies (such as those taken out with a mortgage) can become invalid for staff working in a high-risk area.

Coverage at the beginning and end of the employment contract

Find out precisely when coverage begins and when it ends. It is important to determine whether the staff member is covered even if they are not yet being paid a salary or have yet to be deployed to the location of the assignment. It should also be clear to both the agency and the individual at what point after the end of the assignment coverage ceases.

Premiums

Some insurance companies lower their premiums for individuals working in high-risk areas if the insured person can demonstrate that they have had appropriate security training provided by a recognised or accredited agency. This has already been taken up by many in the journalism profession, and could usefully be explored by the aid sector. While there is no robust data, anecdotal reports suggest that agencies that can demonstrate a serious approach to staff security in their policies and practices may benefit from lower premiums.

Other considerations

Insurance and national staff

International aid agencies vary in practice on insurance cover for their national staff. While some have worked to increase the provision of insurance to nationals, most national staff members of most agencies remain uninsured, and requests for compensation or financial assistance in the case of disease, injury or death are usually dealt with on a case-by-case basis. In many instances it is either not possible to purchase insurance for nationals, or if it is the cost to cover all national hires could be prohibitive. That is no reason, however, to avoid the issue altogether. A country may have a functioning national insurance sector that can be consulted. In other places there will be indigenous practices governing how and by how much staff and their families should be compensated. Even if your international insurance provider does not offer comprehensive coverage for nationals, it may be possible to include them in certain policies, for instance kidnap and ransom.

Self-insurance schemes

In situations where agencies are not able to provide insurance cover for national staff in high-risk areas, some have developed their own internal cooperative insurance system with an insurance pot created with a lump sum from the organisation, and perhaps added to by contributions from participating employees. Medical relief NGOs often provide free healthcare to all staff as a benefit of employment.

Political risk insurance

When the government of Sudan expelled 13 NGOs from the country in 2009, the move cost the agencies involved millions of dollars in lost assets and in the overheads on projects that could not be undertaken. In general, evacuation is very costly (a low-frequency but high-severity event), and some larger aid agencies working in unstable environments have begun to consider political risk and other new forms of insurance products that could provide compensation in such eventualities.

Key points to remember

It may be a cliché, but the importance of reading the small print cannot be over-emphasised. Before policies are purchased, carefully assess the risk and determine what policies and procedures are already in place, and what needs to be added. The objective is to arrive at the right configuration of insurance policies to mitigate the most likely threats. The job is not over when the policy is purchased: agencies must put the necessary administrative protocols in place, in terms of security training and information procedures.

Annex 6
Donor funding and security management

No matter what type of security approaches or strategies aid agencies employ in insecure environments, they will inevitably entail costs. Ensuring that adequate funding is available to enable agencies to operate securely is vital, and a subject on which agencies and their donors should be prepared to have frank discussions. This annex delineates some of the key issues and developments in donor funding of security management and coordination initiatives.

Funding security expenditures

Not all official donor administrations are equally aware of and receptive to the security concerns of operational agencies.[1] Generally speaking, however, the major humanitarian donors are prepared to fund appropriate and justified safety- and security-related expenditures. Explicit references to security management and related expenditures are contained in the proposal guidelines of several official donors, including DFID and USAID/OFDA, and some donors have specific security management and coordination posts, which can provide useful guidance particularly during programme planning and the initial budgeting stages. Donors have also arranged meetings and workshops to advise aid agencies on how to include security costs in proposals. ECHO organised a meeting on 'Risk Management Challenges in Afghanistan' in 2008, for example, and has included security management issues in a number of its Annual Partners' Conferences.

Security-related funding requests usually have to be accompanied by a detailed security plan that includes a context analysis and risk assessment. In order to avoid significant revisions to project budgets once contracts have been signed, risk assessments may describe possible future scenarios – and future needs – should security deteriorate. While donors vary in what they will fund, common areas of expenditure include communications and security equipment, dedicated security personnel, vehicles, physical security upgrades to residences and offices, security assessments and security training. Additional field-level security support such as that offered by private security providers is normally considered on a case-by-case basis.

---

1 By 'official donor' we mean donor administrations working under the auspices of governments (such as USAID or DFID) and intergovernmental bodies (such as ECHO).

There are no uniform budgeting formulae or common expenditure definitions for inputs and activities designed to enhance operational security. Agencies and donors also vary in how they budget for security-related costs. Some include security funding in overhead costs or core support services, while others include it as a separate line item or as a fixed percentage of programme costs. Many organisations would be unable to come up with any security expenditure figure at all, because their security costs are fully integrated, and therefore embedded, within their programme costs. For example, extra vehicles purchased or rented in order for staff to travel in convoys would go into the vehicles/transport line-item; installing gates, bars or alarms would be folded into facilities repairs/maintenance; and the recruitment of new security professionals or additional programme staff would be added to the salaries line.

Several official donors actively encourage greater security awareness and security competencies within the aid agencies they fund, and expect to see security-related expenditures in budgets. Beyond this, however, donors tend not to dictate particular security policies or practices, preferring to leave agencies to determine their own security stance and exercise their own quality control over this area. In part, this is because donors lack the staff time, competence and field presence to exert more direct influence. Donors are also wary of being seen to impose a particular security model on agencies. Getting formally involved in quality assurance would also potentially expose donors to liability claims.

Many donors require visibility for their funding and insist that their logos are displayed on the assets that they pay for, including offices, vehicles and relief items. In some cases this association may be deemed a security threat, particularly if the donor in question is unpopular in the particular context, or if the agency is trying to adopt a low-visibility approach. In such cases an agency may formally request a waiver of the visibility requirement. Donors can be flexible about these requirements when security concerns dictate caution.

Donor involvement beyond funding operational security needs

As both security and humanitarian specialists, security focal points within donor organisations can play key facilitating roles in promoting the security of aid agencies beyond simply funding security-related needs. They can argue for enhanced attention on the security needs of their implementing partners, for example by assuring their colleagues that particular requests are not unreasonable; help to quantify losses due to security incidents, to show the value in investing in security management; conduct discussions with actors on the ground responsible for the security of aid workers (one example of this is bilateral discussions between the US and Sudanese governments); and encourage the compilation and dissemination of good security practice. Official donors also have a role to play in strengthening interagency capacities and competencies, including providing funding for InterAction's Security Advisory Group and the European Interagency Security Forum (EISF). Donors have provided extra-budgetary support for Field Security Officers (FSOs) within the UN Department of Safety and Security (UNDSS), with a particular focus on FSO positions with NGO liaison responsibilities through the Saving Lives Together initiative (see Annex 3). The US government has provided funding to enable FSOs within UNDSS to work full-time on issues of NGO security in Darfur, and to allow UNDSS to augment its capacity to provide services to the community as a whole in Ethiopia, Côte d'Ivoire and Lebanon. An NGO–UNDSS liaison position in New York has been funded with extra-budgetary donor support. Official donors have also funded research to examine evolving challenges in security management and assess current aid agency practice. As agencies often fund programmes with contributions from multiple donors, coordination between donors is important to ensure coherence in security budgeting requirements and guidelines.

Annex 7
Additional resources

There is a growing body of literature on operational security management, encompassing both agency-specific materials and more generic guidance. This annex lists some of the most important sources of information.

General security guides

ECHO, *Generic Security Guide for Humanitarian Organisations*, European Commission Directorate-General for Humanitarian Aid (ECHO) (Brussels: ECHO, 2004).

ECHO, *NGO Security Collaboration Guide*. Commissioned by the European Commission Directorate-General for Humanitarian Aid (ECHO) (Brussels: ECHO, 2006).

David Lloyd Roberts, *Staying Alive: Safety and Security Guidelines for Humanitarian Volunteers in Conflict Areas* (Geneva: ICRC, 2006).

IFRC, *Stay Safe: The International Federation's Guide for Security Managers* (Geneva: IFRC, 2007). Also available in French.

InterAction Security Unit, *Security Risk Management: NGO Approach* (Washington DC: InterAction, 2010).

Inter-Agency Standing Committee, *Saving Lives Together: A Framework for Improving Security Arrangements Among IGOs, NGOs, and UN in the Field* (New York: IASC, 2006).

Security training

Advance Training Program on Humanitarian Action (ATHA): www.atha.se. Provides training in a variety of areas, including security management.

Centre for Safety and Development: www.centreforsafety.org. A non-profit foundation specialising in safety and security for humanitarian organisations worldwide. Organises security conferences and training.

Essential Field Training: www.essentialfieldtraining.org. Provides security awareness training for international aid workers, peacekeepers, government representatives, the private sector and others.

RedR: www.redr.org. Provides training on a variety of topics, including the management of staff safety, training for security guards, field travel safety and the management of staff welfare and critical incidents.

Security Management Initiative: www.securitymanagementinitiative.org. Provides training, information and educational resources on operational security. Based in Geneva.

United Nations: https://dss.un.org (for UN personnel) or http://dss.un.org/asitf (for non-UN personnel). Provides two interactive CD-ROM training courses entitled 'Basic Security in the Field: Staff Safety, Health and Welfare' and 'Advanced Security in the Field'. Also available in Arabic, Chinese, French, Russian and Spanish.

Trends in aid worker security

Aid Worker Security Database (AWSD): www.aidworkersecurity.org. Provides a global picture of major attacks against aid workers since 1996.

Antonio Donini et al., *Mapping the Security Environment: Understanding the Perceptions of Local Communities, Peace Support Operations, and Assistance Agencies* (Medford, MA: Feinstein International Famine Center, 2005).

ECHO, *Report on Security of Humanitarian Personnel: Standards and Practices for the Security of Humanitarian Personnel and Advocacy for Humanitarian Space* (Brussels: ECHO, 2004).

Abby Stoddard, Adele Harmer and Katherine Haver, *Providing Aid in Insecure Environments*, HPG Report 23 (London: ODI, 2006).

Abby Stoddard, Adele Harmer and Victoria DiDomenico, *Providing Aid in Insecure Environments: 2009 Update*, HPG Policy Brief 34 (London: ODI, 2009).

UN General Assembly, *Safety and Security of Humanitarian Personnel and Protection of United Nations Personnel*, UN General Assembly A/64/336 (New York: UN, 2009).

The military and non-state armed groups

Max Glaser, *Humanitarian Engagement with Non-state Actors: The Parameters of Negotiated Access*, HPN Network Paper 51 (London: ODI, 2005).

IASC, *Civil–Military Guidelines and Reference for Complex Emergencies* (New York and Geneva: IASC, 2008).

Abby Stoddard, Adele Harmer and Victoria DiDomenico, *The Use of Private Security Providers and Services in Humanitarian Operations*, HPG Report 27 (London: ODI, 2008).

UN, *Use of Military or Armed Escorts for Humanitarian Convoys: Discussion Paper and Non-Binding Guidelines*, 2001.

Gerard McHugh and Manuel Bessler, *Humanitarian Negotiations with Armed Groups: A Manual for Practitioners* (New York: OCHA in collaboration with the IASC, 2006).

UN, *Guidelines on the Use of Military and Civil Defence Assets to Support United Nations Humanitarian Activities in Complex Emergencies* (MCDA Guidelines) (New York: UN, 2003, revised January 2006). Also available in Arabic, Chinese, French, Russian and Spanish.

UN, *Guidelines on the Use of Foreign Military and Civil Defence Assets in Disaster Relief* (Oslo Guidelines), updated November 2006, revised November 2007. Also available in Arabic, Chinese, French, Russian and Spanish.

People and staff management

Centre for Humanitarian Psychology: www.humanitarian-psy.org. Publishes information sheets on various aspects of staff care.

Alexis Gaul et al., *NGO Security: Does Gender Matter?* (Washington DC: Save the Children USA and the Elliott School of International Affairs, George Washington University, 2006).

ICRC, *Humanitarian Action and Armed Conflict: Coping with Stress* (Geneva: ICRC, 2001). Also available in French and Spanish.

InterAction, *The Security of National Staff: Essential Steps* (Washington DC: InterAction, 2002).

People in Aid: www.peopleinaid.org. Provides policy and practical guidance on a variety of topics related to the management of people in the aid sector, including staff welfare, staff security, mental health and psychological support.

Security and communications

ICT Humanitarian Emergency Platform: www.wfp.org/ict-emergency. Describes best practice in telecoms equipment installation and maintenance and provides some training to humanitarian organisations at headquarters and field level.

Security in-a-box: http://security.ngoinabox.org. A collaborative effort of the Tactical Technology Collective and Front Line, providing guidance on digital security. Also available in Arabic, French, Russian and Spanish.

Security Management Initiative, *Cyber Security for International Aid Agencies: A Primer*, SMI Professional Development Brief 3 (Geneva: Geneva Centre for Security Policy, 2009).

Landmines

UN Mine Action Service and CARE, *Landmines and Explosive Remnants of War Safety Handbook*, 2005. Also available in French, and as a training module, training video and CD-ROM.

Other resources

Aid Workers Network: www.aidworkers.net. Has a resource page on 'safety, security and aid workers'.

International Organisation for Standardisation (ISO) *Risk Management – Principles and Guidelines* (Geneva: ISO, 2009). Also available in French.

Safer Access: www.saferaccess.org. Provides guidance on safety topics such as fire safety, security of laptops, personal trauma kits, the use of boats in relief work and earthquake safety.